Sarah

Also by Trevor Dennis

Lo and Behold! (SPCK 1991)

Speaking of God (Triangle/SPCK 1992)

Trevor Dennis

Sarah Laughed

First published in Great Britain 1994
Society for Promoting Christian Knowledge
Holy Trinity Church
Marylebone Road
London NW1 4DU

British Library Cataloguing-in-Publication Data

A catalogue record for this book is available from the British Library

ISBN 0–281–04689–1

Typeset by J&L Composition Ltd, Filey, North Yorkshire
Printed in Great Britain by the Cromwell Press, Melksham, Wilts

For Celia

and for
Caroline,
Eleanor, Sarah,
Joanna, and Timothy

Contents

Acknowledgements

I did the vast bulk of the work on this book during a period of sabbatical leave granted to me by the Governors of Salisbury and Wells Theological College. Without that sabbatical I would never have begun, let alone finished. To the Governors, therefore, I owe a great deal.

Of course I do not often meet the Governors. I do, however, spend a lot of time with my staff colleagues. We are a small staff, and apart from very friendly relations with one another, have developed thoroughly collegiate ways of working. I am, therefore, a member of a very close knit team of people who know what working as a team means. The support I gain from my fellow members is incalculable.

For the writing of this particular book, however, I owe an even greater debt to the students with whom I have shared my explorations of the Old Testament, and particularly to the women among them. As I acknowledge in my Introduction, they have had a radical effect on my teaching, and it is due to them more than anyone else that I have written the book I have written.

My wife Caroline, and our children, Eleanor, Sarah, Joanna, and Timothy are the ones I have to thank the most, of course, but there is one other person of whom I must make special mention. When I decided to write a book about stories concerned with women, I realized at once that I would need to discuss what I wrote with a woman. Before I began writing I contacted an ex-student of the College and friend of mine, Celia Thomson. She very kindly agreed to help me, and help me she did! She went through the entire manuscript with me, and made innumerable comments which were always sharp and illuminating, and which, in the case of my first chapter in particular, led to radical revision and great improvement (at least, in her opinion and in mine!) of the first draft. Throughout the whole exercise, which for her lasted over six months, not only was she admirably efficient, but she was so encouraging and always renewed my enthusiasm for the next stage of the task. It is in gratitude for all that, and for her friendship, that I have chosen to dedicate the book to her, as well as to my wife and children.

Trevor Dennis
July 1993

Introduction

What does the Bible mean? We might think it easy to answer that question. We might suppose there is only one correct meaning to be found in any particular verse, and that so long as we have a good translation to hand it is not hard to find. We might imagine that the meaning must lie on the surface of the text, waiting to be skimmed off by anyone who can read. But things are not so simple, nor so uninteresting as that. Meaning has to be searched for. We have to dig it out, as we might a seam of gold or silver from the rock. With the narratives and poems of the Bible, there is not just one meaning to be found, not merely a single seam to be excavated, but layer upon layer upon layer. That is one of the reasons why they continue to fascinate, why they are so compelling. No matter how many times we return to the texts, there is always something new awaiting us, some new surprise to come upon, some new glint in the rock we had missed or not reached before.

That way of talking may ring true for us, and yet it is somewhat misleading. For it suggests that somehow meaning is already in the text as some mysterious entity which has been buried by the author or authors, waiting only for our discovery. As we reach a new insight into a particular passage, it can certainly feel as though we have stumbled upon something. However, meaning is not to be found, so much as *created*. Meaning is made, or meaning 'happens', if you prefer, through dialogue with the text. It comes into being in the mysterious process of reading, when text and reader come together.

There may, of course, be some debate about the translation of a passage. Occasionally the Hebrew – or in the case of the New Testament, the Greek – may be corrupt or hopelessly obscure, so that no one can be certain about its original form or its sense. It is true also that the business of translating always involves interpretation, and the creation of something new and different from the original. It is not a matter of simply looking up words in a dictionary. Rhythms will be changed, numbers of words on the page will be altered, nuances, plays on words (the Old Testament has a wealth of those) or rhymes may prove impossible to convey. If for a moment, however, we ignore such complexities as those, there is a sense in which the text is fixed – if not carved in stone, at least trapped in print – and there is a sense in which it is the same for everyone. Whoever we are, wherever we are, if we open our Bibles at the start of Genesis we will read, 'In the beginning God created the heaven and the earth' (at least we will if we are using the King James Version). Ever since 1611, when the King James was first produced, people have read those words; and so long as that translation is used they will continue to do so. It would be exceedingly alarming if one day we were to get up, open our Bibles, and read, 'Once upon a time there was a bear called Sidney.' We would presume someone had played a stupid trick on us or else we had gone mad. There is a sense, then, in which the text is always the same and will always be the same.

But readers are not always the same. And that is why, since meaning happens through dialogue between readers and the text, there has been such a bewildering array of interpretations of the Bible over the centuries, why today different people find different things, and why, if we keep working on the text, our own understanding of it and reactions to it change and develop as we continue to grow and as we find ourselves in new circumstances. The meaning that is created through our dialogue with the text will be profoundly influenced, therefore, by who we are, the times we live in, the society and particular community of which we are a part, by our gender, our age, our beliefs, our values, our preconceptions, our temperament and predispositions, and by the enthusiasms, the concerns and the questions we bring to the exercise.

The last twenty years have seen the flowering of a movement within biblical studies, in which increasing numbers of women have come to see they have distinctive questions to ask of the text and distinctive insights to offer. They have self-consciously brought their own experience and their own concerns to bear upon it. The results have been remarkable, and for many people, men as well as women, they have been liberating. The movement has by no means been confined to the West, though, as we might expect, it has grown particularly strong in the States. It is now of considerable proportions and has attained conspicuous maturity. Writers within it have developed sufficient confidence to criticize the work of their fellow-travellers, as well as that of those outside their number. *The Women's Bible Commentary*, published in 1992 in both the United States and in Britain, is testimony to the progress that has been made.[1] Its forty-one contributors are all women teaching or studying in American universities, seminaries, or rabbinical colleges. Britain also has its fair share of scholars working in the field, and the impact of the movement upon biblical studies in this country, at least at an academic level, is already large and will only increase. Furthermore, on both sides of the Atlantic, and in many other parts of the world, men are being caught up in it and are beginning to play their part. Men, of course, cannot read the Bible as women. The meaning they create in their dialogue with the text will continue to be influenced by their gender. But they can listen to the concerns of women who study the text, and can learn from them new questions to ask of it, new places to look for its treasures, new ways of recognizing its limitations.

For the past eleven years I have been fortunate enough to be teaching Old Testament studies at Salisbury and Wells Theological College. When I first came to the College, and for several years after that, I did not ask of the text the questions I pose in this book, certainly not with the urgency or passion that I do in these pages. That I have changed in my approach I owe partly to books I have read, but much more to the influence of my colleagues, and most of all to that of women among the students I have taught. The issues they have raised in our discussions of the text, the questions they have asked, the insights they have offered, the feelings and reactions they have expressed have had a profound effect upon me, and I owe them a debt far greater than I can adequately acknowledge. To one of them this book is dedicated.

I have written the six chapters with, as one might imagine, great trepidation. The movement in biblical studies of which I have spoken has been initiated by women, and they must remain its leaders. The last thing I wish to happen is for me or any of my fellow men to muscle in on their act and attempt to take it over. That would be fairly typical of us as men, but it would be disastrous. Yet, I am confident that that will not happen. Among women the movement is too strong, and the signs are too clear that it will continue to grow in size and importance. Moreover, their work is safe from anything I might do. I cannot do what they do. I cannot read as a woman, nor write as a woman, because I am a man. I cannot cross the border into their territory. All I can do is come to the boundary fence and listen, attempt to learn, and then on my side of it attempt to apply what they have taught me. Any movement to which I belong as a result will be subservient to theirs. They will continue to pose the agenda, and show the way forward.

Not unnaturally, the women of this movement have been chiefly interested in those passages of the Bible that feature women characters. The historians amongst them have been keen to see what light those texts can throw on the conditions in which women lived their lives in the biblical period. To the evidence of the Bible they have brought material from other sources, from archaeology, from documents from the surrounding cultures, from anthropology and sociology. The literary critics in their number have been concerned to see how women are portrayed in the stories and the poems, the roles they are given to play, how much they have to say for themselves, how many initiatives they are allowed to take, what impact they have on the plots of the narratives in which they are found, or on the development of the poems of which they are a part, and to spot any stereotypes that might be at work. As far as this book is concerned, although we will draw on the work of the historians, especially in our chapter on Eve, our approach will be largely that of the literary critic; we will be interested not so much in what might or might not lie behind the text, as in the text itself in the form it has come down to us.

The Bible is mostly about men. With the exceptions of Ruth, Esther, and the woman in the Song of Songs, women tend to play bit-parts. They come on stage, have a scene to play, or two or more if they are lucky, and then disappear. Yet precisely because the bulk of the material is dominated by male characters, it is vital that we try to do their female counterparts some justice.

The Bible was mostly written by men. The Old Testament does contain at least two songs by women, the Song of Deborah in Judges 5, and the Song of Miriam in Exodus 15 (which was almost certainly much longer than it seems from the text as we have it, as we will argue in Chapter 4), and in the Song of Songs possesses a work of great beauty and power which may well have come from a woman's hand.[2] We will suggest in Chapter 4 that a story in Exodus 1 almost certainly originated in women's circles. Yet even if we suppose there are other female authors we have not detected, we can still be sure that the vast bulk of the biblical material was written by men. It is imperative that we examine what that fact has done to it, what the extent and nature of the male bias is, what the stereotypes are that have been employed; in short, how their gender has affected what the authors have written, the way they have written it, and what they have chosen to say and not to say, and how it has helped to shape their theology, their talk of God. Though we can expect women to be sharper than men in their appreciation of these things, nevertheless, it may be that men can offer some insight also and have some observations of their own to make.

We have chosen for this book five female characters from Old Testament narratives for our discussions, plus a group of women in the first four chapters of Exodus, whose number, since the female attendants of the pharaoh's daughter in Exodus 2 are not identified, is impossible to determine precisely. Three of these women, Eve, Sarah, and Hagar, have been the subject of many studies in recent years. Hannah, Bathsheba, and the women of Exodus 1–4 have not received quite so much attention. Our technique will be to identify with them as closely as we possibly can as we examine the material in which they occur, to look at it from their point of view, to treat the stories as *their* stories, and to persist in doing that even when they themselves are not centre stage. That does not mean we will be going out of our way to defend them. In the case of Eve we will be compelled to point out and condemn the obloquy to which some interpreters of the story have subjected her, but we will not try to rescue her by turning her into a saint. Instead we will attempt to arrive at a sober assessment of her portrayal and to appreciate its finer points, and we will do the same with the women of our other chapters. To do more would be to patronize them, and more seriously to patronize the real women whose stories are reflected in theirs.

One reason why we have chosen these particular women from the Old Testament and neglected some others is a purely practical one: we wish to be able to pay very close attention to the details of the text, while keeping the size of the book within reasonable bounds. None of the women we have selected has a great deal written about her in the text. Eve appears in Genesis 2 and 3 and briefly in Genesis 4; Hagar appears in two stories in Genesis 16 and 21; the limitations of the material about the women of Exodus 1–4 are even more restricted than that title for them might suggest, for they feature only in the second part of Exodus 1, in chapter 2, and then very briefly in chapter 4; Hannah's story begins at the start of 1 Samuel 1 and is over by a little more than half way through 1 Samuel 2. The material concerning Sarah and Bathsheba is more scattered, but in bulk it still does not amount to very much, and we will be able to treat it in the same detail. Alas, with this approach, chapters on Ruth, Esther, or the Song of Songs would have turned out far too unwieldy.

We are aware that with the omission of those three works especially we have not been able to present a balanced picture of the portrayal of women in the Old Testament. For we have left out the two works of some size where women can be said to play the major roles – Ruth and Esther – and in putting aside the Song of Songs have neglected the series of poems in which a woman's voice is heard more clearly than in any other document in the Bible. Yet, of course, we do not pretend to offer any kind of comprehensive discussion. We provide a few glimpses only – nothing approaching the whole picture.

By the end, however, we will have done enough to indicate that the picture is a complex one. We will have discovered a certain male bias in the telling of the story of the Garden in Genesis 2–3, but we will have realized just how much Eve has been maligned by translators, commentators and interpreters; we will have seen how much Sarah truly suffers at the hands of her narrator, as well as those of her husband and her God; we will have been astonished by the honours heaped on the slave-woman Hagar, for all the abuse she too endures, and will have noticed how far the narrator goes out of his way to evoke our sympathy for her; we will have found some true heroines in Exodus 1–4, women who are presented to us as exemplary characters, and two women there whose story probably came originally from women's circles; with Hannah we will have discovered a story which the male narrator takes persistent care to write from her point of view; and with Bathsheba we will have come across an ambiguous figure, whose honour is upheld by the narrator at a crucial stage, but whose character will remain something of a mystery. We will have encountered women in the roles not just of wife and mother, slave, nurse, concubine or mistress, but also in those of companion and co-worker, midwife, conspirator and queen mother, poet, and possibly priest. We will have kept company with an Egyptian slave one moment, and a pharaoh's daughter the next.

We have included within our own text a translation of all the passages we discuss in any detail. That is often taken from the NRSV, or closely based upon it, but sometimes we have offered our own translation, in the hope that it conveys more clearly than the usual versions the nuances, cadences, or sense of the original Hebrew.

There remains one last point we wish to make here, and it is a most important one. This book is an attempt to explore the character of a few Old Testament stories from the basis of particular concerns. Those concerns, which we hope have already become clear enough from this Introduction, and which should certainly emerge plainly from the chapters themselves, extend beyond our desire to achieve some clarity about the biblical text.

They reach into the whole area of the place occupied by women in contemporary society and in the Church in particular. Far more important than the discussion of the details of the biblical text is the question of what we *do* with the text once we have finished our explaining. Eve's story demonstrates the truth of that all by itself. We will in this book find glorious, heart-warming things; but we will also come across what we can only interpret as flaws, insensitivities, and visions of the nature and calling of women which might encourage men to continue to keep them on the margins of power and deprive them of their proper dignity. We will find that the God portrayed in the stories is sometimes himself caught up in the male bias of the text. What then shall we do? This is the most important question of all, and we will try very briefly to tackle it in the course of our 'Final Reflections', when our explorations of the texts are over. All we will do for now is raise the issue of the power the text possesses and of the freedom we enjoy to use it for good or for ill. For these stories might conceivably be used by us to increase our fears, harden our prejudices, and confirm our sense or practice of injustice. Alternatively, we might, whether we are women or men, be fired by them to fight the injustices which women still suffer in our society and our Church, and be enabled by them to come to a clearer understanding of those things within us as well as outside that cloud our vision, spoil our speech and action, and obscure for ourselves and those around us the bright promises of God.

1

Eve: A Woman Much Maligned

(Genesis 2.4b–4.2a; 4.25)

The Garden of Eden has a terrible litter problem. It is knee deep in our prejudices and preconceptions. No patch of ground is more thoroughly spoiled than that on which Eve walks, and the purpose of this chapter will be to do some clearing up. It will not be as easy as it sounds, for no biblical story has been more mistranslated, more misinterpreted than this one. The mistranslations and misinterpretations have been around a very long time, and have taken deep root in our minds. No biblical character has been more misunderstood or more maligned than the woman of the Garden, the woman who comes at the end of the story to be called Eve. Her story, the little story of a strange Garden where she is made and a man is formed also, where she enters into dialogue with a snake, where God performs marvellous acts of creation and walks in the cool of the day, is one of the most subtle and compelling in the Bible, indeed in all literature. It has had a most powerful effect on people's imaginations, beliefs, attitudes and behaviour, and even in these days, when the Church itself neglects the Old Testament so, it is still doing its work, or rather the mistranslations and misinterpretations are still wreaking their havoc. Still the lies that have been told about the woman of the Garden get the better of us, and trap us with their smooth talk as the snake traps her, whispering to us that women are somehow inferior to men, made to be subservient to them, and worse, are dangerous, needing to be kept under men's control. For these reasons alone it is imperative that we look at this story again, and with fresh eyes.

We will have to make a conscious attempt to read the text as if we were reading it for the first time. We will need to recover our sense of surprise, and be prepared to abandon things we thought we knew. We will have to look very hard at the words in front of us, or rather, at points, at the words that are *not* in front of us in our versions, but would be if only the original Hebrew were translated correctly. We will have to peer at them harder, perhaps, than we have ever done before, to see what they say and what they do not say. We will have to make a supreme effort to forget what has been done with the story so often in the past, and to put out of our minds the lies that have been told and are still told about the woman. If we do not succeed in doing that, then she is already judged and condemned before we start.

The task will be a difficult one, but at least we are not the first ones to attempt it. In recent years there have been a number of detailed studies of the story of the Garden which have shed bright light upon it, and done much to strip away the layers of misconceptions and restore the woman to the colours in which she was originally painted.[1] We will be paying close heed to those and making much use of them. They will prove invaluable.

In our exploration of the story, and of the few verses that concern Eve in Genesis 4, we will have five main episodes to consider: the introduction to her creation, the act of creation itself, her being trapped by the snake into eating the fruit of the forbidden tree, the judgement of God upon her, and what she does and what happens to her outside and beyond the Garden. We will at first simply call her 'the woman', for she does not receive her name 'Eve' until near the end of the story. Similarly, the man will remain 'the man', for while he is called *'adam* at the start, it is not clear that the word is being used as a proper name, so we cannot call him Adam until Genesis 4.25.

As we proceed we will reach certain conclusions about the woman (and, of course, about the man). Normally we would not think of anticipating those at this point, but because misconceptions about this particular story are so deep rooted, there is a need for us to do some weeding before we start; we need to shift some of the stinking litter, and clear the air a little, so that when we enter the Garden we can breathe.

So let us now declare a few of the things we will *not* find in the story: the woman's creation will *not* mark her out as inferior to the man; she will *not* be created out of so small and insignificant a thing as one of the man's ribs; in her dialogue with the snake she will *not* emerge as a wicked temptress or dangerous seductress; she will *not* be portrayed as guilty of covetousness, greed or hubris; in eating the fruit of the forbidden tree she will *not* be attempting to become like God or to usurp his power; she will *not* be condemned as the root of all our troubles, and though she will be guilty of disobedience, the man beside her will be no less guilty than she, and possibly more so; God's judgement upon her will *not* place her in a subservient position to the man, indeed will not speak of subservience at all; she will *not* be cursed, and the damaging description of a woman's period as her 'curse' will find no foundation here – the story will make no reference to the menstrual cycle at all; the expulsion from the Garden will *not* be the end of her story, any more than it will be the end of the man's, and there will be some joy to be found for her outside its bounds, short-lived though that will be.

At points we *will* discover a male bias to the story. It is plain even at its very start that it was written by a man, and things are frequently handled from a clear male perspective. In places this results in what we would now regard as a lack of balance, a certain narrowness of vision, a way of writing that we now cannot help finding unsatisfactory. But such bias, almost certainly unconscious on the part of the storyteller, is a world away from the attempts made by some of the story's translators and interpreters to belittle, malign or condemn the woman. Of that there is nothing in the text as it was written. Instead, it makes room for the celebration of woman, for sensitive and poignant comment upon her trials and tribulations, for the dreaming of dreams on her part, and even, though it preaches it so quietly, for revolution.

Prelude

(Gen. 2.4b–20)

In the day that the Lord God made the earth and the heavens, when no shrub of the field was yet in the earth and no plant of the field had yet sprung up – for the Lord God had not caused it to rain upon the earth, and there was no man to work the ground – . . . then the Lord God shaped the man from the dust of the ground . . . (Gen. 2.4b–7a)

That is how the story of the Garden starts. We begin not with the dark mass of water of the beginning of Genesis 1, but with a barren desert – and if that desert is to be transformed, then two things are necessary: rain, and someone to till the soil.

There are two reasons why we should think of that 'someone' as male, one inside the text, one outside it. From the way we have translated the passage, there would seem to be no question about it, but in fact the Hebrew is ambiguous. The word we have translated 'man' is *'adam*, and there is a play on words in the original text, for this *'adam* is made from the *'adamah*, or ground, and there is some justification for Phyllis Trible's translation, 'earth creature',[2] or for Carol Meyers' 'earthling', or her playful suggestion of a 'human' made from clods of the 'humus',[3] or for Mary Korsak's 'groundling'.[4] When Genesis first describes the creation of human beings it does so with the words: 'And God said, "Let us make humankind in our image, after our likeness . . ." So God created humankind in his image, in the image of God he created it, male and female he created them' (1.26a, 27). There the word for 'humankind' is again *'adam*, and quite clearly it does not just mean the male of the species, for the verses end by revealing that the term covers the female also. It can be argued that what Genesis 1 is speaking of is the creation of a single creature, a man-and-woman, and that that is what we have in the Garden story until half-way through, when it is separated into man and woman.[5] Phyllis Trible is careful to point out that the Hebrew term *'ish*, which means quite definitely man the male, is not employed until 2.23, after the woman has herself emerged.[6] It is also true to say that we cannot logically talk of 'male' unless there is also 'female', just as we could have no concept of good without evil.

Nevertheless, in 2.25 and from 3.8 to the end of the story the word *'adam* is used to refer unambiguously to the man of the story, and that makes us suspect it is being used with the same meaning earlier in chapter 2, whatever the demands of our logic might be. Our suspicions are only encouraged by evidence from outside the text. In her book *Discovering Eve* Carol Meyers discusses at length the roles that men and women would have played in the households and village communities of early Israel. She argues that the tasks of working, clearing, terracing and ploughing the land were probably performed by men.[7] So it seems plain that the desert of Genesis 2.5 is desert because of a lack of rain and the absence of male farmers to work the land. At once we are looking at things from a man's (and a farmer's) vantage point. We will have to remember that as we explore what is said about the woman.

But we do not reach the woman quite yet. After the coming of the rains and the remarkable creation of the man, we go straight from the desert to a garden. We might expect the man to have a lot of hard work to do clearing and terracing and ploughing and

sowing, but no. God does the planting, creates a most wonderful
Garden all by himself, and puts the man there. All that man has
to do is keep the Garden in good order. If he is hungry, he can
pick and eat the fruit from all the beautiful trees; when he gets
thirsty, he can fetch as much water as he likes from the continuous
and huge supply provided by the rivers that flow through the place
and go out of it to water the earth. It is an early Israelite farmer's
dream! No wonder the verse which speaks of God 'setting' the man
in the Garden (2.15) uses a Hebrew verb whose usual meaning is
'rest' or 'take it easy'!

But the man's happiness is not yet complete. He is lonely, and
does not have anyone to help him. So God creates the animals and
the birds, and brings them to the man to see if they will do. They
do not. He identifies them all, but as he searches for 'a helper to
match him' (2.18) he finds none. .

It is important for us to linger on that phrase 'a helper to match
him'[8] for a moment, partly because scholars have disagreed over
its translation, and partly because it supplies the reason in the story
for the woman's creation.

Phyllis Trible argues that the word for 'helper' would be better
translated 'companion'.[9] 'Helper', she says, too easily suggests to
us a position of inferiority and subservience, whereas the Hebrew
word behind the second part of the phrase, the one translated 'to
match him', implies that the creature God is looking for will be on
a par with the man, his counterpart not his lackey, his colleague
rather than an under-gardener who just deals with the rubbish and
spreads the manure. She has a point, and a strong one, and we
certainly need to remember that the Hebrew term for 'helper' is
itself often used in the Old Testament to describe one as exalted
as God himself, and almost always refers to one stronger than the
one who needs the help.[10] Nevertheless, as David Clines reminds
us, you cannot get away from the fact that the woman is created
to help the man, to help him in *his* work.[11]

In the end both Trible and Clines are right. The woman is
created to fulfil the man's needs. That is made clear not only by
the term 'helper', but by the fact that God brings her to the man,
in the same way he brought the animals, to see if he thinks she will
do. Again it is clear that the story is written from a man's point of
view. Clines is correct. But if we jump to the conclusion that as
his helper the woman will be the man's chattel, there to minister
to his every whim, then we are quite wrong. The passage is not
as finely balanced as we would like it to be, and the notion of
the woman being created because of the man's need is for us

disconcerting, to say the least. But the man is here given no licence to dominate or oppress. Trible is right, and it is not just the Hebrew word behind 'helper', or the rest of the phrase, 'to match him', that proves her to be so. The evidence of the verses that describe the woman's creation is on her side.

The woman's creation

(Gen. 2.21–5)

> The Lord God caused a deep sleep to fall upon the man, and he slept. Then he took one of his sides and closed up the flesh in its place. And the Lord God built the side he had taken from the man into a woman, and he brought her to the man. (2.21–2)

First, we notice that the storyteller spends just as much time describing the woman's creation as he did the man's in 2.7. That verse was sixteen words long in the Hebrew. If we regard the creation of the woman as beginning in 2.21b, with the words 'then he took one of his sides', and ending in verse 22 with 'he built . . . into a woman', then again we have sixteen Hebrew words. The writer has counted his words and been careful to match the lengths of his two descriptions exactly.

Second, the act of creation is just as intimate and delicate an operation (an apt word to use when it includes a neat piece of surgery on God's part!) as was the man's, and involves considerable effort. In the first one God takes clay, moulds it into the man's body, and then gives him the kiss of life. Now, in the case of the woman, he removes one of the man's sides, sews up the wound, then 'builds' what he has taken into a woman.[12] The woman's creation is even more mysterious than her partner's, but it brings her into just as close contact with the Creator. Both she and the man find their being and their life as a result of God's intimacy, and through his very remarkable manual skill. Something of supreme significance is being said about the value of the human couple, and the features of this passage which suggest that the woman's worth is the same as the man's outweigh the male bias, and almost lead us to forget it is there.[13]

It helps, of course, to have abandoned the usual translation of the woman being created out of the man's rib. The storyteller does not employ an anatomical term. In fact, this is the only place in the Old Testament where the word is applied to a part of the human body. But it is frequently used of the sides of the temple, or the sides of the ark, or the sides of the tabernacle or altar, and those references must be allowed to determine how we translate it here. It is *side*, not rib.[14] God's creation of the woman may defy our imagination, yet his taking a whole side from the man to make her clearly reinforces the sense that her value is as great as her partner's, that she does indeed 'match him', in status as well as in physical form. To speak, without any real justification, of her being made out of the man's rib, is to do her a grave disservice. Translators and interpreters have often assumed that from start to finish the story of the Garden puts her in a subservient position to the man. That is enough to explain the traditional translation, and no doubt lies behind the portrayal of the woman as being made from something as small as a single bone, and one that the man could easily do without. To call it a rib is to undermine the vision which the writer, this counter of words, is trying so carefully to evoke of a mutual and equal partnership between the two newly created human beings.

Our reading of those two verses is supported by the man's reaction to the woman when God brings her to him. The woman opens the man's mouth: we have not heard his voice before. Immediately he breaks into poetry:

> 'Now this one, this time, is bone of my bones
>   and flesh of my flesh!
> This one shall be called "woman",
>   for from man she was taken, this one!' (2.23)

In his commentary on Genesis, Claus Westermann describes this as a cry of joyful surprise, a 'jubilant welcome',[15] and so indeed it is. The man cannot contain his excitement. At last he has found what he was looking for among all those animals and birds that God brought to him before his strange sleep. At last he has found 'a helper to match him'. 'This is the one!' he cries. Notice that it is not her suitability as a helper that he celebrates, but her being the perfect match. He recognizes his side in the woman, and calls her 'bone of my bones', and 'flesh of my flesh'! He greets his other half! He speaks as if he is conscious of what was going on while he was asleep under God's anaesthetic. He knows at once where she has come from. The two of them are made of the same stuff. The woman is not part of the man; she does not belong to him. He could not have his side back, even if he wanted it. She is a new creature, with an identity of her own, the result of God's marvellous 'building'. Yet something has been taken from the man to make her. With her he is complete again. He belongs with her and she with him, and that he at once recognizes in his joke about flesh and bones. She is *exactly* what he has been looking for.

Still using the poetic form of speech, the man cracks his second joke. He has already called the ibex 'ibex', and the white-crowned black wheatear the 'white-crowned black wheatear' (see vv. 19–20; the examples are my own). Now, having already shown remarkable insight into the woman's origins, he has another brainwave: 'this one shall be called *"woman"*,/ for from *man* she was taken, this one!' The Old Testament writers took great delight in plays on words. We have met one before this, in *'adam* being created from the *'adamah*. Unfortunately, they are almost invariably lost in translation. This one, however, still works. The English words 'woman' and 'man' mirror one another, as do their Hebrew equivalents *'ishshah* and *'ish*. Strictly speaking, the word *'ishshah* is not related to *'ish*, but it sounds as though it is, and that was enough for this storyteller, and it is enough for us.

Some commentators, however, insist that to name someone is to assert one's authority over them.[16] They claim that the man was declaring his sovereignty over the animals and birds when earlier he gave them their names. But he was doing nothing of the sort. The creation and naming of the animals is certainly treated from a human, and – since the human being concerned is a man – from a male point of view. Of that there is no question. God makes the animals and birds out of regard for the man's loneliness, as an attempt to provide him with 'a helper to match him'. Yet that itself makes it clear that God brings them to the man not for him to assert his authority over them, but so that he can search among them for a companion. In naming them, all the man does is identify them as possible partners, or rather, since they do not fit the bill, as *im*possible partners. That little episode ends back at square one with the words 'yet for the man he [God] found no helper to match him' (2.20). So now, when he is presented with the woman and names her, he makes no bid for power. He has discovered what he has been looking for. That is all. There is only playfulness, a playful joy. And to prove it, for the first time he refers to himself as 'man'. He is not content to be *'adam*, to take his identity from the stuff, the *'adamah*, from which he was made. Instead he takes it from his relationship with this new creature standing before him, this woman, this *'ishshah*. He knows who he is now. He is *'ish*, man!

However, it is not the details of the text of these verses which most clearly celebrate the woman's worth, but the passage's position in the story. Her creation brings this first half of the story to its climax. Indeed, it represents the high point of the whole story of the Garden. The tale curves upwards from barren desert to this mysterious moment of the woman's arrival and the great joy she brings. Almost at once it begins to slide down again, until the couple find themselves banished to fields which will be little better than the barren land from which it all began. The narratives of the Old Testament often build up to a climax in the middle, and this one is no exception. The woman is the brightest jewel in its crown!

We might, however, be genuinely disconcerted by the woman's silence. We will discover, as we look at other texts beyond this one, that we can often perceive more clearly the value accorded to a particular character in a story by looking at how much they are given to say. Here the man has his playful poetry; the woman has nothing. We know what he thinks of her. We do not hear what she thinks of him. The male standpoint is again evident, certainly. No doubt a woman would have written the passage differently. Yet this woman's time for speech will come, and very soon, as soon as the snake has introduced itself at the start of chapter 3. If the storyteller had made the woman speak before that, in immediate answer to the man, he would have risked spoiling the balance of his narrative. He, this storyteller, was an artist of genius, and storytellers of genius worry about things such as the balance of their narratives. In any case, the man of the story does not invite a response. He does not address the woman. The time for dialogue, let alone embrace, has not yet arrived. He simply cries out to the God who has brought her to him, '*This* is the one!', and God himself has no response to make to that, but to depart from the stage of the story for a while and leave the man and woman to themselves.

The narrator too departs from the scene, or rather he brings it to an end. When next the curtain rises, the woman and the man will be on stage once more, but God's place, in more ways than one, will be taken by a snake. Yet before that, to mark the end of this first act of his drama, the storyteller adds a tiny epilogue in two parts. The first part looks beyond the Garden, yet hints at the passion that was found there. The second returns to the newly created couple, and speaks of the mutuality of their relationship, their security and lack of fear.

That is why [explains the storyteller after the man's exclamation] a man leaves his father and his mother and clings to his woman, and they become one flesh. Now the two of them were naked, the man and his woman, but they were not ashamed. (2.24–5)

In each part we have 'his woman'. In neither do we hear of 'her man'. We are still looking at things from the point of view of the male narrator and the man in the Garden, and no attempt is being made to see what they look like from the woman's or from women's side. That said, what the storyteller is doing in the first part of his epilogue is to reflect upon the power of women over men: the attraction women exert upon men can be so strong that it over-comes the emotional ties between them and their parents. The writer is not talking about men leaving their parents' households to get married and join the households of their brides. In ancient Israel descent was traced through the male line, and property was handed on from father to son. That meant that when a woman married, she left the household of her parents to join that of her husband. The storyteller is not trying to deny what he knew was the universal practice. Instead he is commenting upon the extra-ordinary power of love and sexual attraction,[17] and suggesting with a certain amount of mischief that when a man and woman are united in that love and in sexual intercourse they somehow return to being the one flesh or one creature (the Hebrew term translated 'flesh' could mean that) they once were. When we were discussing God's creation of *'adam* from the *'adamah* we argued that *'adam* should be translated 'man' and not 'man-and-woman', that he should be regarded from the start as male, and not some androgynous creature waiting to be separated into male and female. We would argue that still, but we have to concede that the storyteller comes close to the second view here. He comes close to suggesting the man and woman were created as a single being, that the two 'sides' of this creature were then separated from one another, but that they are joined together again through sexual love.

This brief reflection on such love between men and women contains a hint of passion in the relationship between the man and woman in the Garden beyond what has already been suggested by the man's joyful welcome. Such passion and sexual union may possibly be hinted at again in the second part of the epilogue with its reference to the nakedness of the couple. Yet in chapter 3, when all is spoiled and the couple realize they are naked and are suddenly afraid, what their nakedness signifies is not their readiness for love, but their defencelessness and vulnerability. Here, at the high point

in the story, when the woman and the man are alone with their
creator God, they are naked yet feel secure; they are vulnerable,
yet are not aware of it; defenceless, yet without any sense of having
to defend themselves. They feel utterly safe. But they are not.
They have not reckoned with the snake.

The ensnaring of the woman

(Gen. 3.1–7)

We began this chapter by saying the Garden of Eden was strewn
with litter. We might just as well have compared it to a minefield.
We are about to enter its most dangerous patch. This is the place
where so often the woman's reputation gets blown to pieces. This
is where writers and artists have turned her into the wicked
temptress who leads the man astray in her lustful bid for divine
power. We will have to tread with extreme caution.

The second half of the story of the Garden begins with the
introduction of a new character: 'Now the snake was cleverer than
any other wild animal that the Lord God had made' (3.1). These
are ominous words, but not for the reasons that have often been
put forward in the past. The snake is just a snake, a talking snake
it is true, a storyteller's snake, but still a snake. Christian doctrine
came much later to turn it into the devil. It is not that here; it is
simply one of God's wild animals. But it is the *cleverest*. Does that
mean cleverer than the man and the woman? Alas, it does.

It engages the woman in conversation:

'Did God really say, "You shall not eat from any tree in the
garden?"' The woman said to the snake, 'We may eat of the
fruit of the trees of the garden, but as for the fruit of the tree
in the middle of the garden, God said, "You shall not eat any
of it, nor shall you touch it, or you shall die."' The snake said
to the woman, 'Die? You will not die! For God knows that on
the day you eat it your eyes will be opened, and you will be
like God, knowing good and evil.' Then the woman saw that
the tree was good for food, an attraction to the eyes and a
delight to consider, and she took some of its fruit and ate, and
she also gave some to her man with her, and he ate. (3.1b–6)

For the first time we hear the woman speak. Now she, together
with the snake, takes centre stage, and the man slips so far back

into the shadows of the narrative that we can very easily forget he is there. Not only has the storyteller swung his spotlight upon the woman, but he has changed his own position. He refers to the man now as '*her* man'; no longer is the woman '*his* woman'. He is adopting her stance.

We may fall to wondering why the snake chooses the woman to speak to. The author does not tell us. Some might say it is paying the woman a compliment, that it appreciates that she is the more intelligent and articulate of the two, or else recognizes her as the more ambitious and the one who will be more interested in what it has to offer. Others might claim it realizes she will be more easily led astray. Neither of these suggestions, however, are borne out by the text. The woman does not turn out to be particularly astute or ambitious, while the man just as readily does what the snake suggests. Quite why it picks the woman we do not know. It just does.

It is clearer, perhaps, why it does not formally address them both: dialogues are common in Old Testament narratives, three-way conversations much less so. Yet there is an interesting feature of the Hebrew of these verses which reminds us of the man's presence, and makes us think the snake is really speaking to the man also, or at least is keeping an eye fixed on him as he converses with the woman. In Hebrew the form of verbs for 'you' singular is different from that for 'you' plural. When the snake says 'you' to the woman he consistently uses the plural form, indeed the masculine plural form. The woman, for her part, answers not with an 'I' but a 'we', and when she quotes God's words she too uses the masculine plural 'you' form. What the Hebrew grammar suggests the narrator makes plain after the speaking is done: the woman gives the fruit to her man *who is with her*.

The dialogue begins with what seems a simple question: 'Did God really say, "You shall not eat from any tree in the garden?"' (3.1). It sounds innocent enough, but we must recall what the story has told us so far about the source of food for the human couple. It has told us of God planting trees 'good for food' (2.9); it has had God saying to the man, 'You may freely eat of every tree in the garden' (2.16) – except for the tree of the knowledge of good and evil. There has been no mention of animals to cook, or of wagons of grain rolling in from prairies outside the Garden. By the terms of the story the couple depend for their very survival on the fruit of the trees in the Garden. For the snake to suggest that God might put all that wonderful fruit within their reach and then tell them not to eat it, is to conjure up a picture of a tantalizing, sadistic God, who will not have human beings in his Garden for much longer, because he has effectively condemned them to starve to death.

This disturbing picture does not, however, come into the woman's mind. She catches none of the question's sinister undertones. In her own innocence all she sees is its superficial simplicity, and she gives it a simple, straightforward answer: 'We may eat of the fruit of the trees of the garden, but as for the fruit of the tree in the middle of the garden, God said, "You shall not eat any of it, nor shall you touch it, or you shall die."' This is a fair and accurate summary of the words God addressed to the man after he put him in the Garden (see 2.16–17). The woman makes one addition, 'nor shall you touch it'. It is a most significant one, but it does not have the significance that some commentators have claimed for it. Gerhard von Rad, for example, suggests, 'It is as though she wanted to set a law for herself by means of this exaggeration',[18] and Claus Westermann quotes his statement with approval and then adds, 'One who defends a command can already be on the way to breaking it'.[19] Such aspersions are quite unjustified. If the addition to the divine command *were* reprehensible, then we could not justly blame the woman for it. She was not present when God placed the ban upon the tree. The terms of the story would encourage us to think she has learned about it from the man, and for all we know it is he who has told her the tree should not be touched. In fact, however, those extra words should not make for accusation, but for commendation. For they reveal that the woman recognizes the tree of knowledge of good and evil as holy. She knows, as all ancient Israelites knew, that the holy is dangerous, and that holy things are not to be touched. She understands, as the Israelites did, familiar as they were with the story of Sinai in Exodus 19, or of the unfortunate Uzzah touching the ark in 2 Samuel 6, that touching the holy can mean death. She believes, it seems, that God has put his prohibition on the tree of knowledge for the couple's own good. She may not be as clever as the snake, but she is a considerably better theologian, and so is the man, if indeed she is merely quoting what he has said to her.

Yet the snake rejects her theology: 'Die? You will not die! For God knows that on the day you eat it your eyes will be opened, and you will be like God, knowing good and evil' (3.4–5). With those words the dialogue ends. Tragically the woman has no answer to them, but to take the fruit and eat, and give some to the man. The man, for his part, has no argument to put against them. All he can do in the face of this snake's cunning is to eat what he is offered.

Exactly why the man eats, we do not know. The story does not supply his reasons. Either he does not think at all, and blindly accepts the fruit the woman gives him, or else his motives are the same as the woman's. It is possible, of course, that his motives are worse than hers, though the story does not encourage us to suppose that.

The story does, however, give us the motives of the woman. That it does so is unusual. Old Testament narratives, and the narratives of Genesis in particular, do not generally make people's motives explicit. They usually leave them to our imagination. When they do supply them, therefore, they are asking us to pay them special heed. How ironic, then, and how tragic also, that readers of this story should have ignored them so!

'Then the woman saw that the tree was good for food, an attraction to the eyes and a delight to consider, and she took some of its fruit and ate . . .' (3.6). She has been ensnared by the coils of the snake's smooth words. She should have protested at the way it mocked God's threat of death, and turned it into a lie. She should have denied its cynical portrayal of a lying God who acts not to protect the couple from the dangers of the holy, but to safeguard his own knowledge and power. She should have reminded it that the tree of knowledge was a holy tree, there for God's purposes, not there to be used by the couple like all the other trees. She should have told the snake to get the hell out of it. So should the man. But she does not, nor does he. The snake is cleverer than both of them. Though it does not fill the woman with a lust to be like God – that does not sink in – it does succeed in changing her vision of the tree. In presenting it as something to be used by the couple, it effectively robs it of its holiness for her, and reduces it to the level of the other trees in the Garden.

When we were first introduced to the Garden we heard that 'the Lord God made to grow every tree that is a delight to look at and good for food' (2.9). In explaining the woman's motives, the author recalls that verse by the language he uses. He quotes one phrase from it, 'good for food', and paraphrases another: 'a delight to look at' becomes 'an attraction to the eyes' and 'a delight to consider'. The point is not lost on us. The tree of knowledge of good and evil has now ceased to be anything unusual for the woman, and so naturally she plucks some of its fruit and eats and gives to the man.

There is a mischief and a tragic humour to be found in the contrast the storyteller has created between the vast rewards the snake offers the woman, and the humble gains – no greater than those to be derived from the other trees of the Garden – she seeks by taking the fruit. Yet that mischief and humour have been entirely lost on the vast majority of translators and commentators. The most natural translation of the phrase recording the third of the woman's motives is the one we have given it, 'a delight to consider'. Yet translators have generally had her finding the tree 'desirable to make one wise', and the commentators have then packed into that phrase all the ambition set before the couple by the snake when it promised that if she and the man took the fruit they would be like God, knowing good and evil. In other words they have interpreted the woman's action as if her motives were stated not in 3.6, but in 3.5. They have accused her of arrogance, of hubris, of wanting to usurp God's power. They have found her a most dangerous creature. They have turned her into the snake. But the text will not allow such misogyny. It is verse 6 that gives the woman's motives, and its terms are *not* those of verse 5. It says nothing about becoming like God. It says nothing about knowing good and evil. Twice verse 5 uses the word 'know'. Verse 6 studiously avoids it. The word it does use, the one we have translated 'consider', can, it is true, mean to 'act prudently', to 'have insight', or to 'prosper', but if we allow it to carry such overtones here the mischief of the writer becomes all the greater. For then we see the woman seeking prudence through a most imprudent act; searching for insight, when with a little more of that she would have seen through the snake's smooth talk; aiming for prosperity, when, as it turns out, her action spells her ruin. 3.6 has nothing to do with hubris, but it can have everything to do with irony, and, for all its playfulness, a most tragic irony at that.

There are two more points to consider before we move on to the next section dealing with the woman's punishment. We have touched upon the first of them already, but because the text has been so abused, we must return to it and give it greater emphasis. We mean the part the man plays in all this.

The immediate answer is, very little. It is not until near the end of verse 6, when we are told that he is with the woman, that we can be sure he is on stage. He says nothing, and he does nothing, except eat. 'Aha!' say the woman's accusers, 'but he eats fruit *which is given him by the woman*! There is your temptress, your dangerous seductress!' Let us be quite clear. The text speaks of no temptation, no seduction. '. . . and she also gave some to her man with her, and he ate' (3.6b). *That is all.* There is no egging the man on, nor reluctance on his part, as is portrayed in so many paintings of the scene; no sticking of the fruit in his throat, no explanation here for that curious feature of the male neck we call the Adam's apple.

As Claus Westermann puts it, 'it is not a temptation that is narrated here . . . no temptation was needed in the case of the man; he simply fell into line.'[20] And in falling into line he is not joining the woman in some great act of rebellion. Like her, presumably, he now sees nothing unusual about the tree and so finds nothing wrong in eating the fruit that is offered him. If we insist on blaming one of the couple more than the other, then we should be quicker to accuse the man. For we know for certain that he received the ban upon the tree from God's own lips. It seems both of them have forgotten that prohibition. He has less excuse for doing so. Ironically enough, pushing all the blame on the woman will turn out to be precisely what he tries to do when God confronts him with his crime.

For the woman's and man's eating of the fruit *is* a crime, though the rich language of the Old Testament for sin and transgression is not used in the story. An explicit and quite clear divine command (2.17) has been breached. The fruit was not for eating, and the woman and the man have eaten it. Though some who try to rescue the woman from all blame play down or ignore the fact, there is disobedience here. True, the woman may not have realized what she was doing. True, she has been beguiled by the snake, 'bitten' by its clever, cynical, poisonous tongue. The same things can possibly be said in the man's defence also. But there is no getting away from it. There is disobedience here, and a denial of God's authority. The woman ends up putting more trust in a clever snake than she does in her own judgement, or the man's, about the holiness of the tree. Though she does not take in what it is saying, she puts more faith in its words than in the words of God she understood so clearly, and without a moment's hesitation the man follows suit. Their fault lies in their not continuing to respect the holiness of the holy. They are beguiled into treating it as something to be used for their own purposes. And in forgetting the holy they forget their God.

The punishment of the woman

(Gen. 3.8–19)

When we considered the creation of the woman, we had to pay heed to the man's creation also, and when we came to her eating of the forbidden fruit, we could not ignore the action of the man. Now we have reached her punishment, we will, inevitably, have to say something about the man's. But we will do so in order to illuminate the woman's plight. Our focus will remain on her, as it has been all along.

Before we come to God's pronouncements of judgement, we must look at the more immediate consequences of the couple's disobedience. At once we encounter again the storyteller's playfulness. The eating of the fruit is followed immediately by these words: 'Then the eyes of both were opened, and they knew . . .' Exactly what the snake said would happen! If we imagine ourselves reading this for the first time, we expect it to continue with '. . . good and evil, and became like God'. But instead we are provided with a wonderful example of bathos: '. . . and they knew *they were naked*; and they sewed fig leaves together and made loincloths for themselves' (3.7). All they know is the defencelessness and vulnerability of their humanity, and all they can do to defend themselves is make pathetic loincloths, which God will need to replace with something more substantial when they leave the Garden. So much for becoming like God! So much for the mastery, the omniscience that the snake promised with its talk of knowing good and evil!

The couple's new vulnerability becomes even more evident when God comes on the scene, walking in the Garden in the cool of the day. At once they hide. And God calls to *the man*, to the *'adam*. Suddenly, the woman, who has been so prominent since her creation, far more so than her partner, disappears from the narrative. God speaks to the man as if the woman were not there. It reminds us of the snake talking with the woman as if the man was not beside her. At least when the woman replied to the snake's questions she included the man in her speech: she spoke of 'we', and turned the 'you' singulars of God's original command to the man into 'you' plurals. By contrast the man's reply excludes the woman: 'I heard the sound of you in the garden, and I was afraid for I was naked; and I hid' (3.10). It is still as if the woman was not there. He speaks openly of the breakdown that has occurred in the relationship between him and his God. His speech is also, in its excluding of the woman, a more subtle indication of the breakdown in the relationship between him and his partner. That breakdown is made plain by the man's second speech, when he attempts to defend himself: 'The woman you gave to be with me, she, she gave me of the tree, and I ate' (3.12). The man speaks the truth, of course, but he does not only speak the truth, he accuses. He accuses 'the woman' (that is what she is now to him, not 'bone of my bones', but 'the woman'), and he blames God – 'the woman *you* gave to be with me'. No jubilant welcome now, but rejection and dark accusation. Too many readers of this story have in the past ignored his accusing God, but have relished his accusing the woman. In doing so they have added irony and tragedy to a tale which already has enough of both.

It is at this dark point that God speaks to the woman. Now that she stands accused by the man, God recognizes her presence, and for the first time in the whole story addresses her: 'What is this you have done?' (3.13a). In reply, the woman also speaks the truth, and also accuses: 'The snake tricked me, and I ate' (3.13b). She, too, passes the buck (the serpent will have no one to blame, and, in any case, will be given no chance to defend itself; we have heard the last from that creature already). But she does not accuse God. Nor does she protest against her partner's accusation, and tell God how willingly, how quickly he took the fruit when it was offered him. The man's speech expressed and added to the breakdown in relationships between him and God, and between him and the woman. The woman's speech expresses and adds to the breakdown in the relationship between her and the snake (God will recognize that in his judgement on the snake, when he speaks of putting enmity between it and the woman), but it leaves the other more important relationships unscathed. Is there a hint here that if reconciliation is to be achieved, it will depend more on the woman than on the man?

So we arrive at God's judgements, and at a verse which has caused the woman, and women ever since, more trouble than any other in this entire story. Carol Meyers devotes a whole chapter of her book *Discovering Eve* to it, and subjects every single word of its Hebrew text to the most minute analysis.[21] Our translation and interpretation owe a great deal to her work, though we will depart from her at one crucial point.

God underlines the formality and the solemnity of his judgement by slipping into poetry:

'I will increase, yes increase your toil and your pregnancies;
    in the midst of toil will you have children.
But for your man shall be your desire,
    and for you he will be irresistible.' (3.16)

The judgement on the man in the next three verses speaks of back-breaking work in the fields, of an unremitting battle waged against a cursed and recalcitrant soil and its thorns and thistles, in order to grow enough food to eat. It has long been recognized that those lines present a brilliant summary of the typical plight of the Israelite hill-farmers, and the problems they had to contend with.

What Carol Meyers has demonstrated is that the verse concerning the woman equally well sums up the plight of those hill-farmers' wives. In the village communities of early pre-monarchic Israel, households made up of extended families, or multiple family groups (such as brothers living together with their families), or a mixture of both, were virtually independent and self-sufficient units. Within the household some tasks were shared among the women and men, some divided between them. Overall the women played as important a part as the men in keeping the households going and in helping them to flourish. The women's life, like the men's, involved a great deal of drudgery, and their work was made more difficult by frequent pregnancies, with all the dangers and almost inevitable grief those brought with them. The average lifespan for a man was forty years; that for a woman thirty. Large families were counted a great blessing, and the survival of the households depended on them. Yet women must have longed for some rest from their work and their pregnancies and child-rearing. But if they decided to have no more children, their desire for their husbands, especially their sexual desire, got the better of them.

This, almost certainly, is the background to and the sense of God's judgement on the woman. We have to jettison parts of the usual translations of the verse, together with the interpretations of it which have held sway for so long. The verse is not about the pains of childbirth, and, more importantly, it is not about any subordination of women.

Far too often these lines have been seen to provide men with a licence to dominate women, a licence, what is more, issued by God himself. It has been used to keep women in their place, a place largely defined by men. Or else both men and women have found its notions abhorrent, and in rejecting it have sometimes rejected the whole story of which it is a part, or even the whole Bible, as hopelessly patriarchal. That is why it is so important to get it right. That is why Carol Meyers is justified in spending over twenty-six pages of her book discussing it.

For the first half of the verse, the majority of translators and commentators offer something akin to the NRSV's

> 'I will greatly increase your pangs in childbearing;
> in pain you shall bring forth children . . .'

But a single Hebrew noun lies behind that translation's 'pangs' and 'pain' in this verse, and its 'toil' in the next, when it deals with the judgement on the man. There it has

'cursed is the ground because of you;
in *toil* you shall eat of it all the days of your life . . .'

That 'toil' quite clearly refers to back-breaking work. There is no good reason to think the Hebrew term means anything different in the case of the woman. Further, Carol Meyers has shown that the Hebrew word translated 'childbearing' by the NRSV (and by other versions) does not mean childbirth, but pregnancy, and that the one in the second line usually rendered as 'bring forth', or in other versions 'give birth to', does not refer specifically to the birth process, but to the business of 'having children' in the sense of becoming or being a parent.[22] These first two lines, then, do not offer comment on the pains of labour and childbirth, but represent, in terms even more pithy than those used to describe the lot of the man, a sharp and sensitive summary of the hardships endured by the women in the villages of early Israel, and quite probably by very many of them throughout the biblical period. With a few brilliant strokes of his pen the writer captures those aspects of their lot that could so easily break their spirits and which eventually broke their bodies.

Having done that, he explains in the second part of the verse how women are trapped in their life of unending toil, unable to break free and find rest. In the case of the man, his drudgery will never come to an end, because of the curse laid upon the ground he works. In the end it will kill him. For the woman, what will trap her is the strength of her sexual desire for her husband. Her life is to be made especially arduous by continual pregnancies and continuous child-rearing. There, in the view of this storyteller, will lie the chief source of her 'toil'. But if she wishes to stop having children, her sexual drive will get the better of her. In the passionate love poetry of the Song of Songs the same very rare term for 'desire' is used once (7.11). There it refers to the love of the man for the woman, and is presented as a cause for huge celebration, like the woman's passion for him. Here in the Garden we had a similar view of sexual desire hinted at in the verses immediately following the woman's creation and the man's welcome of her (2.24–5). But now we are shown a darker side of it. The Song of Songs expresses the elation of those who have fallen passionately in love, and Genesis 2.24–5, and 2.23 also, echo that joy. Now Genesis 3.16 reflects on the harsher aspect of long-established married life, and upon the consequences of their continuing sexual passion for women who had no access to contraception.

It is, of course, in our translation of the last line of God's judgement upon the woman, in our 'for you he will be irresistible', that we depart so far from the usual translations, and where we even leave Carol Meyers behind. The familiar versions have 'he will/shall rule over you' (RSV, NRSV, NIV), 'he will/shall be your master' (NEB, REB), 'he will lord it over you' (JB), or 'he will dominate you' (NJB). Carol Meyers has 'he shall predominate over you'.[23] All of these translations, with the exception of Carol Meyers', presuppose that the storyteller, or rather the poet as he is at this point, is referring in general terms to the subservience of women to men. There are at least two reasons why that is not so. The first is supplied by a verse in the Cain and Abel story which follows in the very next chapter of Genesis, and the second has to do with how Hebrew poetry works.

We have already remarked that 'the very rare' Hebrew noun used for 'desire' in the third line of 3.16 also occurs once in the Song of Songs. In fact the only other place we find it in the whole of the Old Testament is in the Cain and Abel story, and in a pair of lines which play with this second half of 3.16. Genesis 4.7 tells of God's warning to Cain when he is in danger of being overcome with anger for his brother and is plotting to kill him. The latter part of it reads:

> 'If you do not do good,
>   sin is crouching at the door.
> For you will its desire be,
>   but you must master it.'

The Hebrew word we have translated 'master' here is the same as the one that lies behind our 'irresistible' for 3.16. In his speech to Cain, God is quite clearly speaking of a powerful force that Cain must resist; he must not allow it to get the better of him. In the Garden story at 3.16 the woman's sexual desire is presented as a force comparable in its power to Cain's desire to kill his brother, but in her case there is no command to get the better of it, instead a prediction that she will not be able to do so. It will be too strong for her, as in fact Cain's murderous hatred will be for him. Her husband will 'master her', not in the sense that he will overrule her and demand sexual intercourse of her when she is reluctant (that is Carol Meyers' interpretation[24]), but because she will find him quite irresistible.

That explains why the woman's punishment does not refer to any subservience to the man. The way Hebrew poetry works makes plain that the verse *cannot* have such meaning. Throughout the Old

Testament its poetry is generally made up of pairs of lines, or rather of pairs of half-lines. The genius of the poetry lies in the ways in which these pairs are combined with others, and also in the subtle movements within the pairs themselves. A second half-line will carry forward the thought or the image introduced in the first; it will clarify it further, perhaps, intensify it, look at it from a different angle. A good example is provided by the first part of 3.16 itself:

> 'I will increase, yes increase your toil and your pregnancies;
> in the midst of toil will you have children.'

The second line, or half-line in the Hebrew, picks up the language of the first, and by that very repetition adds emphasis to it, but also carries the thought further, and moves from pregnancy to parenthood. The movements are small and subtle. There is nothing dramatic or ostentatious about them, nor do they introduce any thoroughly new thought. That is precisely how Hebrew poetry works within its pairs of half-lines, with small crescendos, subtle variations on a theme. Of course new thoughts, new themes can be introduced, but only by moving from one pair of half-lines to another. It is *virtually inconceivable* that within a single pair of half-lines an Israelite poet could shift from considering the sexual desire of women to any notion of their general subservience to men. That is far too large a jump to make within such a small space.

Once we understand the movement of Hebrew poetry, we have to say that it is all but impossible to read the last part of 3.16 the way it has been read for so long. If we then ask why such a misreading should have held sway all this time, we can only suggest the answer lies in the layers of misogyny that have been heaped upon the text. The notion of the woman as the wicked temptress has so dominated interpretations of the story that translators and commentators have been only too glad to see 3.16 as talking of her being kept in check and under man's control.[25]

Ironically enough, even if our reading of the verse is quite wrong, and our versions and the general run of commentators are right, even if we accept something as blunt as the Jerusalem Bible's translation of the last half-line, 'yet he will lord it over you', the passage still gives no encouragement to those who would seek to keep women under the authority of men. Indeed, *quite the reverse.* For these lines, together with those where God pronounces upon the snake and the man, are meant to encapsulate what is *wrong* with life. They are meant to 'explain' why life for snakes and for human beings is so very hard. They occur towards the end of a story which dreams a fine dream of what life could be like, at least for human beings if not for snakes, if only they could manage to remain obedient to God. On one level such a story is designed to help people come to terms with their lot. But outside the book of Ecclesiastes the Old Testament is decidedly short on fatalism, and much longer on prophetic passion and the call for change. Genesis 2–3 is meant to stir the will, as well as the mind and the emotions. It is meant to help men dream of a life where work is a matter for celebration and not for cursing, and to strive towards a society where that is possible for all. It is designed to enable women to long for a life which is not dominated by drudgery and continual pregnancies and the rearing of small children, and to work for a society in which those longings are fulfilled for all. No one would wish God's judgement on the man in 3.17–19 to mean that all attempts to turn the drudgery of men's labour into fulfilling, self-satisfying work are against the will of God, and to my knowledge no one has done so. No one, therefore, should try to turn God's judgement on the woman, however it is translated and understood, into a justification for the unnecessary hardships women have to endure. Far from supporting the *status quo*, these verses on the woman's and man's plight quietly preach revolution.

There are three other features of 3.16 which invite brief comment before we move on: its length, the way it is introduced (or rather *not* introduced), and the absence of any language of curse.

First, it is much shorter, indeed only half the length of the judgement pronounced upon the snake, or the one delivered upon the man. If we still wish to find the woman the true villain of this piece, then we may think this fact rather curious.

Second, it lacks any reminder in its introduction of what the woman has done. The snake is told, 'Because you have done this . . .' (3.14); the man is reminded (for the second time, the first being in 3.11) that he has disobeyed a divine command (3.17). But God does not point to the woman's own disobedience, he does not underline the gravity of her act. It is as if he accepts her as one more sinned against than sinning, as one who was tricked into taking the fruit, as indeed she was and as she said she was. Again, she hardly emerges from this part of the text as the evil temptress of the familiar stereotype.

Finally, while the snake is cursed, and the man is condemned to working cursed ground, the judgement on the woman contains no curse at all. Her punishment lacks a dimension, an awesome dimension, that both the snake's and the man's have. She, indeed, will be the one who first restores the language of joy and blessing to the narrative, as we shall see in the next section of this chapter.

The woman's return to joy

(Gen. 3.20–4.2a, 25)

The woman's honour and dignity can be rescued in their entirety from the lines declaring her punishment. Immediately God ceases speaking, however, the male bias of the story reasserts itself. The man names his wife, and calls her Eve (3.20). The narrator, with another play on words, explains the name: 'because she became the mother of all living' (in the Hebrew the words for 'Eve' and 'living' are similar). When we came earlier to the man's calling the newly created woman 'woman', we rejected any notion that he was asserting his authority over her. Now we cannot be so sure. It would be comforting to find Eve (we can call her that now) giving the man a name in the next verse, but we do not. The man remains simply 'the man', and as the text of the NRSV makes clear, *'adam* does not become the proper name Adam until suddenly it appears in that form in 4.25. The verse leaves us with disconcerting questions: Is the man's naming Eve a further indication of the breakdown of their relationship? Does he now bid for an ugly power over her that goes far beyond that given him by the strength of her sexual desire? If it is, and he does, then even more disconcertingly the narrator has God coming in on the act. In the final verses of the chapter, where the expulsion from the Garden is described, the woman is entirely absent from the text. Verses 22–4 speak only of 'the man'. Once more, it is as if the woman were not there. We cannot explain her disappearance from these verses by saying that only the man is expelled. As we all know, and as many great artists have poignantly portrayed, Eve is driven out along with him. We can only talk of an unconscious male bias in the writing, unless we suppose the storyteller has left the woman out of the story, as he did for a time when the couple first hid themselves from God, in order to indicate how much things are spoiled and all awry. In the end we cannot penetrate the author's mind here. Yet we will notice in our subsequent chapters, with the exception of the one on Hagar, that God seems much more ready to have direct dealings with men than with women. This may be enough to explain why in 3.9 he calls only to the man, and why now, in 3.22–4, his speech and action should leave the woman unmentioned. Perhaps we can see the influence of the Israelite cult at work here, a cult which was led and almost entirely staffed by men, and which therefore taught people to think primarily of men as the mediators between God and his people, and as the ones he was used to dealing with.

Yet still, if we return to the woman's new name, we find it double-edged. It may symbolize a bid by the man for power over her, but what a name it is! 'Mother of all living'! It is more a title than a name, and the grandest of all titles, too. It is a title fit for a goddess, and, indeed, 'mother of all living' is a phrase applied by Ben Sirach to Mother Earth (Sirach [or Ecclesiasticus] 40.1). No wonder, then, that once outside the Garden, and after conceiving and bearing her first child, she should greet her son's arrival with the joyful cry, 'I have created a man just as the Lord did!' (4.1b). Our translation, 'just as . . . did' is an attempt to interpret a single, two-letter Hebrew word, whose sense is not entirely clear. Most probably Eve is comparing her bringing her son into the world to God's own creation of the man in chapter 2.[26] She too is a creator!

In fact, this verse takes us back to chapter 2 in more ways than one. Eve's joy echoes the joy the man expressed when he first saw her. The verse begins with the words 'Now the man knew his wife Eve and she conceived and gave birth to . . .' (4.1a). His 'knowing her' (a beautiful and profound euphemism for sexual intercourse, common in the Old Testament), reminds us of the narrator's comment after the man's welcome of her, when he referred to a man clinging to his wife and their becoming one flesh. 'Knowing' in chapter 3 was dangerous, and came to mean fear, defencelessness, the ruining of relationships. Now it means pleasure, joy, and the couple's returning to one another. So this verse takes us back not just to chapter 2, but to its triumphant climax, to the point in the story, the *only* point in the story, when all was well. It would seem that things outside the Garden will not be so bad after all, despite the fact that the male standpoint is so evident, with the man taking the initiative in 'knowing' Eve, and with her being described as 'his wife'. And the next verse begins with the birth of a second son! But if our hopes are now high, then let us remember the names of these children. They are Cain and Abel.

There is one more mention of Eve, at 4.25: 'Adam knew his wife again, and she bore a son and named him Seth, for she said, "God has set for me another seed in Abel's stead, for Cain killed him."' Another play on words (Seth is similar to the Hebrew word for 'set'), and another cry of joy. In the Hebrew of the verse as we have it the play on words does not quite work, and it looks as though the reference to Cain and Abel might have been added as an afterthought.[27] Without it Eve's joy is unalloyed. In the final form of the verse it is dulled by dark memories of the loss of her second child at the hands of her first. Though she now does the naming of the child,[28] balancing, to some extent, Adam's naming of her, we are not back in Eden after all. Chapter 5, as if to rub this in, lists the descendants of Adam, and tells us of his death and how long he lived, but does not mention Eve at all. Her name will occur only twice more in the entire Bible: in 2 Corinthians 11.3 and in 1 Timothy 2.13, both passages where she finds herself maligned, and which together bear much responsibility for the cruel treatment she has received over the centuries, and for the misunderstanding that has so often hidden her story from our sight. Adam's name, beyond Genesis 5, will be used twelve times, and Paul will coin his doctrine of Jesus as the New Adam. No New Eve.[29]

2

Sarah: A Woman Caught up in God's Promises

(Genesis 11.29–23.20)

Scholars generally refer to Genesis 12–50 as 'the patriarchal narratives', or 'the patriarchal story'. It is easy to see why. The chapters are primarily concerned with the male ancestors, the founding fathers, the patriarchs of the people of Israel, that is with Abraham, Isaac, Jacob, and Joseph and his brothers. God plays the most significant part in their story, but they, at least Abraham, Jacob, and Joseph and his brothers, have the biggest supporting roles. They have more lines to speak than anyone else, more things and a greater variety of things to do; they are on stage for longer and more frequent periods than any other characters. Nevertheless, the titles 'patriarchal story' or 'patriarchal narratives' hide from our view the remarkable parts played by other 'minor' characters, and, in particular, encourage us to neglect the importance of the roles played in these chapters by women. Genesis 12–50 is concerned with a family, a particular household. As we noticed in Chapter 1, women played highly significant roles in the households of ancient Israel. It is hardly surprising, therefore, that Genesis should tell us a good deal about the likes of Sarah, Rebekah, Rachel and Leah.

We would do better to call Genesis 12–50 'the ancestral narratives',[1] so as to do the main female characters greater justice. After all, Sarah, Rebekah, Rachel and Leah all play parts as large as, if not larger, than the second of the patriarchs, Isaac. Nevertheless, as we examine the chapters in which Sarah features, we will notice a huge disparity between the amount of space devoted to her and that given to her husband Abraham. While we will inevitably spend most of our time on those stories which have her on stage, we will also have to pay heed to those stories in which she is *not* present. Along the way we will encounter two passages which feature her together with her Egyptian maid Hagar. Hagar will be the subject of our third chapter, so we will be analysing those particular stories twice. However, we will try to avoid repeating ourselves unduly. In Hagar's chapter we will be looking at things from Hagar's point of view; in this, we will be looking at them from Sarah's.

Neither Sarah nor Abraham carry around with them as many of our preconceptions as did the woman and the man of the Garden of Eden. Nevertheless, the image of Abraham as the exemplary man of faith has come to dominate our thinking about him, and Sarah sometimes basks briefly in his glory. Because of what passages such as Romans 4, Galatians 3 and Hebrews 11 have to say about Abraham, it is hard for us to approach the text of Genesis with an open mind. We know already what to think. But if that is the case, then either we are in for some surprises, or else, clinging to our prejudices, we will miss what the stories are trying to tell us. For in truth, Abraham is far from being a saint in Genesis, and the same goes for Sarah. Abraham was turned into a saint by the Jewish theologians of the period between the Old and New Testaments, and sometimes Sarah was given something of a halo herself. That thinking had a profound influence on the writers of the New Testament, and led to the two-dimensional pictures of Abraham and Sarah we find in the Epistles. In Genesis itself they are fully rounded characters, subtly drawn, with their strengths matched – one is tempted to say *more* than matched – by their weaknesses. They are, in a word, all too 'human' there, and the narrator rarely tells us explicitly what to make of them. Sometimes, by the way he writes his story, he points us in a certain direction, but still he leaves much of the work to us, and allows us to form our own judgements. The New Testament passages have their own value, of course, and their own importance. But we must put them aside as we approach Genesis, put out of our minds any notions of patriarchal or matriarchal sanctity, and allow Sarah and Abraham to doff their haloes.

A barren woman

(Gen. 11.27–12.3)

Sarah, or rather Sarai as she is for the present (and will remain until 17.15), first appears in a short passage (11.27–32) which tells us of Abraham's, or Abram's, origins (he will not become Abraham until 17.5). We are informed that Abram had a father called Terah, who lived in Ur, and that he had two brothers, Haran and Nahor; that Haran had a son called Lot, and that Abram and Nahor also 'took wives'. The name of Abram's was Sarai, that of Nahor's Milcah. We are given the names of the father and sister of Milcah. We are told nothing of Sarai's parentage or siblings. We are told only one thing about her, and yet it is of such significance that it will help to determine the course of the narrative for the next nine chapters: 'Now Sarai was barren; she had no child' (11.30). As is usual in the Old Testament, the lack of children is put down to the wife, not the husband. As is typical of Hebrew narrative, the bare outlines of such a momentous statement as this are not coloured in. Though her barrenness is underlined by the 'she had no child', and by the reminder in the next verse that Terah had a grandson in Lot, Sarai's own feelings are not touched upon. The narrator leaves them entirely to our imagination. Not until chapter 16 will they begin to come to the surface of the text. Then we will know something of her pain.

The full significance of Sarai's condition does not become clear until, with the start of chapter 12, Abram receives the famous command and promises of God:

> 'Go from your country and your kindred and your father's house to the land that I will show you. I will make of you a great nation, and I will bless you, and make your name great. And be a blessing!² I will bless those who bless you, and the one who curses you I will curse, and in you all the families of the earth shall be blessed.' (12.1–3)

The promise of becoming a great nation and gaining a great name depend in the first place on Abram having a child, and, since in ancient Israel the inheritance of a family was passed on through the male line, a male child. Without such a child, and children after him, the promise of a land will not mean much either, for after Abram's and Sarai's death it will have nobody in it, or else it will only have the wrong people. And in a culture where children were regarded as one of God's greatest blessings, it would also seem strange for a childless man to be a source of blessing for all the families of the earth. So it *all* depends on Abram having a son. And Sarai is barren. Either, then, she will not be the child's mother, and Abram will have to find another wife, or God will have to heal her barrenness. Not until the middle of chapter 17 will we discover which of those options God has in mind. For the time being let us notice once more Sarai's plight. *Everything* depends on Abram having a son, and she, his wife, cannot give him one. God's promises to Abram represent, if we look back to Genesis 1–11, his new initiative for the redemption of the world, his most important creative act since the creation itself.[3] In that great venture Sarai can, it seems, play no part for the present, except, through her barrenness, to obstruct its fulfilment. Is that why the promises are not given to both Sarai and Abram, but only to Abram? It will turn out to be more complicated than that, but for the moment we can notice that there is no mention of Sarai in those extraordinary verses at the start of chapter 12. God will repeat the promises many times to Abram and will expand upon them (in 12.7; 13.14–17; ch. 15; 17.1–22; 18.10–14; 21.12–13, and 22.1–18), but not once will he address them to Sarai. The particular promise that is most pertinent to her, she will have to overhear!

'Say you are my sister'

(Gen. 12.10–20)

'So Abram went, as the Lord had told him' (12.4). With those fine words the narrative continues. Yet if they put Abram on a high pedestal of obedience and faith, all too soon we find ourselves caught up in a story which knocks him on to the floor and puts a pharaoh's boot on his back for good measure.

With divine guidance he has 'taken' Sarai and Lot and the rest of his entourage straight into the Land of Promise. Before the end of 12.5 they are in Canaan. Only five verses later, however, they are out of it again, and on the borders of Egypt. Famine has driven them there, as it will Joseph's brothers at the other end of the ancestral narratives. That Egypt, the one in which Joseph and his brothers settle, the one to which Jacob comes to die, will for their descendants turn out to be the land of bondage, the very opposite of the land to which they have been called. Its pharaohs will prove themselves tyrants of the worst kind. This Egypt, Abram's and Sarai's Egypt, has a pharaoh whose righteousness will put the 'righteous' Abram to shame. This Egypt will bring Abram a harsh and well-earned rebuke, but send him away a rich man. This Egypt will be the place where Abram sacrifices Sarai on the altar of his own fear and self-interest. It will be the place where their marriage very nearly comes to an end, and Abram puts the bright promises of God in great jeopardy. It will also be the place where God comes wielding great plagues to rescue Sarai from the pharaoh's embrace, as in the early chapters of Exodus he will arrive again in similar fashion to rescue his people, and will then find the pharaoh in office considerably more difficult to deal with. Thus this little story at the start of the ancestral narratives will foreshadow the events that lie at the heart of the Old Testament's gospel. Sarai will 'play the part' of the trapped Israelites, but if there is a villain of this piece, then it is not the pharaoh, but Abram, her husband.

It begins on the Egyptian border. Abram is afraid:

> . . . he said to his wife, Sarai, 'I know well that you are a woman beautiful in appearance, and when the Egyptians see you, they will say, "This is his wife"; then they will kill me, but they will let you live. Say, please, you are my sister, so that it may go well with me because of you, and that my life may be spared on your account.' (12.11–13)

Claus Westermann tries to explain that Abram's fear is readily understandable.[4] With famine at his back and the mighty Egypt in front of him, Abram feels immensely vulnerable. Sarai's presence only makes things worse for him, for he knows that the country is ruled by a pharaoh so powerful that he can have any woman he likes at the drop of an eyelid. And so he resorts to a trick: 'Say, please, you are my sister.' 'The ruse', says Westermann, 'is the only weapon left for the powerless given over to the mighty.'[5] Quite so, but what a trick it is, and see how the narrator presents it to us! Though he does not tell us what Sarai feels about it – she has nothing to say and no initiative to take in the whole story – he goes out of his way to emphasize that Abram's motives are those of fear and self-interest alone, and are upheld at Sarai's expense: '. . . then they will kill *me*, but they will let *you* live . . . so that it may go well with *me* because of *you*, and that *my* life may be spared on *your* account.' As we said when we were looking at Eve's story, the storytellers of Genesis do not generally tell us the motives of their characters. Here Abram's motives are quite clearly stated, *three times!*

If Abram is vulnerable, what of Sarai? If Abram is powerless, then how much power does Sarai have? Abram has no thought for her and for what might happen to her. He has no thought for his marriage. He shows, indeed, no concern for the promises of God that he carries down to Egypt with him. He still has no son, the son on whom everything depends, and how will he gain one when his wife is taken away, as surely she will be, by Egyptians believing his story about her being his sister? What then? There will then be no point to any curing of her barrenness that God might have in mind. Abram will have to take another wife. Has he thought of that? Has *Sarai* thought of that? Still the story tells us nothing about her feelings. Abram does what he likes with her, and thus cruelly mimics what he fears the pharaoh might do.

Abram's trick works . . . and the worst, or very nearly the worst, happens. The Egyptians do indeed notice Sarai's beauty, and they believe Abram's story. But instead of pursuing her themselves, they take reports of her to their pharaoh, and sing her praises in his throne room. As a result she is 'taken' into the pharaoh's household. This is the third time since she has been introduced to us in 11.29 that Sarai has been 'taken', and this 'taken' is particularly alarming, not just because it further underlines her powerlessness, but because we will soon learn that it means the pharaoh has 'taken' her for his wife.

It is alright for Abram! As the male of the family who has surrendered his 'sister', he gets a huge bride price from the pharaoh: 'And for her sake he dealt well with Abram; and he had sheep, oxen, male donkeys, male and female slaves, female donkeys, and camels' (12.16). He hoped it would 'go well' with him if Sarai said she was his sister. Well, it most certainly has! There is something of a rags to riches story about this, and there is also a somewhat coarse and very male humour at work. Look what the 'simple nomad' has got from the pharaoh! All this from the greatest king in the world! And what a price he gets for his lovely 'sister'! We have been taught over the years not to expect humour in the Bible. In fact, there is plenty of it, at least in the Old Testament, and I feel sure it is intended here. Yet, if we persist in looking at this story from Sarai's angle, we will not find it funny at all, and if we do not, then we are in the best of company, because God himself does not see the joke. God takes things very seriously, with the deadly seriousness of 'great plagues', which he inflicts upon the pharaoh and his household. The pharaoh does not see the divine hand in these calamities, but he is inspired enough to realize at once the reason for them, to understand Sarai's true status, and to realize that all unwitting he has committed adultery. He summons Abram. 'What is this you have done to me? Why did you not tell me that she was your wife? Why did you say, "She is my sister," so that I took her for my wife?' (12.18–19a).

Abram's initial fears were exaggerated. The Egyptians he has encountered have not been men driven by lust and violence. Their pharaoh is a just and honourable man, who responds to divine prompting with supernatural insight. Yet now, surely, he has much to fear. He stands before the most powerful monarch in the world, accused of the most terrible deception, and responsible for the most appalling suffering having been inflicted upon the king and his household. Surely now he will die, Sarai will find herself a widow in a foreign land, and God will have to start all over again in his plan to redeem his world. But no. The story has one more surprise for us: 'Now then, here is your wife, take her, and be gone' (12.19b). With those curt commands, even more terse in the original Hebrew (literally translated it is, 'Here, your wife. Take, and go!'), Abram is sent packing, and he and Sarai and his entourage are expelled from Egypt, as the Israelites will later be ordered out of it at the Exodus (see Exod. 12.31–2, which has the same 'take . . . and go'), and as the man and woman were expelled from Eden. The story-teller does not allow Abram to respond to the pharaoh's questions. Like the man in the Garden, he might have said, 'I was afraid.' Like the snake in the Garden, he is certainly guilty of a most fearful deception. Like the woman in the Garden, he has been asked, 'What is this you have done?', and like her he has had no answer to give. The storyteller does not pass judgement upon him. Having written the story as he has, he does not need to. And we will find Abram doing it again, and, if he is to be believed, again and again!

And still Sarai has not said a word. Still she has not done anything, only had things done to her. Still she is to be 'taken'. It would be good to think of her as the calm centre of this stormy narrative, the innocent and heroic victim of men's machinations. But the text does not allow us even to do her that service. Innocent she is, certainly, for when the pharaoh summons Abram he confronts him with what *he* has done, and does not accuse Sarai at all. And God comes riding into Egypt on his black horse with the specific purpose of rescuing her. We cannot, however, call her 'calm' or 'heroic', for we have no evidence to go on. Her fears, her reactions, her faith are completely neglected. She has no power here even to evoke our admiration.

Another ruse turns sour

(Gen. 16.1–6, 15–16)

It is not until chapter 16 that Sarai appears again in the narrative. Meanwhile Abram has been extremely busy. He has sorted out a

serious conflict between his herdsmen and Lot's; he has settled
with his nephew what parts of the Promised Land each of them
should live in; he has had the extent of the land that his descendants
will occupy confirmed by God, and has walked the length and
breadth of it to stake his claim upon it; he has himself settled in a
place called Mamre; he has built his third altar; he has gone on a
daring raid to rescue Lot from capture; he has been met on his
triumphal return by the king of Sodom and has played the part of
the magnanimous hero; he has been blessed by Melchizedek,
priest-king of Jerusalem (called Salem in the text); he has had his
second vision of God, and his first dialogue with him; he has taken
part in an awesome ceremony in which God has made a covenant
with him and has declared himself under solemn obligation to fulfil
his promises; most important of all, as far as Sarai is concerned,
he has been assured by God that he will have a son of his own,
though he is not informed who the mother will be. In all this Sarai
has played no visible part. She has not been on stage, nor been
mentioned at any point.

When she emerges again at the start of chapter 16, we are
reminded at once of the way she was introduced to us in chapter
11: 'Now Sarai, Abram's wife, bore him no children' (16.1). We
are back to where we began, and still the narrator persists in seeing
things from Abram's angle. Indeed his emphasis seems to have
shifted further away from Sarai since the first mention of her
barrenness. The 'she had no child' of 11.30 has now become '[she]
bore him no children'. His wording reminds us of the importance
of a child for Abram, but encourages us to forget how significant
one would be for Sarai. Yet in the very next verse, for the very first
time, she is allowed to act on her own initiative and to speak. 'She
had an Egyptian slave-girl whose name was Hagar. Sarai said to
Abram, "See, please, the Lord has stopped me from bearing
children; go, please, to my slave-girl; it may be that I shall be built
up through her"' (16.1b–2). Even when she was on stage in the
story of Abram's trick in Egypt, she remained deep in the shadows
of the men surrounding her. Then we could scarcely make out her
outline; now she steps out into the open, and we begin to see her
features.

'The ruse is the only weapon left for the powerless given over to
the mighty.' That was Claus Westermann's comment on Abram's
trick in Egypt.[6] It might be ours now on Sarai's own ploy.
'The mighty' are no longer the pharaoh and the lustful, violent
Egyptians of Abram's fantasy. The threat to Sarai is more subtle
than that. For her now 'the mighty' are her husband, her God, and

the narrator. See with what caution and what great courtesy she speaks!

We must be careful not to exaggerate the brightness of the light these stories cast on the position of women in ancient Israel. We must not jump to the conclusion that their only role and function was to bear children, especially male children, to their husbands. Nevertheless, as 16.1 has reminded us, in *these narratives* that is what Sarai is there for. From God's first declaration of his promises to Abram at the beginning of chapter 12, through to the birth of Isaac in chapter 21, the stories are dominated, implicitly or explicitly, by the theme of an heir, a son – or rather by the theme of his absence. Though she does not learn of God's promises until chapter 18, Sarai is caught up in them from the beginning. Her role and function are limited to those the narrator has given her, and her position with regard to her husband, though not as subservient as we might expect, as we shall soon see, cannot fail to be affected by the dominant position that he occupies in the narrative as a whole.

In the face of all this might, Sarai at last attempts to gain some power for herself. Despairing of ever conceiving a child of her own, she offers her husband her slave-girl Hagar, in the hope that she might be 'built up' through her. Her despair is understandable. As we learn from 16.3, she and Abram have already been in Canaan ten years. How long they were married before that, the narrator does not tell us, but we do not need him to do so. Ten years and more is a long time to wait, an agonizingly long time, as many couples will still testify. Sarai, in her offer of Hagar, is not showing a lack of faith. She is simply being realistic. We might ask why she has not come up with the plan before this.

Interestingly enough, her plan is beginning to have a contemporary ring about it. The question of the surrogate mother is now on our agenda also. But while for us it is a relatively new one to consider, for the people of ancient Israel, and other nations in the Ancient Near East, it was not a question but an established practice.[7] Genesis has further cases to offer. In chapter 30, for example, the barren Rachel gives her maid Bilhah to her husband Jacob, while his other wife, Leah, realizing she is too old to conceive any more, gives him her maid Zilpah.[8] The children of such unions were counted as the offspring not only of the husbands who fathered them, but of the original wives whose slaves the natural mothers were. So now, in this story, any child born to Hagar will count as Sarai's child. That is why she hopes that she will 'be built up' through her. If Hagar has a child, Sarai will at last be able to shake off the status of the barren wife.

That is what she *hopes* will happen. But, like the snake in the Garden, hope can deceive, and as it turns out, Sarai's plan quickly goes awry. Hagar does at once conceive, and she will give Abram a son. But Sarai gains only further humiliation, as we shall soon see, while the son does not turn out to be the one who will inherit the promises of God, the one on whom everything depends. It transpires that Sarai's ruse is something of a red herring as far as the larger narrative is concerned. For that reason some commentators have censured her for a lack of faith, for trying (after more than ten years of waiting!) to force the pace of God's purposes, instead of continuing to wait patiently for him to give her a son. John Calvin, in his sixteenth-century commentary, did so,[9] and in 1956 the German scholar Gerhard von Rad was still able to comment on Sarai (and Abram) falling into 'severe temptation'.[10]

Let us get a few things straight. Let us return to reading these stories as if we were reading them for the first time, not knowing what the outcome will be. It is easy, then, for us to see Sarai not as obstructing the purposes of God, but as trying the only thing she can think of to remove the obstacle of her barrenness from the path of their fulfilment. Though she has not heard the promises of God, it is as if she understands them, and wishes to serve them. Interestingly enough, one Hebrew word of verse 2 would appear to back up that interpretation. It is the one we translated as 'I shall be built up'. Our versions tend not to translate it so literally, and the NRSV is typical, with its 'I shall obtain children'. Such a paraphrase does not allow the Hebrew to ring the bells it might. As Sharon Jeansonne has pointed out in her book *The Women of Genesis*, the term 'build up' is used elsewhere of establishing a people.[11] At first sight it seems from 16.2 that Sarai is thinking only of herself. That one word in the Hebrew text hints that she has larger (very much larger) purposes in view. One thing is certain: for all the conflict it produces, her ruse does not seriously threaten the purposes of God – unlike Abram's trick in Egypt.

However, it does pay Hagar's needs as little heed as Abram paid Sarai's in chapter 12; it results in the humiliation of its perpetrator, as happened in the earlier story; Sarai is rebuked by the narrator, as Abram was rebuked by the pharaoh; and the passage finds an ending in another expulsion.

At first, as happened at least for Abram in Egypt, with all his slaves, sheep, oxen, donkeys and camels, things go remarkably well. Sarai 'takes' Hagar (this is the first time Sarai has done the taking; hitherto others have taken her) and gives her to Abram 'as a wife'. Then the story goes on: Abram 'went in to Hagar, and she conceived' (16.4). It is all so simple. Sarai has been waiting for a child for well over ten years. Now what seems to be the first act of sexual intercourse between her husband and her maid results in conception (and will end up producing a son!).

Elsewhere in the Old Testament such notice of conception is usually followed straightaway by the news of the birth. Not this one. We will have to wait until the end of the chapter for Hagar's child to be born, and meanwhile we are allowed to dwell on her pregnancy. At once things go wrong for Sarai: '. . . and when she [Hagar] saw that she had conceived, her mistress became contemptible in her eyes' (16.4b). When Sarai gave Hagar to Abram as his secondary wife, she gave her a status far higher than the one she enjoyed as her slave. But she assumed that her own status would be enhanced by any child born of their union. Now that Hagar is pregnant, the reality of things turns out to be very different. Hagar has turned the tables on her. The utterly power-less foreign slave has shown what female power there is to be found in fertility, and what degradation lies in barrenness. Sarai is now far beneath her. The Hebrew verb used to express Sarai's loss of status, her becoming 'contemptible', is the same one as the poet of the Book of Job uses to describe Job's sense of his smallness in the awesome presence of his God (see Job 40.4). No wonder, then, that all the bitterness of her years of unfulfilled longing, all her sense of failure, and all her disappointment at the dashing of her new hope come spilling out in dark words of accusation: 'Then Sarai said to Abram, "May the violence done to me be on you! I gave my slave-girl to your embrace, and when she saw that she had conceived, I became contemptible in her eyes. May the Lord judge between you and me!"' (16.5). At last we hear her pain, and it is now greater than before. In the conception of her ruse (the only thing she could conceive) she glimpsed for a moment, for the first time, some hope, a way out. Now it has left her even more degraded. Her feelings are summed up in the word 'violence'. My Hebrew dictionary explains, somewhat quaintly, that it often refers to the 'rude wickedness of men, their noisy, wild ruthlessness'.[12] It is the term used in Genesis 6.11 to describe the lamentable state of the earth before the Flood. There it is precisely because of the world's 'violence' that God decides to go within a hair's breadth of ending it all. Hagar may be the one who is pregnant, but by the use of that word 'violence' the narrator suggests it is Sarai who is left feeling as if she has been raped.

And Abram only makes things worse. He does not appear to hear her accusations. If he does, he does not respond with anger, nor seek to defend himself. He does not seem to hear her pain. If he does, he gives her no comfort, no embrace, no love. He remains detached, aloof both from her and from his new wife. He reminds Sarai that Hagar is still her slave-girl. She can do with her what she likes. His detachment is most cruel, and results, not surprisingly, in more cruelty: 'Then Sarai dealt harshly with her [Hagar], and she ran away from her' (16.6b). As is often the case in the more sophisticated narratives of the Old Testament, tragedy is laced with irony. The Hebrew word for 'dealt harshly' is the one the narrator put in the mouth of God just a few verses before our story, at 15.13, when he was telling Abram of the oppression his descendants would suffer at the hands of the Egyptians. Hagar, we remember, is an Egyptian. Her people will get their own back. We have God's word on it.

For Sarai, and for the rest of us, this particular scene is at an end. When the curtain goes up again we find ourselves in the desert with Hagar, and in the extraordinary territory we will cover in our next chapter. Yet before we leave this part of the story, we must see how it ends. Hagar returns, and the narrator concludes with these words: 'Hagar bore Abram a son; and Abram named his son, whom Hagar bore, Ishmael. Abram was eighty-six years old when Hagar bore him Ishmael' (16.15–16). Sarai does not appear in these verses at all. The narrator has left her alone in her bitterness. She hoped at the beginning of the story that she might be built up by Hagar's child. But this Hagar has born Abram a child, not she. She hoped at the start that a child from Hagar might 'cure' her of her own barrenness. Now, at the story's end, the narrator thrice underlines her inability to have children by thrice telling us that Hagar has given birth to a son. Sarai *will* have her barrenness taken away. But she will have to wait another fourteen years.

Sarah's big moment

(Gen. 17.15–16)

Sarai has her next entrance in chapter 18, and she will then reappear as Sarah. Chapter 17 is almost entirely taken up with God speaking to Abram, or Abraham, as he is now renamed. As soon as he appears to him, he identifies himself as God Almighty, and Abram prostrates himself before him, as well he might. Then God declares: 'No longer shall your name be Abram, but your name shall be Abraham; for I have made you the ancestor of a multitude of nations. I will make you exceedingly fruitful; and I will make nations of you, and kings shall come from you' (17.5–6).

Surrounding this speech is repeated talk of covenant, between God and Abraham and between God and Abraham's particular descendants, the Israelites; the promise to them of the land of Canaan is renewed; and the practice of male circumcision is solemnly introduced as the mark to be worn by Abraham and his male descendants, an indelible reminder to them and to God himself of the binding agreement between them.

Then the passage proceeds with yet more solemn promises:

'As for Sarai your wife, you shall not call her Sarai, but Sarah shall be her name. I will bless her, and moreover I will give you a son by her. I will bless her, and she shall give rise to nations; kings of peoples shall come from her.' (17.15–16)

The commentaries tell us that, in fact, 'Sarai' is probably just an old form of 'Sarah', and that the two names mean the same thing. Yet for the narrator and his hearers the change must have been more significant. It is possible they thought the name Sarai meant Mockery.[13] Certainly Sarah means Princess.

So now, for the first time, Abraham and we, the readers of the story, learn that Sarah will have a son. The 'mockery' of her barrenness will soon be over, and instead she will have – indeed already has – the status of a princess. Moreover, the child to be born to her will be the son that we have been waiting for ever since the story began. The twice repeated 'I will bless her' takes us back to God's first pronouncement of the promises to Abraham in chapter 12, and echoes their language. Since Genesis 1 the talk of 'blessing' has been laden with fertility, and so here. Sarah will be able to perform the role for which the narrator has created her. At last she will be able to play her part in the fulfilment of the promises of God. At last she belongs to the world of those promises. She is no longer an outsider. How tragic, then, that at this, her great moment, she is not on stage! Such fine words have been spoken, such momentous words have issued from the mouth of God, and she is not there to hear them!

The bias of the chapter reveals itself in other ways, too. Verses 15–16 balance verses 5–6, but they do not achieve equilibrium. Sarah will only have one child, and even that she will bear for her husband, not for herself. Abraham, by contrast, will be made 'exceedingly fruitful' (he already has Ishmael, of course, and after Sarah's death he will marry another wife, Keturah, and have *six* children by her; 25.1–2). God does not speak of making a covenant with Sarah, and there is no mention of any equivalent to circumcision for her and her female descendants. They will not bear God's mark upon their bodies, nor carry the sign of his everlasting commitment.

And if the narrator is biased, so is Abraham! To all the fine promises of the first part of the chapter he does not react. He does not think it at all ridiculous that he should be the ancestor of a multitude of nations. But as soon as Sarah's name is mentioned, he falls on his face with laughter. 'Can a child be born to a man who is a hundred years old? Can Sarah, who is ninety years old, bear a child? . . . O that Ishmael might live in your sight!' (17.17– 18). Of course, the idea that they will have a child at their age *is* absurd! When the child is born, his birth will break all human rules and be quite astonishing, utterly miraculous. Yet Abraham laughs prostrate before his God, in the attitude of worship. His laughter, for all that it is understandable, comes uncomfortably close to blasphemy. It is also prophetic. For God responds by saying: 'No, but your wife Sarah shall bear you a son, and you shall name him Isaac . . . my covenant I will establish with Isaac, whom Sarah shall bear to you at this season next year' (17.19, 21). In Hebrew, Isaac means 'he laughs'. Sarah will bring Laughter into the world, she will bring laughter to Abraham (for again, twice, it is said she will bear *him* a child). Whether she will laugh herself – and if so, for how long – remains to be seen. For the moment, we must rest content with the new information these two verses give us, about the name the child will have, and the time of his birth. Sodom and Gomorrah will be destroyed before that time comes, and Abraham will put God's whole plan in the greatest danger once again. But first Sarah needs to learn what God has in mind for her.

'No, but you did laugh'

(Gen. 18.1–15)

Once more God appears to Abraham, but this time in disguise. The Hebrew makes things clearer than our English versions. 'The Lord appeared to Abraham by the oaks of Mamre, as he sat at the entrance of his tent in the heat of the day. He looked up and saw three men standing near him' (18.1–2a). That is how the NRSV has it. In the Hebrew original the word for 'appeared' in verse 1 is the same verb as the one for 'saw' in verse 2. Thus the Hebrew shows more plainly what is going on: what is actually there in front of Abraham is God himself; what he *sees* is three men. In chapter 17 he knew who he was talking to. Now he does not, and what is more he never penetrates the disguise.

Still finding it hard to break the idol of the righteous Abraham, we may find it hard to see that at points the narrator of Genesis turns him into something of a buffoon. In Egypt, in chapter 12, he wears the dress of a comic character, despite his cruel treatment of Sarah – of course, comic characters are not always nice. He plays the part there of a country bumpkin, who, not reckoning with the possibility of divine intervention, tries to pull a fast one on the sophisticated Egyptians and gets a severe ticking off from the pharaoh for his pains. In chapter 23 he will wear nearly the same costume, and be taken for a very long ride when he buys a burial plot for Sarah from the clever men of Hebron. Now here, in chapter 18, he sits at the entrance of his tent sucking straw and tinkling the bells on his toes.

At first the story proceeds as if it were simply a tale of fine oriental hospitality, and God says and does nothing to suggest that he is not what he seems to be. Abraham greets the 'three men' with supreme courtesy. He runs to meet them, he bows low to the ground, he addresses one of them as 'My Lord' (there is a marvellous ambiguity and irony about that, of course: he has, by accident, given God the name by which he was most often called![14]), he refers to himself, twice, as their servant, and he entreats them to stop and rest while he fetches them 'a little water' and 'a morsel of bread' – he cannot allow them to think they are causing him any trouble, or that he is blowing the trumpet of his own generosity. Then all is hustle and bustle. He rushes into the tent – one is sorely tempted to say 'the kitchen' – to find Sarah. 'Quick! Three measures of best flour! Knead it and make cakes!' (18.6). There is a delicious but highly disconcerting contrast, which is even more obvious in the Hebrew, between the elaborate formality of his earlier courtesy and these curt, breathless orders that he gives to Sarah. This is no way to talk to a princess, even if you do happen to be married to her! Sarah is treated no better than the slave who has to prepare the rest of the meal, and roast the calf that Abraham chooses from his herd. Like the slave, she does not speak, she remains on the outskirts of the action, hidden from the view of the 'men', as etiquette dictates. When the meal begins, and Abraham waits on his guest(s), her vast pile of cakes (the quantity of flour Abraham ordered her to use was quite enormous!) does not get a mention, only the calf, and the curds and milk that Abraham has himself supplied.

So far, if not entirely good, then fairly unremarkable, except for the size of the meal – a whole calf, as well as all those cakes and the curds and milk – and except, of course, for the fact that we know that the guests are God himself. But then the dialogue suddenly becomes mysterious. 'Where is your wife Sarah?' (18.9). How do 'they' know her name is Sarah? Well, *we* know the answer to that. It does not occur to Abraham to ask! 'There, in the tent,' he says, thinking he is being straightforward. Nor does he fall to wondering why his guest(s) should enquire after his wife. No one in these narratives has asked after her before. Suddenly *we* begin to think that Sarah might not be so much on the edge of this story as we imagined. Does God's question indicate why he has turned up for dinner? Has he really come about Sarah? Is she really at the centre of the story, even though we cannot see her, hidden away as she is in the tent? This God has paid Abraham so much attention. After his fine words of 17.15–16, is he now turning his attention to Sarah? It would seem so, for he responds to Abraham's 'in the tent' by saying: 'I will surely return to you at lifetide,[15] and your wife Sarah shall have a son' (18.10). Who has been making promises of a son to Abraham, but God himself? Who was it who assured him in the previous chapter that Sarah would have a child the following year, if not the same God? Yet still Abraham plays the buffoon. Still the penny refuses to drop. Indeed, the story moves away from Abraham and his reaction; its spotlight swings round, and for the first time its beam catches Sarah.

> And Sarah was listening at the tent entrance behind him. Now Abraham and Sarah were old, advanced in age; it had ceased to be with Sarah after the manner of women. So Sarah laughed to herself, saying, 'Worn out as I am, shall I have pleasure? And my husband is old!' (18.10b–12)

It is only her third speech since she was first introduced in chapter 11, and it is her most famous. There are a number of things about it for us to notice. First, it would seem that Abraham has not told her the glad tidings that God conveyed to him about her in chapter 17! We may laugh about a lack of communication between the aged husband and his wife, but when we return to seeing things from Sarah's angle, Abraham's silence seems intolerably cruel. She has been waiting for years and years to hear the news that Abraham was given in chapter 17. Now she has to hear it, quite obviously for the first time, from the lips of 'a stranger'. Indeed, and this is our second point, she has to *over*hear it! That detail of the story, so central to its plot, is of such significance that we need to dwell on it a little.

The etiquette of Sarah's time demands she keep hidden in the tent when her husband entertains 'male' guests. On one level her having to overhear God's promise should not surprise us, however much it might offend our own sensibilities. Yet, as we set the tale in its larger context, we cannot fail to remember how often God appears to or speaks with Abraham, and to notice that he has never yet appeared to or spoken with Sarah. At the very end of this story she will have her one and only dialogue with him. She will say to him what amounts to two words in the Hebrew; he will say just three to her. Why should all this be the case? Why should the narrator have written the story like this? We cannot be sure, for we cannot get inside his mind, or ask him what his reasons were. We can only suppose that we are again witnessing the influence of the priests and the cult of ancient Israel upon the text.[16] Though some women were prophetesses, though some took part in the cult as musicians or occasional composers of sacred music, though the two references we have to women serving at the entrance to the Tent of Meeting (see Exod. 38.8 and 1 Sam. 2.22) may indicate that a few played a far more significant role than they are generally given credit for, the priesthood in Israel was confined to men, and Israel's worship was run almost entirely by them. Within the cult, therefore, the task of mediating between God and his people was done exclusively, or almost exclusively, by men. This may be the reason why a male storyteller – for, as in the case of the Garden story, it is abundantly clear he was male – should describe his God as having so much to do with Abraham and so very little with Sarah. As we shall see in our next chapter, God does appear to and speak directly with Hagar, but on both the occasions when that happens there is no man on the scene. Whatever the reason for the huge imbalance in the story, it is one of its features we need now to find shocking. We need now to shake ourselves free of the influence of the male-dominance of the cult of ancient Israel, and to use these stories of Sarah and Abraham to expose and condemn the prejudices and practices within the contemporary Church and our society that still keep so many women in Sarah's place behind the tent-flaps, in a position of having to overhear.

Third, to return to our comment on Sarah's laughter, we notice that she, too, sees nothing odd about the stranger's knowing her

name, or being able to predict she will have a son. She has her own
contribution to make to the comedy of the story. The penny does
not drop for her either. But then she is not used to speaking with
God and hearing him make such promises. All this is new for her.
Finally, her laughter is every bit as understandable as Abraham's,
if not more so, but does not approach blasphemy as his did. We
now have the additional information, for Sarah herself gives it to
us, that she is past the menopause (that is what the text's quaint
reference to it having 'ceased to be with' her 'after the manner of
women' means), and a broad hint that for her and Abraham sexual
intercourse is a thing of the long gone past. That makes the
promise of a son even more preposterous. (See how skilfully the
narrator prepares the ground, step by step, for the miracle of
Isaac's birth!) Of course Sarah laughs, but she, unlike her
husband, does not know who she is listening to. She does not mean
to mock the promises of God. She does not laugh in his face, or
rather hide her laughter at his feet.

Yet, as so many commentators have noticed to Sarah's cost, her
laughter meets with divine rebuke. 'No, but your wife Sarah shall
bear you a son' was God's response to Abraham's incredulity and
his proposing Ishmael as the child of the promises. Abraham's
laughter remained unchallenged. With Sarah things are different:
'The Lord said to Abraham, "What's this? Sarah laughed and said,
'Shall I indeed bear a child, now that I am old?' Is anything too
wonderful for the Lord? At the set time I will return to you, at
lifetide, and Sarah shall have a son"' (18.13–14). In challenging
one and not the other the text is not even-handed. We must not
suppose, however, that somehow Sarah's laughter must after all be
more reprehensible. Still the narrator does not tell us what to
think. Still he leaves us to form our own judgement on the basis
of the pointers he has chosen to include. God's response to Sarah
here is only one of his pointers. The others we have already
discussed, both with regard to this passage and the one in
chapter 17, and the conclusions we drew from them need not be
altered.

Sarah is, even at this stage, so near to the end of the story, still
having to overhear. Her rebuke is not addressed directly to her,
but to Abraham. God continues to talk with him 'man to man',
and has the courtesy (to Abraham, that is, not to Sarah) and
the duplicity to alter Sarah's words. He omits any reference to
Abraham's lack of sexual prowess and the absence of any sexual
relations with his wife. Sarah's 'Worn out as I am, shall I have
pleasure? And my husband is old!' is reported to Abraham in the

form, 'What's this? Sarah laughed and said, "Shall I indeed bear a child, now that I am old?"'!17

Yet the rebuke brings Sarah out into the open, and results in the only dialogue with God that she is given in all these many chapters. 'But Sarah lied, saying, "I did not laugh"; for she was afraid. And he said, "No, but you did laugh"' (18.15). Sarah's fear is the only clue we are given in the story that she at least has penetrated God's disguise. We might think that the words of God's rebuke gave the game away right enough. But if we are expecting Abraham, to whom the speech was addressed, to fall to the ground in worship, or at the least to start quaking in his sandals, we are disappointed. We are not told of his reaction. The obtuseness he has displayed in the story this far encourages us to think of him as a buffoon to its end (though if he is, he will cease to be one as soon as the next scene begins). Sarah, however, like the man in the Garden, is suddenly afraid; like him, she finds herself in an entirely unfamiliar and most awkward position, yet turns, not to accusing God, as the man did, but to lying. She tries to withdraw her laughter. But God is not having that. The son that is to be born to her will be called Laughter. God cannot withdraw his promise just to save Sarah's blushes. Laughter must be born, will be born. Laughter cannot be denied so easily. 'No, but you did laugh' – and, we might add, 'you will again'.

Unless, of course, Abraham ruins everything. One and a half chapters later, he does his best!

'She is my sister', *again*!

(*Gen. 20.1–18*)

'While residing as an alien in Gerar [a town in the south of Canaan], Abraham said of his wife Sarah, "She is my sister." And King Abimelech of Gerar sent and took Sarah' (20.1b–2). We might have thought we had come a long way since chapter 12, and yet here we are back almost where we began. In truth things are much worse now, and Abraham's conduct beggars our belief. Though his treatment of Sarah in Egypt was intolerably cruel, though he showed no concern for the future of the promises of God, at least neither he nor we could be certain that Sarah was to be the mother of the child on whose birth so very much depended. It was not clear then quite how much was at stake. But now we know, and so does he. We know, and he knows, not only that Sarah is to have the child, but that she is to give birth to him next spring. It is almost as if he is doubting his own ability to father the child, and is resurrecting the old ruse to get Sarah impregnated by one of the men of Gerar. If such speculation seems preposterous – and, it is true, it is given no explicit support by the text – then we can claim, in mitigation, to have been driven to it in a desperate attempt to explain Abraham's behaviour. Later in the story, when he is attempting to excuse himself before Abimelech, he will tell him, 'I did it because I thought, "There is no fear of God in this place, and they will kill me because of my wife"' (20.11). The same old story. If we believe Abraham – and not all commentators do (the narrator typically leaves us free to decide for ourselves) – then once again he is intent only on saving his own skin, and cares nothing for anyone or anything else. Our own 'preposterous' suggestion is almost easier to take than Abraham's own excuse, for at least we allow him some thought for the fulfilment of the purposes of God, and even, in a curious way, for Sarah and the ending of her barrenness.

We were able to claim for the Abraham of the Egypt story that he could be seen as a comic character. Not so in Gerar. For comedy to work, the writer must evoke our sympathy for his or her comic characters. They may be seriously flawed, but they must not be beyond the pale. The narrator of chapter 20 does nothing to encourage us to be sympathetic towards Abraham. Quite bluntly, without any speech, any introduction, any explanation as yet, he says in 20.2, 'Abraham said of his wife Sarah, "She is my sister."' And, as David will one day send for and take Bathsheba, so Abimelech sends for and takes Sarah.

Everything seems to be ruined: Abraham's reputation, and the prospect of a son being born to him and Sarah; the fulfilment of the promises of God, and the development of Sarah in the narrative that has brought her out into the open as a character in her own right. That development, seen in chapters 16 and 18, did not amount to very much, but it was a start. Now she slips back into the shadows, and becomes less discernible than she was when she was cooking or hiding in the tent at Mamre. Again she is allowed no speech. At one point, when Abimelech is defending himself to God, he quotes her, and puts into her mouth what in the Hebrew is two words: 'Did he [Abraham] not himself say to me, "She is my sister"? And she herself said, "He is my brother"' (20.5). Near the end of the story Abimelech, unlike the pharaoh of chapter 12, addresses her: 'Look, I have given your brother a thousand pieces of silver; it is your exoneration before all who are with you; you are completely vindicated' (20.16). We must be grateful for small mercies, but small indeed they are. The first of them shows Sarah joining in Abraham's deceit. We may say she is only obeying orders, and indeed the story makes it quite plain that that is what she is doing. It makes it quite clear, as we see from verse 16, that no blame or guilt belongs to her. Yet that very reassurance is disconcerting. The narrator protests too much. His words remind us of the stereotype of the wicked temptress, the seductress who leads men astray. Subtly they hint that in the depths of our minds Sarah is guilty until she is found innocent. It seems churlish to say it, when the storyteller has gone out of his way to defend Sarah, but it would have been better if he had remained silent, and let the details of his tale speak for themselves. They would have preserved Sarah's innocence well enough, without allowing us to imagine she was in any need of defence.

We have already touched upon some of the similarities between this story and its counterpart in chapter 12, and upon some of the differences. Others are not hard to find. Again God has to intervene, this time much more quickly, in order to ensure that Abimelech does not have sexual intercourse with Sarah and so become by mistake the father of the child of the promises. No sooner has the king sent and taken Sarah, but God appears to him in an alarming dream, telling him she is a married woman. When he protests he took her in all innocence, God readily accepts his defence, but threatens him and the rest of his household with death if he does not return Sarah to her husband forthwith. The next morning he summons Abraham and rebukes him even more severely than the pharaoh did. Abraham seems to have learned nothing from the events in Egypt. He still has no defence to offer, but this time he makes it anyway. Part of it we have discussed already, his fear that the godless men of Gerar would kill him as soon as they saw his wife. (We need to forget for the purposes of this story that, according to its context, Sarah was very nearly ninety years old at the time!) That fear is as groundless as were his fears in Egypt. It insults the men of Gerar, and is nothing more than racial prejudice. Abimelech himself, like the good pharaoh before him, is an honourable and god-fearing man.[18]

The rest of Abraham's defence we need to linger on a while, for of all the details of this extraordinary story, it is perhaps the hardest to swallow:

'Besides, she is indeed my sister, the daughter of my father but not the daughter of my mother; and she became my wife.

And when God caused me to go astray from my father's house,
I said to her, "This is the kindness you must do me: at every
place to which we come, say of me, He is my brother."'
(20.12–13)

As we remarked at the start of Sarah's story, we were given no
details of her parentage. This is the first we have heard about her
being Abraham's half-sister. Is Abraham lying to get out of a tight
corner, as Sarah herself did when she denied her laughter? We
know from the story of Tamar in 2 Samuel 13, a story we will come
to later in this book, that such a marriage as Abraham describes
was not forbidden (see 2 Sam 13.13). But do we believe him? If
we do, then we must, I think, believe the rest of his speech. We
must believe that he is for the first time expressing his true feelings,
his resentment about his being called to leave the city of Haran,[19]
when he accuses God of causing him to 'go astray' (for that is what
the Hebrew means – the verb is the same as the one used, for
example, in Isaiah's 'All we like sheep have gone astray'; Isa. 53.6).
More importantly, we must believe that he has been playing his
cruel game with Sarah over and over again, at '*every place*' to which
they have been! If we do believe that, then Sarah is surely one of
the most abused women in the Bible.

Abimelech responds to these excuses by giving Abraham huge
presents! He gives him sheep and oxen, and male and female
slaves. Only the donkeys and camels are missing this time, but the
king more than compensates Abraham for their absence with that
fabulously large heap of silver, and his equally remarkable gift of
land. 'My land is before you', he says; 'settle where it pleases you'
(20.15). No expulsion this time. The gifts are not given as a bride
price either, as they were by the pharaoh. They are given, with
astonishing magnanimity as well as stunning generosity, to make
amends. They are given to restore Abraham's and Sarah's honour,
at least that is how others will understand their purpose.[20] They
are really gifts for Sarah, at least one of the most valuable of them
is: a gift to declare her innocence, a gift to compensate her for the
grievous wrong that has been done to her by her husband, and by
the unwitting Abimelech when he took her for himself. For the
king continues with words we have quoted already, but must now
quote again: 'To Sarah he said, "Look, I have given your brother
a thousand pieces of silver; it is your exoneration before all who
are with you"' (20.16). As Claus Westermann comments, 'He
hands the money . . . to Abraham because by the rules governing
such a society the wife cannot acquire it.'[21] It remains a present

for Sarah, a gift fit for an abused princess. By calling Abraham her 'brother', he shows, unless of course he is being sarcastic, that he believes the terms of her husband's defence. In that case he believes, presumably, that Sarah has already had to endure the rejection, the humiliation, the danger she has suffered in Gerar in town after town. A large pile of silver can never make up for that, but it is the best this Canaanite king can do. It would put Abraham to very great shame, but he cannot be put to any more than the story has heaped on him already.

If we read this story in the Hebrew, there is one word that sticks in our minds as we leave Gerar behind us. It occurs near the end of Abraham's defence of himself, at the point where he is reporting to Abimelech what he told Sarah to say whenever they came to a new place: 'I said to her, "This is the *kindness* you must do me: at every place to which we come, say of me, He is my brother"' (20.13). The Hebrew term for 'kindness' is *hesed*. It is often used in the Old Testament of relations between human beings, but it is also very commonly applied to God. It is hard to translate, and it is impossible to convey all its nuances in a word or a phrase. It speaks of mercy, kindness, love, fidelity, a love that will persist in the midst of great danger, and in the face of great provocation and rejection. It is often translated 'steadfast love', and when it is used of God it tells of his enduring commitment to his people more powerfully than any other word. With what bitter irony, then, does the narrator of chapter 20 put it on the lips of Abraham, even as he is justifying his rejection of his wife!

And in all this Sarah remains silent, and is allowed to take not a single initiative.

The birth and death of Sarah's joy

(Gen. 21.1–14)

Chapter 20 represents, for Sarah, one of the two lowest points in the narratives in which she appears. The beginning of chapter 21 marks her triumph, and in two verses captures the brief moments of her joy. The passage begins with bare, rather formal, almost cumbersome speech: 'The Lord visited Sarah as he had said, and the Lord did for Sarah as he had promised. Sarah conceived and bore Abraham a son in his old age, at the time of which God had spoken to him' (21.1–2). The word we and many of our versions have given as 'visited' also means 'pay attention to', and one is

tempted to translate, 'The Lord *paid attention* to Sarah'. It is only
the second time he has done so, at least openly, above the surface
of the text. Beneath it he has rescued her from the clutches (the
word is not just being used metaphorically!) of two kings. But only
on the occasion of her laughter have we *seen* him attending to her,
instead of dealing with her husband. Her Egyptian slave, Hagar,
will receive much more attention from him, as we shall see. Of
course, Abraham cannot conceive and bear a child. Whatever we
heard when Sarah laughed, that *is* too wonderful for the Lord! So,
at long, long last, it is Sarah's turn. She conceives, and gives birth
to a son.

Yet even now the story is being told from Abraham's point of
view. Even now she bears *him* a child, and as the passage proceeds
with its dry, flat speech, it is he who names the boy, although in
early Israel it was more usually the mother who did the naming;[22]
and it is he who circumcises him on the eighth day, although it is
not unknown in the documents for a woman to perform that rite,[23]
as we shall see in our fourth chapter. And the narrator reminds us
how old Abraham is when Isaac is born; he does not remind us of
Sarah's equally remarkable age.[24]

Yet the balance of the narrative is quickly restored, for it
continues with this: 'Now Sarah said, "God has made laughter for
me; everyone who hears will laugh with me." And she said, "Who
would have ever announced to Abraham, 'Sarah is suckling a
child!'? Yet I have borne him a child in his old age!"' (21.6–7).
Now the language gets the colour back in its cheeks! These are
words to remember Sarah by! They represent only her fifth
utterance, and there will be but one more. Alas, that one will be
laden with fear and will give vent to bitter ruthlessness. Here there
is only joy and surprise and a newborn laughter. We are a world
away from the derision of Abraham's laughter in chapter 17, and
not much closer to the laughter of Sarah's own disbelief. Here, and
here alone, Sarah is fulfilled.

She has brought Laughter into the world (of course, all the talk
of laughter is a play on the meaning of Isaac's name). True, she
has not escaped the man's world in which she lives. She still
recognizes that her purpose is to bear Abraham a son, not to give
a child life for the two of them together. She is not there to serve
her own needs. She knows that. And yet she cannot contain her
joy. Back in chapter 16 it was, 'The Lord has stopped me from
bearing children'; now it is, 'God has made laughter for me.' Her
new cry echoes the surprised delight of Eve when Cain was born.
We have never heard Sarah speak like this before. She has a power

here we are not used to. And this remains true, despite the fact that the final author of the text has almost certainly robbed her of an important function.

We cannot be certain how this story reached its final form. But we can notice how strange it is that the one who 'explains' the name of the child, as Sarah does in verse 6, is different from the one who gives him his name. Invariably in the Old Testament those two functions are performed by the same person. We have already come across an example of it in Eve's naming Seth and then saying, 'God has appointed for me another child instead of Abel.' It looks very much as though in an earlier stage of the tradition it was Sarah who named her son after all[25] – as if the male bias of the text were not strong enough already!

Eve's joy, however, was very short-lived, destroyed by terrible conflict. Sarah's meets with a similar, and similarly swift, fate. The rejoicing continues, but only for one more verse.

Isaac grows and is weaned, and Abraham makes a great feast to celebrate the event. Archaeological discoveries at burial sites in Israel have demonstrated what we might have guessed, that infant mortality rates could be appallingly high.[26] Children were generally not weaned until they were in their third year, and so the feasting was chiefly to celebrate their surviving the most dangerous period of their lives.

But the relief, the sheer joy of Isaac's feast, quickly evaporates. 'But Sarah saw the son of Hagar the Egyptian, whom she had borne to Abraham, "Isaacing". So she said to Abraham, "Cast out this slave-woman and her son; for the son of this slave-woman shall not inherit along with my son Isaac"' (21.9–10). What did Sarah see? We cannot be sure. The Septuagint, the Greek translation of the Old Testament, whose version of Genesis was probably composed in the third century BCE, adds to the end of the first sentence the words, 'with Isaac her son'. That has led most of our versions and commentators to say that what Sarah saw was Ishmael 'playing' with Isaac. If play it was, it may not have been innocent. When Isaac is grown up, Abimelech, the king of Gerar, will see him 'playing with his wife Rebekah' (26.8), and there the context will make it clear that their 'play' is of an overtly sexual nature. But should we follow the Septuagint here? The Hebrew word for 'play' comes from the same root as the name Isaac. When we read the Hebrew of verse 9 aloud, we cannot fail to be struck by the pun. Verse 8 ends in the Hebrew with Isaac's name, *yitzhaq*; verse 9 ends with *metzaheq*. One commentator suggests we should translate *metzaheq* as 'Isaacing',[27] that is not playing *with* Isaac, but *playing*

Isaac. This is Isaac's feast, his big moment. But Ishmael cannot help but seek to attract the attention and the honour of the occasion to himself. He, after all, is the elder of the two boys, and as such can consider himself the rightful inheritor of the bulk of Abraham's land, and of the wealth and fine promises that go with it.[28] No one has told *him* that he is not the heir Abraham and Sarah and God have been waiting for. Only Abraham and God, and we, the readers of the narrative, know that.

We can now more readily understand Sarah's reaction, and why it will meet with divine approval.

Sarah begins with the old jealousies of chapter 16. That story's conflict between her and Hagar was left unresolved. Now the bitterness which has been simmering for these past fourteen years once more breaks out, and is so strong she cannot bring herself to give either Hagar or Ishmael their names. They are simply 'this slave-woman and her son'. Hagar is not even 'my slave-girl', as she was in the earlier story, but Abraham's. And yet, ironically, in her very rejection of Hagar, Sarah assumes her full authority as her mistress, and orders Abraham to get rid of her. In chapter 16 Sarah gave Abraham some plain speaking. But this is the first and only time we see her giving him a command.

Yet chapter 16 is not enough to explain the strength of Sarah's feelings at this point, or the particular reasons for her action. Then Sarah was barren. Now she has a son of her own to defend. She may not know of God's plans for Isaac. God has never communicated them to her, and Abraham, to judge by the evidence of chapter 18, has not been especially forthcoming either. For the same reasons, we can presume she does not understand what God has in mind for Ishmael. All she knows is that Isaac has an elder brother, that he is the son of the Egyptian woman who for so long rubbed salt into the wound of her sterility, and that, if things are left to themselves, he will inherit the bulk of Abraham's wealth and power. Already in Genesis we have seen an elder son kill his brother in the story of Cain and Abel. Later in the book we will witness the threat posed to Jacob by his elder brother Esau; and we will hear much about the attempts to get rid of Joseph by his older brothers. One has to be very careful of older brothers in this book. When Sarah has waited so long for Isaac to be born, when his conception and birth have so far exceeded her expectations and given her such surprising joy, can we ourselves be surprised when she is determined at all costs to defend him from the one who represents such a potent threat? God, as we know, has his own plans for Isaac that must not be put in jeopardy. He has his own reasons for wanting Ishmael, and Hagar with him, out of the way. Sarah's bitter rejection of them serves him very well. 'Whatever Sarah says to you,' he tells Abraham, 'do as she tells you' (21.12).

Yet while we can explain Sarah's action well enough, we cannot escape its cruelty and its tragedy. 'Cast out this slave-woman . . .' is her last speech. With those words she leaves the narrative, and she only re-enters it to die, and for Abraham to mourn her and weep over her, and find a burial place for her body (ch. 23). Her harsh words remind us of the expulsion from Eden, where the same 'cast out' appeared in the text (3.24). The narrator allows her no chance to redeem herself, no opportunity to make amends.[29] There will be no healing of the conflict between her and Hagar as there will be of the one between Jacob and Esau. There will be no time for the kind of reconciliation that will take place so movingly between Joseph and his brothers. In more ways than one this story reminds us of the tale of Cain and Abel.

A deafening silence

(Gen. 22)

We have very nearly finished with Sarah. There is only one more story to be mentioned. It is the most powerful of all those concerning Abraham, and, indeed, one of the most remarkable in all Scripture. We all know how it begins:

> After these things God tested Abraham. He said to him, 'Abraham!' And he said, 'Here I am.' He said, 'Take your son, your only son Isaac, whom you love, and go to the land of Moriah, and offer him there as a burnt offering on one of the mountains that I shall show you.' (22.1–2)

All we wish to ask is this: where is Sarah?[30]

God talks of Abraham loving Isaac, but it was Sarah who expressed so much joy at his birth. All along, it has been Sarah whose eyes have been focused on that birth. It was she who suggested the child might be born through Hagar. When God appeared to Abraham in disguise, but came really for Sarah and her sharp ears, all his talk, all Sarah's talk, was about this son. And she it was who perceived so clearly the threat from Ishmael, and was so quick and so determined to protect Isaac from him. God has now commanded Abraham to take the child who is *her* son also and slit his throat.

And Abraham gets up early in the morning and prepares for the journey to the land of Moriah, and leaves with the fire and the knife and the wood for the burnt offering, and the sacrificial victim, her son. Has he told her where he is going? Has he said anything to her about what he is about to do? Has God made his own attempt to explain things? We do not know. The story does not tell us. Sarah is not even mentioned once from beginning to end. Neither God's previous record of communicating with Sarah, nor Abraham's, would lead us to think she knows anything at all. Though Isaac is saved from death at the last second, it seems from the text that he does not return home with his father.[31] If Abraham has any explanation to offer Sarah for the boy's absence, we do not hear it. It would seem she never sees him again, for six verses after Abraham's return we learn of her death.

Chapter 22 represents for Abraham the passing of the most severe test that God could set him. On one level it is his moment of greatest triumph, the achievement which above all has contributed to his lasting reputation as a righteous man. For Sarah it is the second of the two lowest points in all the narratives in which she appears.

She does not share in her husband's glory. She has no chance here or anywhere else in her story to prove herself a woman of conspicuous faith and obedience. God has made no demands of *her*, just as he has never given her any promises. In all the chapters we have been looking at, the issue of *her* faith, *her* obedience, *her* righteousness has never once been raised. In these ancestral narratives she is an abused woman, and in the end, after an all too brief moment of joy, a wholly tragic character.

3

Hagar: A Persecuted Madonna

(Genesis 16.1–16; 21.8–21)

Where does Hagar's story begin? In Genesis 16, or Genesis 12? She does not come on stage until chapter 16, but there she is described as an 'Egyptian slave-girl', and we have heard about Egyptian slave-girls before. They were part of the bride price the pharaoh gave to Abram, to compensate him for the loss of his 'sister', Sarai. Sharon Jeansonne suggests that by using the same term for slave-girl in 16.1 as he used in 12.16 the narrator is trying to tell us something.[1] Certainly the rabbis thought the story of chapter 12 explained how Hagar came to be in Sarai's service. Not content with that, they claimed that Hagar was the pharaoh's own daughter![2] By their token Hagar is a princess from the most exalted of royal families, who finds herself slave to the wife of a nomad from an obscure part of her father's empire, thanks to his payment of an absurdly large bride-price which the same nomad had tricked out of him, and which he, the pharaoh, had very soon lived to regret. By their token she comes on stage already a princess, playing the part of a slave to a barren woman who is yet to become one, for Sarai will not be renamed Sarah until chapter 17.

Alas, there is nothing in the text to support the notion of Hagar's royal blood. If there were, then there would be a further dimension to Hagar's two stories, another bitter ingredient in her humiliation and suffering, yet more pathos and poignancy for us to discover. In truth, however, the text does not need the rabbis' brilliant speculation. Its delineation of Hagar's plight is sharp enough already, while, on the other hand, it has waiting for her a status and privileges that far exceed those that any princess might expect, and which are nowhere accorded to her mistress.

The silence of the abused

(Gen. 16.1–6)

We have already covered the first part of chapter 16 in our discussions about Sarah. Some things about Hagar have been said already, and need not be said again. But still we must go back to these verses and explore them afresh from Hagar's point of view.

'Now Sarai, Abram's wife, bore him no children' (16.1). That is the cue for Hagar to be introduced. She arrives in the narrative as a possible answer to the problem of another woman's barrenness. Once again we must resist the idea that the only thing women were considered good for in ancient Israel was bearing and rearing children. As we said in our previous chapter,[3] that was far from being the case. It is a matter of the limitations of the narrative. For the narrator, Sarai's role is to bear a child. That is Hagar's primary role also, at least to start with.

The passage reminds us immediately of Sarai's status. She is Abram's wife. When Hagar is introduced, at once we learn her status also. She is Sarai's Egyptian slave-girl. She is a foreigner, a slave, with, we might suppose, no rights or power of her own. Much will depend on her relationship with her mistress. She is her personal servant,[4] and life might be bearable for her if Sarai treats her with some kindness and sensitivity. If she does not, then she will have no means of redress, unless, of course, God comes to her rescue.

Yet she has a name. We know what to call her. So often in Old Testament narratives, characters who appear in just one or two scenes remain anonymous. Hagar is not merely given the dignity of a name, but, as we shall see, will acquire the unique honour of bestowing a name on God himself. If 'an Egyptian slave-girl' seems to put her firmly in her place, then 'whose name was Hagar' hints already that that place may not turn out to be such a lowly one as we might expect.

For the moment all we see is Hagar's powerlessness. 'Go, please, to my slave-girl,' says Sarai to Abram. 'It may be that I shall be built up through her' (16.2b). Hagar's name is not used here. Instead Sarai reminds Abram of the woman's status, and of who she belongs to. Her mistress may give us a hint of a concern for the fulfilment of the promises of God,[5] but she has none for Hagar. Hagar is not consulted. She has no say in the matter. She is only a slave, and slaves are there to do what they are told. Hagar will, Sarai hopes, conceive and give birth to a child, but if she does, the child will not count as hers. Hagar will have to hand the child over to Sarai, and having done that, will have to continue living with her and serving her needs. For herself, Sarai hopes that she will be 'built up' if Hagar has a child. She entertains no hopes for Hagar beyond the pleasures of sexual intercourse and the pains of childbirth. Hope is not for the likes of an Egyptian slave. Chapter 15 has just spoken of Sarai and Abram's descendants becoming slaves in Egypt and being oppressed there for four hundred years (v. 13). That might only reinforce our sense of Hagar's helplessness and increase our sense of foreboding.

Yet, as we saw in our last chapter, the tables are quickly turned, and Hagar's fecundity exalts her above her still barren mistress. The narrator and Abram have decided what roles these women will play in this story. They have put them in a situation where conflict is to be expected. We should not be surprised by it now that it occurs.[6] Its predictability, however, does nothing to lessen the tragedy of it for both women. For Sarai the results are further bitterness, a deeper sense of her own failure, a greater despair, and the practice of a harsher cruelty. As for Hagar, she finds that her new pride, her new status and power are a sham, a cruel charlatan. For they only make things worse. They lead to Sarai treating her so harshly that she has to escape. The treatment is condoned by Abram. 'Your slave-girl is in your power; do to her as you please,' is all he says to Sarai when she confronts him with the conflict that has arisen (16.6a). His speech amounts to just seven words in the Hebrew. In its brief simplicity it encapsulates Hagar's plight. It sums up what it means for her to be a slave. The cruelty that immediately ensues sums up what it means for her to be a slave in that particular household. Neither her mistress, nor her mistress's husband, the man whose child she bears in her womb, have once used her name in their speaking to one another. She has not been Hagar to them, simply a slave-girl. She has been given no words to say, no initiative to take. She conceives, she realizes she is pregnant, and she runs away. These are the only things she does. Everything else is done to her.[7]

A first meeting with God

(Gen. 16.7–16)

Next, however, the scene changes, and suddenly we see what part Hagar is playing in the story. The narrator follows her out into the wilderness, and finds her beside a spring of water on the way to Shur (16.7). Shur is either a place near the Egyptian border, or a reference to the border itself and its defensive forts.[8] It seems Hagar is going home. But the narrator and we, the readers of his masterly story, are not the only ones to find Hagar. She is found also by 'the messenger of the Lord'.

Exactly who he might be will not become entirely clear until the end, but already we have a clue. Hagar, a slave, has been subjected to unusually harsh treatment, and has fled from her oppressor. She has escaped into the wilderness, and now there is talk of water. To those who know the story of the Exodus from Egypt, all this sounds remarkably familiar. In Genesis 12 we found Sarai playing the part of the enslaved Israelites.[9] Now, with supreme irony, the *Egyptian* Hagar is playing the same role. Unlike Sarai, however, Hagar has come to 'Sinai', not only to the desert of that name, but to its place of meeting, the place where God is encountered and new promises are made and new demands given. When the people of Israel come to Sinai they will be given, not long after the Ten Commandments, the following instruction: 'You shall not wrong or oppress a resident alien, for you were aliens in the land of Egypt. You shall not abuse any widow or orphan. If you do abuse them, when they cry out to me, I will surely heed their cry . . .' (Exod. 22.21–3). The Hebrew word for 'abuse' twice used there is the same as the one behind the 'dealt harshly' of Sarai's treatment of Hagar in 16.6. It occurs earlier in Exodus, in that book's very first mention of the enslavement and oppression of the Israelites in Egypt (see Exod. 1.11–12, where the NRSV translates it as 'oppress').[10]

Hagar may not be a widow, though the man who is her husband (for Sarai gave her to Abram 'as a wife') took no care of her when she found herself so threatened by her mistress. She may not be an orphan child, though she is every bit as vulnerable as one and in as much need of protection. She *is* an alien, though no longer a resident one. But God is not pedantic. 'If you do abuse them . . . I will surely heed their cry.' That is what he will say to his people. Here, though Hagar has not yet uttered a sound, he is as good as his as yet unspoken word. He pays her heed. At the end it will be quite plain that 'the messenger of the Lord' is none other than God himself. For the moment he hides himself in the narrator's pious periphrasis.

'And he said, "Hagar, slave-girl of Sarai, where have you come from and where are you going?"' (16.8a). For the first time someone other than the narrator has used Hagar's name. The questions he asks of her recall the one that will be asked of Elijah when he too comes to Sinai: 'What are you doing here, Elijah?' (1 Kings 19.9, 13). But the question to Elijah is high comedy, designed to prick his paranoia and deflate his absurd ambition.[11] God's question to Hagar lacks such playfulness. He reminds her that she is Sarai's slave. He wants to know what she is doing there, on her own, in the desert.

Whose side is God on? We do not know that yet. Has he come to rescue Hagar, as he will rescue his people from the oppression of the Egyptians, as he will vow to rescue the widow and the orphan? Surely it is one of the distinguishing marks of the God of Israel that he always takes the side of the oppressed? That is the nature of the God of the Exodus, of the God of the torah, and of the God of the prophets. Or has this God come only as a spy, to find out why this slave is not about her duties? In short, is he the God of hope and revolution, or the God of the *status quo* who works in the interests of the powerful?

Hagar replies to his question, 'I am running away from my mistress Sarai' (16.8b). She speaks the truth, but she does not speak the whole of it. She does not tell him why she is running away. She does not tell of the abuse, the harsh treatment, the cruelty. And yet God catches their dark undertones beneath her words. 'Return to your mistress, and suffer harsh treatment beneath her hand' (16.9). The NRSV has, 'Return to your mistress, and submit to her.' But that is far too tame for the Hebrew, which again uses the strong verb of the 'dealt harshly' of verse 6, the same verb as the 'abuse' of Exodus 22.22–3, or the 'oppress' of Exodus 1.11–12.

God's commands to Hagar represent one of the darkest, most unnerving moments in all Scripture. It seems he has revealed his true colours. Here, at least, he seems to be in favour of the *status quo* and on the side of the oppressor, a defender of the interests of the Sarais of this world against its all too vulnerable Hagars. If the story were to end here, it would surely be intolerable.

But it does not, and its image of God has other, brighter facets to it. 'The messenger of the Lord also said to her, "I will so greatly multiply your offspring that they cannot be counted for multitude"' (16.10). This is the by now familiar language of the promises. In 12.2 God declared to Abram, 'I will make of you a great nation'; in 13.16 he told him, 'I will make your offspring like the dust of the earth; so that if one can count the dust of the earth, your offspring also can be counted'; in 15.5 he brought him outside his tent and said, 'Look toward heaven and count the stars, if you are able to count them . . . So shall your descendants be.' So far in the ancestral narratives Abram has been the only person to hear such talk. God will repeat his promises to his son and his grandson, to Isaac (see 26.2–6, 24), and to Jacob (28.13–15; 35.9–12; 46.3–4), but to no one else. Even the great Joseph will have to receive them at second hand from his father (see 48.3–4). Hagar, then, is one of just four people in Genesis to hear the language of promise from God's own lips, and she a woman, a slave, an Egyptian.[12]

She is, indeed, one of only three women in Genesis to engage in dialogue with God. The other two are the woman in the Garden and Sarah. But Sarah's conversation amounts only to this: 'I did not laugh'/'No, but you did laugh'; and Eve's to this: 'What is this you have done?'/'The snake tricked me, and I ate' – and to that God responds with his judgement upon her. In both of those cases God's language is that of accusation and judgement. There is promise, right enough, in his 'No, but you did laugh' to Sarah, for, as we have seen, it effectively renews his commitment to her bringing a son called Laughter into the world. Nevertheless, promise is only whispered in what is much more loudly a rebuke. There is a hint of accusation, as we have also just discovered, in God's initial questions to Hagar, 'Where have you come from and where are you going?', and fearful judgement in his, 'Return to your mistress, and suffer harsh treatment beneath her hand.' Yet in her case, and her case alone, God does not stop there. With Hagar he is not content with accusation and judgement. Indeed, the vast bulk of his speech to her is concerned with promise, for he continues:

'Now you have conceived and shall bear a son;
   you shall call him Ishmael,
   for the Lord has given heed to your being so harshly treated.
He shall be a wild ass of a man,
   with his hand against everyone,
      and everyone's hand against him;
   and he shall live at odds with all his kin.' (16.11–12)

There are a number of annunciation scenes in the Bible, and this is the first of them. God's solemn announcement of the birth of Ishmael is echoed by words of his to Abraham in 17.19–21:

'Your wife Sarah shall bear you a son, and you shall name him Isaac. I will establish my covenant with him as an everlasting covenant for his offspring after him. As for Ishmael, I have heard you; I will bless him and make him fruitful and exceedingly numerous; he shall be the father of twelve princes, and I will make him a great nation. But my covenant I will establish with Isaac, whom Sarah shall bear to you at this season next year.'

There is a further parallel to be found in Judges 13.3–5, when 'the messenger of the Lord' announces the birth of a son to the unnamed wife of Manoah (the son is not named there either, but turns out to be Samson), and a much more famous one in Isaiah, where the prophet is speaking to Ahaz, king of Judah: 'Therefore the Lord himself will give you a sign. Look, the young woman is with child and shall bear a son, and shall call his name Immanuel' (Isa. 7.14). But, of course, the most striking parallel of all is in Luke's Gospel, when the angel Gabriel announces to Mary the birth of Jesus:

'You will conceive in your womb and bear a son, and you will name him Jesus. He will be great, and will be called the Son of the Most High, and the Lord God will give to him the throne of his ancestor David. He will reign over the house of Jacob forever, and of his kingdom there will be no end.' (Luke 1.31–3)

There are a few other formal annunciations in the Bible. There are the brief predictions of Isaac's birth in Genesis 18.10 and 14; an anonymous prophet announces the coming birth of king Josiah in 1 Kings 13.2, addressing his words to an altar in the presence of king Jeroboam; David reports to Solomon a prophecy he had once received about his birth (1 Chron. 22.9–10); and Zechariah receives from an angel word of the birth of John the Baptist (Luke 1.13–17). Matthew also has his own annunciation scene, when 'an angel of the Lord' appears to Joseph, and tells him of the birth of Jesus (Matt. 1.20–1).

We begin to see from these parallels how very surprising is the honour which is bestowed upon Hagar (and upon Ishmael too) in Genesis 16. For a start, annunciations are a rare commodity in the Bible – we have listed *all* the significant occurrences – and Hagar's is the first of them. In only three cases, those of Hagar, Manoah's wife, and Mary in Luke, is the promise of a son made to the one who will be the mother of the child (although Sarah overhears in Genesis 18, the words are addressed to her husband). In only four cases does God make the announcement himself. God speaks with Abraham in Genesis 17, and again in chapter 18 (though, as we have seen, in the second passage Abraham does not realize who he is); and Judges 13, like Genesis 16, makes it plain by the end that 'the messenger of the Lord' is God himself (see vv. 6, 18, and especially 22). Thus only two women in the entire Bible receive annunciations from God himself, Hagar and the unnamed wife of Manoah. When Luke came to write his Gospel, he took the patterns for his two annunciation scenes from their stories. The announcing of John the Baptist's birth is clearly modelled on the second of them, though, interestingly enough, Elizabeth, John's mother, does not appear on its stage, and is only mentioned by name. For the appearance of Gabriel to Mary, Luke took the Hagar passage. Hagar, then, turns out to be the Mary, the madonna of the Old Testament,[13] or one of them at least, for Hannah will be another.

In one sense, if we compare her to Mary, the honour done to Hagar is the more remarkable. By the time Luke's Gospel was written the Jews had filled their heavens with a host of angelic beings, who were independent from God and had their own function as mediators between him and human beings, and sometimes, as in Gabriel's case, their own names.[14] Though Gabriel comes trailing God's glory behind him, so that Mary is disturbed by his speech, he is not God himself. God, for that moment at least, keeps his distance and allows the angel to bridge the gulf between them. Mary does not react in the way Hagar soon will with her cry, 'Have I really seen God, and remained alive after seeing him?' (16.13).

In his words to Hagar, not only does God pay Hagar a singular honour, he also shows a new concern for her plight. Our rather cumbersome translation of the final part of 16.11, 'for the Lord has given heed to your being so harshly treated', is an attempt to convey another echo in the Hebrew. The single word behind 'your being treated so harshly' comes from the same root as the 'dealt harshly' of verse 6, or the 'suffer harsh treatment' of verse 9. In verse 9 God's response seemed itself to be intolerably harsh, and to add abuse to abuse. Then he spoke words of judgement. Now, however, he slips into the language of salvation. At the Burning Bush God will assure Moses, 'I have observed the *misery* of my people who are in Egypt . . . and I have come down to deliver them from the Egyptians, and to bring them up out of that land

to a good and broad land, a land flowing with milk and honey . . .'
(Exod. 3.7–8). Later Moses will instruct those who will farm that
same good and broad land what to say when they bring their
harvest offering to God: 'When the Egyptians treated us harshly
and *afflicted* us . . . the Lord heard our voice and saw our *affliction*'
(Deut. 26.6–7). The Hebrew word for 'misery' in the first passage
and the ones for 'afflicted' and 'affliction' in the second belong to
the same root as Hagar's 'harsh treatment'. So the text invites us
to compare God's salvation of Hagar to his deliverance of his own
people. But in what will Hagar's salvation consist? Not in escape
from oppression, for already she has been ordered back to her
tyrant of a mistress. Not in the gift of a good and broad land, for
she and her son will not have a land of their own. Ishmael will be
the ancestor of the bedouin desert tribes, who will live on the
borders of the territory of the Israelites and be in continual conflict
with them and their other neighbours. No, her salvation will be
her son, a son whose name will be a constant reminder to her of
the heed God once paid to her misery. For Ishmael means in the
Hebrew, 'God hears'.

We might think God's promises concerning Ishmael amount to
something more akin to a curse than a blessing. We can compare
them to the blessing the dying Isaac will pronounce upon Esau in
Genesis 27.39–40, remembering what a poor thing that will be
beside the one he has just given to Jacob (see 27.28–9). Certainly
the conflict promised to Ishmael and his descendants will recall
Hagar and her own plight. We have already seen her at odds with
Sarai, and will do so again. Like mother, like son, we might say.
Yet Ishmael and his people will also remind us of the defiance
Hagar showed when she knew she was pregnant, and which she
will demonstrate a second time at the very end of her story.

> 'He shall be a wild ass of a man,
>   with his hand against everyone,
>   and everyone's hand against him;
>   and he shall live at odds with all his kin.' (16.12)

Claus Westermann describes this verse as a tribal saying which
must have originated among the Ishmaelites themselves, and is
surely correct when he calls it a 'jubilant, defiant affirmation of
predatory, bedouin life'.[15]

So far in this encounter with God, we have been able to compare
Hagar, the Egyptian slave-woman, to the patriarchs who received
God's promises and to Mary the mother of Jesus. But the verse we

now come to in her story allows her a role which no one else at all plays in the whole Bible: she gives a name to God. 'So she named the Lord who spoke to her, You are El-Roi' (16.13a). Now the identity of the 'messenger' is out in the open for us all to see. He is the Lord himself, Yahweh, the God who will be the God of Israel. Hagar calls him El-Roi, 'The God of My Seeing', that is, 'The God who Sees Me.'[16]

Westermann comments, 'That is not to say that Hagar gives to a hitherto nameless divine being a name that sticks to him everywhere and always . . . but Hagar says: "For me he is, whatever else he may be called, the God who sees me, i.e., the one who came to my aid in my distress." '[17] He is quite right. The name El-Roi occurs nowhere else in the Old Testament. It is Hagar's name for God, and Hagar's alone. It arises out of, and speaks eloquently of, her own private encounter with him. Though many others in the Old Testament will find that God comes to them when they are in just such a dire need or distress as hers, none has exactly Hagar's experience. Each encounter with God is unique. Each leaves its own mark upon the one whom God meets. Only in Hagar's case, she leaves *her* mark on God. He goes on his way with a new name.

Let no one underestimate how extraordinary this naming is. We had to examine the parallels to Hagar's annunciation scene in order to appreciate how remarkable hers is. So here we must briefly consider two other passages to demonstrate the singularity of Hagar's act, and the extent of her daring.

After wrestling with God all night at the river Jabbok, Jacob names the spot, Peniel, or 'The face of God' (Gen. 32.30). After coming so close to sacrificing Isaac, but being given a ram to slaughter instead, Abraham names the place, 'The Lord Sees' (22.14).[18] Abraham's name is very close to the one Hagar gives God. Yet, like Jacob, Abraham names the *place* of encounter. Neither of them dares to name the God who has met them there. Elsewhere Abraham calls *upon* the name of God (12.8; 13.4; 21.33), but that is a very different exercise. Moreover, Hagar does not name her God as an aside, or declare his identity to herself after he has left the stage. She names him to his face: '*You* are the God who Sees Me.' The phrase the narrator uses for the naming is the usual one in Hebrew narrative. It is the same as the one used, for example, when the man in the Garden named his wife Eve, or Eve herself named her third son Seth. Soon it will be used for the naming of Ishmael, and again for the naming of Isaac.

This astonishing story is nearly at an end, but it has one more surprise still in store for us. Hagar has one more thing to say: 'Have I really seen God and remained alive after seeing him?' (16.13b). Unfortunately, the second part of this question in the Hebrew is unintelligible. There are places in the Old Testament where the text as we have it is clearly damaged or corrupt, and this is one of them. The 'and remained alive after seeing him' is a translation of Wellhausen's attempt to arrive at the original form of the text.[19] If we follow his lead, then Hagar's astonishment is similar to Jacob's at Peniel: 'For I have seen God face to face, and yet my life is preserved' (Gen 32.30). It reminds us of Isaiah's reaction when he has a vision of God in the temple in Jerusalem: 'Woe is me! I am lost, for I am a man of unclean lips, and I live among a people of unclean lips; yet my eyes have seen the King, the Lord of hosts!' (Isa. 6.5). The huge sense of awe that could overwhelm the ancient Israelites in the presence of their God is nowhere more powerfully expressed than in the words that God speaks to Moses when he asks to see his glory: 'You cannot see my face; for no one shall see me and live' (Exod. 33.20). They are echoed by Manoah near the end of the annunciation scene in Judges 13: 'And Manoah said to his wife, "We shall surely die, for we have seen God"' (13.22). To say 'and remained alive after seeing him' is precisely what we might expect Hagar to say in the circumstances. For the circumstances are quite clear: she has seen God. On *that* score the Hebrew presents no difficulties. So, without any doubt at all, Hagar joins a very select band of people in the Bible of whom it is said plainly that they 'see' God. Abraham is not among them. Three times the narrative has God appearing to him (12.7; 17.1; 18.1), but none of those passages say in so many words that he saw him. The great Moses sees him, together with his brother Aaron, his nephews Nadab and Abihu, and seventy of the elders of Israel (Exod. 24.9–10). Yet at the Burning Bush, Moses hides his face, for he is afraid to look upon him (Exod. 3.6), and though on Sinai God speaks to him 'face to face, as one speaks to a friend' (Exod. 33.11), when he asks to see his glory, God shields him with his hand as he passes by, so that he sees only his back and not his face (Exod. 33.18–23). It is possible to say that Sarah sees him when he comes to the tent in the form of three men, for, as we know, her fear may indicate she has penetrated the disguise. Jacob, Manoah and his wife, and Isaiah 'see' him, and so does Amos (see Amos 9.1), Ezekiel (Ezek. 1.4–28), Job (Job 42.5) and Daniel (Dan. 7.9–10). Mary, the mother of Jesus, does not see him, for only God's messenger, Gabriel, meets with her, and in fact it is not clear from Luke's story that she does more than hear his words. For

New Testament counterparts to Hagar's vision, we have to turn to the story of the Transfiguration (Mark 9.2–8 and parallels), to Luke's stories of the stoning of Stephen (Acts 7.55–6), or the conversion of Paul (Acts 9.3–5; 22.6–8; 26.13–15), or to the experience of the writer of the Book of Revelation (Rev. 1.12–18).

Yet Jacob has to leave Peniel, and go on to the meeting with Esau which he so much dreads. Peter, James and John have to come down the mountain away from the bright glory of its summit, to be confronted at once by noise and argument, by the helplessness of their fellow disciples when dealing with an epileptic boy, and by Jesus' own exasperation and his accusing them of belonging to a 'faithless generation' (see Mark 9.14ff. and parallels). So, now, after all this, after all *this*, Hagar must return to Sarai and Abram. For the moment we hear nothing more about Sarai's treatment of her. We are told that she bears Abram a son, and that he names him Ishmael. But that is enough for her to be brought down to earth with a cruel bump. For was she not promised by God that *she* would name the child? As Phyllis Trible says, Abram's action 'strips Hagar of the power that God gave her'.[20] She is no longer a madonna. She is back in the costume of the slave. We hear nothing about any joy of hers at Ishmael's birth. Her mistress, by way of contrast, will make the welkin ring when Isaac is born. We have come back to where we began, and if, when the curtain rises on Hagar's third scene, we find ourselves in the company of Abraham and Sarah also, as indeed we do, then Hagar's future, at least in the short term, looks bleak.

Rejection

(Gen. 21.8–14)

Our worst fears are fulfilled. As we have seen already, the conflict between Hagar and Sarah (as she is now) breaks out with renewed ferocity at the feast made to celebrate Isaac's weaning. The first clash between them was provoked by Hagar herself. This one is sparked off by her son. Hagar is not involved at all. She is not a Rebekah. She does not egg Ishmael on to claim his rightful place in the family as the elder son, as Rebekah will one day be the power behind Jacob's throne and engineer a plot to secure for him all Esau's privileges. Yet she is at once caught up in the punishment: 'Cast out this slave-woman with her son' (21.10). Though she asserts her authority as Hagar's mistress by ordering Abraham to get rid of her, Sarah demonstrates by her choice of words that, as far as she is concerned at least, the relationship between them is already at an end. Though Hagar was told by God to return to her mistress, Sarah here cannot find the grace to acknowledge her as her slave. She has already rejected her before she opens her mouth. The order to expel her simply makes the rejection audible and seeks to make the break final. It will succeed.

In the first story Sarai appealed to God to judge between her and her husband, and, by implication, called on Abram to exercise his authority and put Hagar in her place. Abram, so unresponsive to Sarai's accusations, so deaf to her pain, nevertheless was quick to recognize the unspoken claim upon him and at once restored Hagar to Sarai's control. He remained aloof, unfeeling. Now, however, with the relationship between his two wives broken beyond repair, he cannot shrug off his responsibilities so easily. Then no son was yet born to him. Now he has two to think of. 'The matter was very distressing to Abraham on account of his son' (21.11). As Sharon Jeansonne points out, it is not clear which son he is so concerned about.[21] Most commentators assume he means Ishmael. But it could be that Sarah has made him aware of the threat Ishmael poses to Isaac. One thing seems clear: he is not concerned about his wife Hagar. He does not appear to spare her a thought. He rejected her before by putting her back in Sarai's hands. Now he appears to reject her again. Yet God responds to his distress by imputing to him feelings for Hagar that he has not expressed: 'But God said to Abraham, "Do not be distressed because of the boy and because of your slave-woman; whatever Sarah says to you, do as she tells you, for it is through Isaac that offspring shall be named for you"' (21.12). Who are we to believe, God or the narrator? Though God suggests Abraham's first thoughts are still for his son (it remains unclear which son), are we to think Abraham is distressed for Hagar after all? Are we to suppose that he who, in the words of the psalmist, 'knows the secrets of the heart' (Ps. 44.21) is aware of the man's true feelings for the woman who is still his wife? Or is he reminding him that he *ought* to be concerned for her, just as he will suggest to Jonah that he ought to feel sorry for the plant destroyed by the worm when clearly the prophet has no pity for it at all?[22] Again, we cannot be sure. But we can and should be disconcerted by the way God refers to Hagar. Like Sarah, he does not use her name. Even when God is talking of her, her anonymity continues to underline her lack of status, her powerlessness, her not counting for anything. God, *this* God, the one who met her in the desert and heaped astonishing honours upon her, does not even remind Abraham that she is his wife. He gives her the bitter title Sarah gave her in her fear and anger: he calls her Abraham's 'slave-woman' (notice he does not call her Sarah's slave; it would seem he also recognizes the completeness of the breakdown of their relationship). Phyllis Trible's comment is fair: 'If Abraham neglected Hagar, God belittles her.'[23] Indeed, as God's speech proceeds, we see that though he might imply at the start that Abraham ought to be concerned for Hagar, he himself thinks only of Isaac and Ishmael. He reassures Abraham that the promises are still safe with Isaac, and that those he made with regard to Ishmael[24] will also be fulfilled. There is no assurance about Hagar. She is yet further diminished by the end of the speech.[25] She was promised in the desert that God would multiply *her* offspring. Now he promises that Ishmael will be the ancestor of a nation because he is *Abraham's* son. As Abram handed Hagar back to Sarai in the first scene, as God in the second issued her with the dark command to return to her mistress's abuse, so now, in the third, God tells Abraham to obey Sarah's orders, and again puts Hagar at her mercy. Once more God seems to be on the side of the oppressor. When Hagar and Ishmael are expelled and sent away to die in the desert, it is not just Sarah and Abraham who are responsible for their plight, but God also. He appears to add his cruelty to theirs.

However, once again, when Hagar and her son are on their own, God will come to their rescue. Quickly he will resume his normal guise and be the saviour of the oppressed. Why once more this change in him? Why this alarming inconsistency? I believe the answer is to be found in his promises and the limits they keep.

When he is in the presence of Sarah and Abraham, God inhabits the world of the promises to them and their descendants, and is bound by them. Though he has fine things in store for Ishmael also, the richest of his blessings are reserved for Isaac and the people that will eventually spring from him. The land of Canaan will be for them, not for the Ishmaelites. The covenant and the relationship it expresses will be with them, not with the bedouin. Only the people of Israel will be given his torah at Sinai. Only they will be given a David, and the promise that his dynasty will last for ever. There is an exclusiveness about these promises of God which cannot be denied, and so long as she keeps company with Abraham and Sarah, Hagar will find herself excluded. She does not belong to their world. She does not have a place in the brightest of their promises. The story of the people of God will go on without her, and after the end of Genesis 21 will not spare her another thought.[26] In *Lo and Behold!* we said this of Esau: 'He remains a bystander on the edge of God's purposes, and one who has suffered grievously that those purposes might go forward.'[27] After Hagar's story is over we might well say the same of her.

But we have not yet reached the end of it, nor are we quite at the end of this scene. First we must hear of Abraham's reaction to God's speech and of the immediate outcome for Hagar and Ishmael: 'So Abraham rose early in the morning, and took bread and a skin of water, and gave it to Hagar, putting it on her shoulder, along with the child, and sent her away. And she departed, and wandered about in the wilderness of Beer-sheba' (21.14). In the very next chapter Abraham will again get up early in the morning and make elaborate preparations for travel. Following a command he has received from God, he will take Isaac with him and journey for three days towards what he is certain will be the boy's death. At the last moment 'the messenger of the Lord' will call to him from heaven and save the child. He will look up and see a ram, and will sacrifice that in Isaac's stead. Hagar's last scene will contain further anticipations of that story, but in the preparations for her departure we have one already. She, too, is leaving as a result of a divine command, though the command has not been issued to her directly – it was Abraham who was told to do whatever Sarah told him. Thanks to Abraham she takes with her bread and water, the symbols of life, not the fire and the knife and the wood for sacrifice that Abraham will take for Isaac's death. Hagar's supplies represent the only tokens of love – or is it merely pity? – that Abraham ever gives her. Like the loincloths the woman and man make for themselves in the Garden, they will turn out to be pathetically inadequate. Abraham will go on a fearsome journey. Hagar and her son are sent away to a fearsome place, notorious for its harsh conditions and lack of water. But they will not go on a journey. In her second scene we found her on the way to Shur. She was on a particular route, and one which was for her the way home, the way back to Egypt. Now she and her child have nowhere to go. When God sends Abraham to the land of Moriah to sacrifice his son, he has a particular purpose for him in mind. He is testing him to discover where his true attachments lie. God is instrumental in sending Hagar and Ishmael out into the desert of Beer-sheba, but he has no immediate purpose for either of them. They are but bystanders on the edge of his larger purposes, and for the time being can only wander aimlessly about until the food and water and they themselves are exhausted.

Their wanderings bring to mind another range of stories. In the book of Exodus the Israelites will be sent away[28] from Egypt, and will also find themselves wandering in the desert, and will soon become desperately short of water. Hagar's last scene, like her second, will echo those stories also.

A second encounter with God

(*Gen. 21.15–21*)

The start of the scene could not be more stark. The narrator does not bother to describe her wandering about with her child. He does not tell us how far they went, or how long they were able to carry on. With the sureness of touch of a master storyteller, he brings us straight to the point where the crisis reaches its climax. The water runs out.

> When the water in the skin was gone, she cast the child under one of the bushes. Then she went and sat down opposite him a good way off, about the distance of a bowshot; for she said, 'Do not let me look on the death of the child.' And as she sat opposite him, she lifted up her voice and wept. (21.15–16)

In *The Women's Bible Commentary*, Susan Niditch reminds us of the associations in literature between fertility and water. They represent, she suggests, 'ancient intuitive acknowledgements of our watery origins on earth and in mother, and of the source of life upon which we continue to depend'.[29] In the case of Genesis she directs our attention to the story of Rebekah meeting Abraham's servant beside a well, when he is searching for a suitable wife for Isaac (24.10–27), and to that other well where Jacob falls in love with Rachel (29.1–12). She also points us towards the two scenes of Hagar in the desert. We will recall that in chapter 16 God met her 'by a spring of water'. That water did indeed remind us of fertility. She was carrying Ishmael in her womb at the time, and she received a promise from God that he would multiply her offspring so that they would be far too many to count. Now, however, in the apparently arid desert of Beer-sheba, a lack of water seems to spell an end to all that. Hagar's period of fertility appears to have come to an end. She is not on the way home now, and there is no convenient spring. The end of the water surely means death for her, for her son, and for the promises that God gave her beside the spring. The Hebrew of verse 15 already has the smell of death about it. When it says she 'cast' her son under a bush, it uses a verb which is commonly used elsewhere in the Old Testament for the throwing down of dead bodies. Hagar casts Ishmael aside as if he were a corpse. But how different is this 'rejection' from those she herself has suffered! It is a token of her love for the child, not of her contempt. It is an expression of concern, not only for herself and her own feelings, but for the boy also. She can do no more for him. Any power she had has now gone with the water. All she can do is put him in the shade and sit waiting for his death where she will not be able to see or hear too much. She is not at all concerned for her own plight, beyond her grief at the loss of her child. So concentrated is her attention on Ishmael, that we have to use our imaginations to realize that she is sitting waiting for her own death also. She shows the selflessness of the mother whose child is in grave danger, and who quite forgets any threat to herself.

The insertion of the detail of 'the distance of a bowshot' seems curious at first sight. Everything else in the narrative plainly contributes to the pathos of the scene and to the sense of impending tragedy. This alone seems superfluous. But it is not. After this scene is over, the narrator will tell us what becomes of Hagar and her son. It turns out that Ishmael will become 'an expert with the bow' (21.20). Hagar's sitting at that particular distance is thus prophetic. Just as Abraham's and then Sarah's laughter at the prospect of their having a child reassured us that Isaac, 'Laughter', would be born against all the odds, so Hagar's putting a bowshot's distance between her and Ishmael hints to us that they have a future after all. Yet we only pick up the hint once we get to the end of the story! For the moment, if we are looking for straws to clutch, all we have is the child's name, Ishmael, 'God Hears'. But in these verses his name is not used.

'For she said, "Do not let me look on the death of the child"' (21.16). That is Hagar's only speech in this whole chapter. In the company of Sarah and Abraham, she was given nothing to say, as was the case in the opening scene of her story. God will soon come to her again, but this time she will not engage in dialogue with him. She will, in fact, have nothing more to say. These words of utter despair, in which she cannot bring herself even to speak her son's name, are the last ones we hear from her lips.

But they are not to be the last words of her life. The story continues with, 'And God *heard* . . .' The Hebrew, following its usual custom, puts the verb before the subject: 'And heard God . . .' The word for 'heard' and the first two letters of the word for God spell out Ishmael's name. Curiously, Ishmael is not named directly at any juncture in the scene, but this play on his name is the point on which it all turns.

And God heard the voice of the boy; and the messenger of God called to Hagar from heaven, and said to her, 'What troubles you, Hagar? Do not be afraid; for God has heard the voice of the boy where he is. Come, lift up the boy and hold him fast with your hand, for I will make a great nation of him.' (21.17–18)

The story of Hagar was especially attractive to the seventeenth-century artist Rembrandt, and he devoted an etching and a number of drawings to her, most of them depicting the moment of Abraham's dismissal, or else dealing with this encounter with 'the messenger'. As we might expect, Rembrandt shows the messenger as having a human form with wings, and as coming down from the sky. In fact, the narrator reveals to us by the way he introduces the encounter that the one meeting with Hagar is again God himself, for it is he who hears the crying.

One of Rembrandt's most eloquent treatments of the scene shows his angel reaching out to touch the distraught Hagar on the shoulder. With the other arm he points to a well of water, which soon we and Hagar will discover has been there all the time. Rembrandt has so positioned the figures that the angel seems about to embrace her in his arms.

He has, alas, used artist's licence. In Hagar's first encounter with God, he came so close that she could 'see' him and even give him a name. This time he keeps his distance, as again he will when Abraham has the knife poised at Isaac's throat. Hidden from our sight in the periphrasis, 'the messenger of God', he keeps himself from Hagar's view also, and calls to her from his own domain. His wide universe of hope and promise reaches out to the small world of her despair and transforms it, but there is no longer the intimacy of their first meeting. The promise that Ishmael will become a great nation is repeated, but there is no dialogue, no expression of awe and astonishment on Hagar's part, no daring to give God a name. When we recall how few parallels we could find in the biblical literature for her first encounter, we realize that this one is also quite remarkable. Here, too, God does Hagar very great honour. Nevertheless, this encounter, for all Rembrandt could do with it, lacks the immediacy, the terror of the first, and leaves its awesomeness understated.

In one important respect Rembrandt's drawing is true to the

biblical text. He shows his angel paying heed to Hagar. Ishmael is asleep (another bit of artistic licence) in the bottom right-hand corner, but the angel's attention is focused on the mother, and it is to her that he is speaking. Some commentators and translators have taken too much notice of the fact that God hears the crying of her son. Indeed, some of them have found the shift from the mention of Hagar's weeping to God's responding to Ishmael so abrupt that they have declared the Hebrew text of the end of verse 16 corrupt, and have altered it to make Ishmael lift up his voice and weep.[30] Instead of 'And as she sat opposite him, *she* lifted up *her* voice and wept', they have 'And as she sat opposite him, *the child* lifted up *his* voice and wept.' Thus, as Phyllis Trible remarks, they have robbed Hagar of her grief.[31] Rembrandt in a few lines gives it wonderful expression, and so keeps closer to the text than does the Septuagint (the ancient Greek translation of the Old Testament), the RSV, the JB, or such commentators as Gerhard von Rad and Claus Westermann!

By responding to the little boy's[32] cries (21.17), God is only directing his concern to where Hagar's own attention is focused. The mother is anxious not for herself, but for her child. Hagar in her grief is self-effacing, and God acknowledges that. By paying heed to the child, he *is* paying heed to the mother, and that he makes plain by his addressing his speech to her. Yet, as Phyllis Trible notes,[33] his arrival in the story does mark a shift away from Hagar to her son. We can see that most clearly if we compare the end of verse 17 with its parallel in Luke's Gospel. For, although Luke found the pattern for his story of the annunciation to Mary most especially in Hagar's first meeting with God, he based some of the details on this second scene. After Gabriel's initial greeting, Luke's story proceeds as follows:

'Do not be afraid, Mary, for you have found favour with God. And now, you will conceive in your womb and bear a son, and you will name him Jesus. He will be great, and will be called the Son of the Most High . . .' Mary said to the angel, 'How can this be . . .?' The angel said to her, 'The Holy Spirit will come upon you . . .' (Luke 1.30–5)

Hagar's story also has 'Do not be afraid', but continues with, 'for God has heard the voice of the boy'. While Luke keeps our eyes focused on Mary, the narrator in Genesis turns them away from Hagar towards the son. While Luke allows Mary to speak, the storyteller here has Hagar remain silent.

But, of course, there is a crucial difference between the two scenes. Mary does not have a boy dying beneath a desert bush. Hagar 'listens to a deity who is concerned primarily with her son,' says Phyllis Trible.[34] That is too simple. In Hagar's circumstances, if God were to be 'concerned primarily' with her, then she would surely tell him to stop worrying about her and go and help her son. We have already seen where her own mind is fixed, and at the end of the scene we are given further evidence pointing in the same direction. When, after he has finished talking with her, God opens her eyes and shows her a well nearby, she goes and fills the skin with water and gives Ishmael a drink. There is no mention of her quenching her own thirst. God attends to her needs as much as Ishmael's when he tells her to go across to the child and lift him up and hold him tight. He continues to attend to her when he promises again that Ishmael will become a nation. To a mother of a child on the edge of death, that is fine music to the ear! She can resume her role as the boy's mother; for a second time, through the gift of water, she can give him life; once more she can dream the dreams about him that God first put in her head before he was born. What seems at first sight a shift in the story that diminishes Hagar, ends up leading to the restoration of her dignity and her proper authority, and then the re-emergence of that defiance which we glimpsed briefly in her first scene. For her story ends with this: 'God was with the boy, and he grew up; he lived in the wilderness, and became an expert with the bow. He lived in the wilderness of Paran; and his mother got a wife for him from the land of Egypt' (21.20–1). Three quarters of the talk is about Ishmael, and reflects the experiences the Israelites were to have of the bedouin. At first it seems Hagar has disappeared from the narrative altogether. It appears that only Ishmael counts for anything, that in the end the narrator and his God are interested only in him. But at its very end the story returns to her and to her initiative.

In the company of Sarah and Abraham she could take no initiative at all, except once to run away. In her first encounter with God she was able to give him the name El-Roi. In the desert for a second time, she took over the running of the story. She put Ishmael aside in the shade, she went and sat down where she could not see him die, she spoke her grief, she lifted up her voice and wept. When God answered from heaven he encouraged her to continue in this vein, and enlarged her acting on her own initiative into the exercising of true freedom. Before he entered the story, she could take decisions for herself, but still had no more power than when she was a slave of Sarah's. All she could do was wait for her son's death, and make her own a little more bearable. She had simply exchanged one harsh mistress for another. Instead of Sarah, she was at the mercy of the desert. With the lifting up of her son, the taking of his hand, the putting of water to his lips, she has at last become a free woman. She will have no more to do with slavery. She will have no more to do with Sarah or Abraham. This time there is no divine command to return. The desert changes from a place where she and Ishmael are sure to die to one where they can live and thrive. Though they have no Promised Land, the wilderness becomes their home, and eventually, in taking a wife for her son from Egypt, she returns to her own roots and allows her own people to help determine the character of the nation that will spring from her.

Although Rebekah will be behind Jacob's being sent by Isaac to find a wife among her people (see Gen. 27.46–28.5), no other woman in the Bible will choose a wife for her son. It will be Abraham who secures, through the good offices of his trusted servant, that same Rebekah as a wife for Isaac (24.1–67).

In the two scenes set in the desert Hagar plays several roles that elsewhere are played by Abraham or by the Israelites of the Exodus. The embryo in her womb in the earlier of them, and the child riding on her shoulder in the second, has no father to care for him. Hagar and Ishmael, alone together in the desert, constitute a one-parent family. And so Hagar the mother must there perform the roles of the father also. For that reason it is not surprising that she enjoys some privileges that belong elsewhere to Abraham, and sometimes apes or foreshadows his actions. Nor is it so remarkable that she should in the desert gain a status and an honour that Sarah, her mistress, nowhere receives, for Sarah never appears in the narrative away from the company of men.

Yet let us not fail to underline the significance of the roles she plays, or the extraordinary nature of the particular honour she achieves. We have said enough already about the privileges heaped upon her, but a few final remarks must be made about her roles. She is not simply father to her son as well as mother. She reminds us of a particular father, the one who is the father of her own child, the one who is destined to be the father of the people of God. If Abraham has any counterpart in these narratives, it is Hagar, the Egyptian slave, not Sarah. It is Hagar to whom God appears, and who speaks with him and receives his promises. It is Hagar whose second encounter with him will so clearly anticipate the story of the binding of Isaac and what, in the judgement of the narrator, is Abraham's finest hour. And not content with giving her Abraham's part, the narrator has her play the Israelites themselves, and in a way that looks forward to the events that will lie at the heart of their gospel, those of the Exodus. God will hear their cries also; he will come to their rescue; he will provide them with water when none is to be found (see Exod. 15.22–5; 17.1–7; Num. 20.2–11). Hagar will not repay him with bitter complaints and accusations as they will, and the selflessness she shows when Ishmael is dying of thirst will put them to shame.

Susan Niditch says of Genesis 21, 'While reading this story one has the distinct feeling it is being told from Hagar and Ishmael's point of view'.[35] I do not share her feeling until the last scene in the desert, but there it is surely supported by the text, which in its few masterly lines allows us to come so close to their hopelessness, and finally to rejoice with them in their triumph.

In telling Hagar's story the narrator has carefully ordered his plot and his words so that they will readily evoke our sympathy for her and her son. And yet he has included it in a narrative that traces the origins of the Israelite people, and will soon record how grievously they suffer at the hands of Hagar's own people, the Egyptians. His generosity is yet one more surprise this astonishing tale has to offer its readers.

4

Unsung Heroines: The Women of Exodus 1–4

Anyone familiar with the Bible has heard of Sarah. A great many people not familiar with it have still heard of Eve. Admittedly, Hagar may not be so well known, though she has received a great deal of attention from scholars in recent years, and long ago became a favourite subject of painters and artists who chose to illustrate biblical scenes. Shiphrah, Puah, and Zipporah, however, have a very long way to go before they become household names! They are the subject of this chapter, along with the mother and sister of Moses, a pharaoh's daughter with her female attendants, and the other six daughters of a Midianite priest called Reuel or Jethro (Zipporah is the seventh and becomes Moses' wife). Here, for the first time, we will meet some true heroines.

Setting the scene

(Exod. 1.1–14)

The Book of Genesis ends most movingly with reunion and reconciliation. Joseph is reunited with his brothers and then with his father, and though the brothers' fear of him returns once Jacob is dead, it quickly evaporates as their own pleas for forgiveness and Joseph's magnanimity and wisdom together create reconciliation. As Joseph prepares to die at the close he declares a promise. The whole family are now in Egypt, but Joseph assures them: 'God will surely come to you, and bring you up out of this land to the land that he swore to Abraham, to Isaac, and to Jacob' (Gen. 50.24). The Book of Exodus describes that coming of God.

It begins on what might seem an optimistic note. After rehearsing the names of Jacob's sons (there is no mention of his daughters, though we know he had some[1]) and passing on beyond their generation, it continues with: 'the Israelites were fruitful, they swarmed, they multiplied and grew exceedingly powerful, so that the land was filled with them' (Exod. 1.7). This is Genesis language, the language of the promises, and even more conspicuously the language of creation. In Genesis 1 God said, 'Let the waters *swarm* with *swarms* of living creatures' (v. 20), and to the human-kind, created in his image and likeness, he said, 'Be *fruitful* and *multiply* and *fill the earth*' (v. 28). Later he promised Abraham that his descendants would be as numerous as the stars in heaven (15.5; 22.17), as the particles of dust on the earth (13.16), or those of the sand on the seashore (22.17), and become a '*powerful*' nation (18.18). All seems to be going according to plan. His promises, together with the bright designs of his creation are finding fulfil-ment. There is only one snag. The descendants of Abraham are in the wrong place. The land promised to them is Canaan, and they are in Egypt.

Genesis 1.28, after speaking of humanity being fruitful and multiplying and filling the earth, continued with the words, 'and subdue it; and have dominion . . .' The word it used for 'earth' is the same as the one for 'land' in Exodus 1.7. When he first gave his promises to Abraham, God declared, 'I will make of you a great nation . . . and make your name great' (Gen. 12.2). The Hebrew terms employed there suggested an independent nation state, with its own monarchy of fine renown,[2] and they were later reinforced by God's prediction in Genesis 18.18 that Abraham would become 'a great and powerful nation'. In echoing these passages so deliber-ately the narrator of Exodus has struck a note to alarm the hearts of the Egyptians. Will these descendants of Jacob subdue *their* land and have dominion over *them*? Will they set up their own king and become an independent nation in their midst? These are the questions which the narrator has begged for them. Now that we hear them too, the paranoia of the pharaoh becomes more understandable.

Now a new king arose over Egypt, who did not know Joseph. He said to his people, 'Look, the Israelite people are more numerous and more powerful than we. Come, let us deal wisely with them, or they will increase and, in the event of war, join our enemies and fight against us and escape from the land.' (1.8–10)

This pharaoh does not know Joseph. That makes all the difference. He does not know the man who rescued his own people, the Egyptians, from famine.[3] He does not know the one who, in fact, if Genesis is to be believed, brought back the whole earth from the brink of death through his wisdom, foresight and efficiency (Gen. 41.57 tells us that 'all the world came to Joseph in Egypt to buy grain, because the famine became severe throughout the world'.) Thus he does not know of the one who averted the greatest crisis for the world of the Genesis narrative since the Flood, and brought some fulfilment at long last to God's promise to Abraham that through him all the families of the earth would find blessing. He does not know the one who, according to Genesis 47.13–26, established for him the basis of his enormous wealth and power. He is ignorant of the man who could perceive the purposes of God underlying the events in Egypt, and knew what was going on.[4] Not knowing all this, he is terrified, and finds it impossible to keep things in perspective.

'Look,' he says, 'the Israelite people are more numerous and more powerful than we.' Such is the paranoia of the dictator or the absolute monarch. His claim is absurd on both its counts. And yet – and here we see the playfulness of this storyteller – his fear that the Israelites might join his enemies and fight against him and escape from the land will be fulfilled. He has got just one thing wrong. He should have spoken of an enemy, not enemies. The one who will 'fight' against the Egyptians and who will engineer the Israelites' escape will not be a foreign invader, but God.[5]

His terror finds a ready outlet in violence and oppression. The stories of the first half of Exodus are a delicious mixture of the plausible and the implausible. The reports that appear from time to time in our newspapers and on our televisions mean that the pharaoh's ploy and his reasons for it ring bells whose sound is alarmingly familiar. The Israelites are too numerous and their loyalty to the state cannot be counted upon. So the powers that be try to break their spirits and their backs with unremitting forced labour, and attempt to make their conditions so harsh that they will stop breeding so successfully. With an irony that has its own cruelty, the Egyptians set them to work building supply cities. When Joseph made plans for the storage of grain in advance of the coming famine,[6] all benefited, both Egyptians and non-Egyptians. His storehouses were sources of life. Now the pharaoh's store-cities are meant to spell death for the Israelites, who will, we can be quite sure, enjoy none of their bounty.

Yet the promise of God that the descendants of Abraham would become as many as the stars, or the particles of dust on the earth, or the grains of sand on the seashore, cannot be defeated so easily. 'The more they were oppressed, the more they multiplied and spread . . .' (1.12). Alice Laffey aptly comments, 'What other sources of stimulation, pleasure, and human accomplishment' did they have?[7] As so often happens, oppression ends up working against the oppressor, and produces the very opposite of what is intended. And as we might also have predicted, the violence and fear of the pharaoh and his minions turn out to be infectious, and the whole Egyptian people go down with the disease. We are told they come to regard the Israelites with a sickening dread and loathing (the Hebrew verb near the end of v. 12 can and probably does mean both things). Such racial hatred makes them more than willing allies of their king: 'The Egyptians became ruthless in imposing tasks on the Israelites, and made their lives bitter with hard service in mortar and brick and in every kind of field labour. They were ruthless in all the tasks that they imposed on them' (1.13–14). The Hebrew text is particularly striking. Five times in these two verses it uses a root which refers to slave labour, twice it ends a sentence with the word 'ruthlessness'. Thus, with the greatest skill and without any sensationalism, the narrator underlines the Israelites' plight.

He does not tell us directly of the outcome of this treatment. He maintains a poignant silence on the subject, and moves straight on to the pharaoh coming up with a second and much more drastic plan. We are left to conclude that his people's eager co-operation in his ploy has proved as fruitless as his own initiative, or else again has only made things worse. He now decides to go beyond slavery to genocide.

Shiphrah and Puah, heroines of the resistance

(Exod. 1.15–21)

'Now the king of Egypt said to the midwives of the Hebrews, one of whom was named Shiphrah and the other Puah . . .' (1.15). Thus we come to the first two of the women we are considering in this chapter. They are given no more introduction than that, but in several respects it is most remarkable.

Before we examine the features of verse 15 itself, we must make sure we pay sufficient heed to the point where it falls in the story. That place is already very dark, full of fear, cruel exploitation and violence. Already we have seen things get worse for the Israelites, and now we can expect them to get worse still. We have seen the Israelites put on the rack by the pharaoh. We have seen them being stretched more ruthlessly by his people. We can now expect there to be a further intensification of their pain and of the violence of their oppressors. Shiphrah and Puah could not enter the narrative at a more sinister moment.

Yet there is one more thing to remember about storytellers, and about those of the Old Testament in particular: they frequently take delight in leading their readers or hearers up the garden path. A development in a story may mark a continuation and intensification of what has gone before, or else it may represent a twist, a point where suddenly, without warning, things change course and are never quite the same again. Sometimes, in the more sophisticated stories, there is both a crescendo *and* a sudden change of key. The beginning of the Book of Exodus presents us with just such a story.

Before, however, we see how it proceeds, we must return to verse 15 itself, and the manner in which Shiphrah and Puah enter the narrative.

The first thing to notice about them is that they are both named. That is perhaps the most astonishing detail of all. They appear in a large narrative unit which has its beginning at the start of Exodus 1, and its ending at 14.31, after the dramatic crossing of the Sea of Reeds. It has a cast of untold millions. The main parts are played by God, Moses and two pharaohs. Aaron looks at first as though he might join their company, but ends up with nothing very much to do and very little to say. After him come a number of people who play bit-parts of varying importance, and then hordes of extras. Besides Shiphrah and Puah, there are, in order of appearance, a number of Egyptians in charge of the Israelite slave-gangs, Moses' father, his mother, his sister, the daughter of the first pharaoh (together with her female attendants), an Egyptian who is killed by Moses, a Hebrew man being beaten by that Egyptian, and two Hebrews fighting with one another. A pastoral interlude brings on stage a priest of Midian called Reuel (or Jethro, as he is called elsewhere in the unit, and beyond in Exod. 18), his seven daughters (among them Zipporah), a gang of nasty shepherds, and a son born to Zipporah and Moses named Gershom. Back in Egypt we are introduced to the elders of the Israelites, to more Egyptian

overseers, and to Israelite supervisors set in immediate control of
the labourers, and then to 'the wise men and sorcerers', or
'magicians', of the second pharaoh's court, and to others of his
advisers. The extras consist of all the countless Egyptians who
join in the pharaohs' cruelty and who suffer from the plagues God
sends on the land, the soldiers and chariot-drivers of the second
pharaoh's army, the Israelite people, who themselves are enough
to 'fill the land', and then vast numbers of animals and insects.
There are the flocks belonging to Reuel or Jethro, those belonging
to the shepherds who drive his daughters away from the well, the
snakes which emerge from Moses' and Aaron's rods and their
unfortunate Egyptian counterparts, the domestic animals of the
Egyptians and the Israelites, the Egyptian war-horses, and finally
the creatures responsible for four of the plagues, the frogs, the
gnats, the flies, and the locusts. If we discount the list of the twelve
sons of Jacob in the prologue to the narrative, and leave aside the
genealogy in 6.14–25, then we discover that apart from God, who
names himself, there are just seven characters who are named.
Shiphrah and Puah are the first of them, and the rest are, again in
order of appearance, Moses, Reuel or Jethro, Zipporah, Gershom,
and Aaron. Particularly conspicuous by their absence from that list
are the two pharaohs. They retain throughout the anonymity of the
enemy, and, precisely because they are not identified, wear the
garb of the archetypal tyrant, and belong to any age that recognizes
it for what it is.

It is not simply their having names, nor even the initiatives they
will take and the particular things they will do and say, that ensure
that Shiphrah and Puah step out from the pages of the narrative
as colourful individuals. The narrator has thrown the spotlight full
on them by having only two of them. In an obvious sense that
number is ridiculous. It is one of the story's more implausible
details. No two women could begin to help with all the deliveries
there must have been among the Israelites, and indeed their speech
to the pharaoh suggests they might do duty among the Egyptian
women also. For the storyteller, however, such implausibility was
of no consequence. It is equally inconceivable that the midwives
would have an audience, indeed *two* audiences, with the pharaoh
himself, instead of with one of his relatively minor officials. After
all, we do not find women of any kind anywhere else in Exodus
walking the corridors of power as they do. But that did not matter
either. The narrator was interested in composing a lively, compelling tale. There was much greater drama to be had in the midwives'
meeting with the great pharaoh himself, and his readers (or might

it here be *her* readers? – we will return to that possibility at a later stage) would find it much easier to engage with them and identify with them if there were only two, and not a whole crowd of them filling the pharaoh's throne room.

Strangely, however, though the narrator takes so much trouble to flesh out these two characters, he or she does not make clear whether they were Hebrews or Egyptians. The Hebrew text is ambiguous, and could either mean they were midwives who were themselves Hebrews, or that they were women, presumably Egyptian, who served as midwives among the Hebrews. Ultimately the ambiguity cannot be resolved, and that means we will have to give two readings of this story, not just one.

We suggested that Shiphrah and Puah come on stage at a most ominous moment in the action. Our worst fears are at once fulfilled, if not exceeded: 'The king of Egypt said to the midwives of the Hebrews . . . "When you act as midwives to the Hebrew women, keep an eye out for the stones;[8] if it's a son, kill him; if it's a daughter, she shall live"' (1.16). The pharaoh's order is extremely abrupt, the language utterly stark in its horror. There is no courtesy about his speech, no attempt at diplomacy, nor could there be any. We are reminded of 'the massacre of the innocents' in Matthew's Gospel, of Herod's ordering all children in and around Bethlehem who were two years old or under to be killed (Matt. 2.16). Yet the pharaoh's command is even more terrible than that. Herod wishes to make sure one particular child called Jesus is dead, and though he does not care how many children die in the process, the scale of his slaughter is strictly limited. Furthermore, though Matthew does not explain who carried out Herod's orders, we can safely presume he used his own soldiers. This pharaoh's designs are much more ambitious than Herod's, and he chooses *midwives* to do his work. Shiphrah's and Puah's role was to deliver, to help to bring to life, to lead out of pain into joy. The pharaoh commands them to become his agents of death.

It is not entirely clear what the pharaoh is trying to achieve. The scene does not introduce any new motives on his part, so we might assume that they are the same as led him to his policy of enslavement and forced labour. If they are, then he is cutting off his nose to spite his face. As Brevard Childs comments, 'Ordinarily a ruling nation, particularly in the Ancient Near East, would not think of destroying its labour supply.'[9] Cheryl Exum exposes further layers of absurdity. She finds it incongruous enough that in his first ploy the pharaoh should be determined to reduce the Hebrew population, when apparently he needs the labour of their males to build his store-cities. With regard to his second plan, she points out that it neither serves his immediate purposes (that is, if they are the same as they were before), 'nor represents the logical way to control overpopulation, which would be to kill females'.[10] Yet violence has its own fascination, and dictators of this pharaoh's sort obey their own logic. Everett Fox's comment is a fair one, although it does not address all the points that have been made: 'The story does not describe a rational fear, but paranoia – paralleling the situation in Nazi Germany of the 1930s and 1940s, where Jews were blamed for various economic and political catastrophes not of their own making and were eliminated from a society that could have used their resources and manpower.'[11] He is right to remind us of the Holocaust here. His statement itself makes plain that the parallel between it and the events in Egypt is far from exact. Nevertheless, we do well to ponder on the fact that the people whose very identity is now bound up with memories of the Holocaust should in Exodus begin their history as the intended victims of genocide.

This new plan is much more drastic than the pharaoh's first one, and so represents an intensification of what has gone before. It also marks a new strategy, a change of direction on his part, for which the earlier measures did not prepare us. In that respect it is a twist in the course of the narrative. Yet the shift it contains is as nothing compared with the one provided by Shiphrah's and Puah's reaction. 'But the midwives feared God; they did not do as the king of Egypt commanded them, but they let the boys live' (1.17). The language is as simple and straightforward as that of the pharaoh's command. The narrator does not underline their defiance or their heroism. But he does explain their motive: they 'feared God'. These two women are surrounded by fear. The narrative has already spoken of the fear of the pharaoh and his people. It will go on to tell us of the fear of the two Hebrews fighting with one another, when Moses intervenes; of Moses' own fear as he flees for his life from the pharaoh, and as he faces God and his terrifying demands at the Burning Bush; of the fear of the Israelite foremen as the tyranny of the second pharaoh threatens to destroy them and their people; of the fear of that pharaoh and his officials when plagues rain down upon them; and of the fear of the Israelites caught between the Sea of Reeds and the pursuing Egyptian army. Twice we are told in the course of their short scene that Shiphrah and Puah 'fear' God. But their fear is unlike that of all the rest. It is different even from the fear that overcomes Moses at the Burning Bush, as we can see if we compare the results of the two. Moses' fear is disabling, and runs counter to the declared purposes of God. It makes him squirm and wriggle and protest or raise objections to what God is asking of him. Indeed, no one in the entire Bible is so persistent in protesting against a divine commission as Moses is in that scene.[12] His fear and that of all the rest is sheer terror. The fear of Shiphrah and Puah is not that at all, but a sense of awe and the mark of where their loyalty lies. It does not turn them to flight or feeble protest, nor to accusation or violence. It enables them to defy the pharaoh *without fear*, and then, as we shall soon see, to confront him with astonishing bravado and make a fool out of him. Because of their fear of God, they owe the pharaoh no allegiance and they show him none. They refuse his hideous stratagems. They refuse to wear the uniform of his death squads underneath their midwives' garb. They do not tell him to his face that they will not do as he commands. Such overt disobedience would no doubt have cost them their lives, and he would simply have sought others to do his dirty work. They simply go away and carry on doing their work as they have always done it.

If, however, an oppressive regime such as the one in Egypt is to carry out its purposes, it must have clear lines of communication and an efficient network of informants. We are not told of these. We do not even hear of the pharaoh being informed. The pace of this narrative is too quick for such details. All we are told is that the midwives are summoned by the pharaoh to explain themselves. 'So the king of Egypt summoned the midwives and said to them, "Why have you done this, and allowed the boys to live?"' (1.18). They now find themselves in the utmost danger. We may recall the case of an earlier pharaoh summoning Abram to explain why he had claimed Sarai was his sister. But that pharaoh turned out to be a just and honourable man. This one, we know already, is a merciless tyrant who is driven by paranoia.

Shiphrah and Puah, however, do not bat an eyelid: 'The midwives said to pharaoh, "But these Hebrews are not like Egyptian women. They are bursting with life! By the time the midwife gets to them they have given birth!"' (1.19). With these words, the only ones Shiphrah and Puah have to say, the audience ends. We do not hear directly of the pharaoh's response. The two women do very well out of it all, as we shall soon discover, while the pharaoh himself moves on to another plan of action which does not rely on any midwives for its execution, but instead demands the co-operation of 'all his people'. We must presume he believes the women's excuse, and allows them to go free. Otherwise their survival and his change of tack make no sense.

Again we recall the comment Claus Westermann made with regard to Abram's deception of the Egyptians and their pharaoh in Genesis 12: 'The ruse is the only weapon left for the powerless given over to the mighty.'[13] In this particular case, according to Brevard Childs, the pharaoh is characterized as 'the wicked fool who is duped by the clever midwives',[14] and later in his commentary he writes, 'the frail responses of two women have succeeded in outdoing the crass power of the tyrant'.[15] Less soberly, Cheryl Exum remarks: 'They respond with a defense which would strain the gullibility of any pharaoh.'[16]

To their apt comments we would add an observation of our own. Surely the women's response amounts to a midwives' joke! In the past serious-minded commentators from Augustine to Calvin and beyond have worried themselves very silly about the women telling a transparent lie and then getting rewarded by God (as they do at the end of the scene).[17] Some more recent commentators have not got the joke either, so that Brevard Childs is able to say, 'The response of the midwives is so clever as to have convinced not only Pharaoh, but a number of modern commentators who accept its veracity on face value.'[18] Even such an astute critic as Carol Meyers can use this verse as evidence that Israelite women had easy deliveries![19]

Surely we will misunderstand this passage if we do not catch its humour. Cheryl Exum hints at it, as we have just seen, but it is Jonathan Magonet who brings it out into the open. First he draws our attention to how the midwives speak of the mothers they attend: 'The Egyptians they mention are referred to as "women", the "Hebrews" are not dignified with such a title – they are not like our (refined) Egyptian ladies!' Next he comments on the unusual Hebrew word *hayot*, which the midwives apply to the Hebrew mothers, and to which we have given the rather free, but suitably vulgar translation, 'bursting with life'. *Hayot* is, he explains, 'an unusual form of the verb meaning "to be" or "to live". But the form in the Hebrew is almost identical with the word for "animals", *hayyot* . . . these women are so "animal-like", that before the midwife can get there, they have "dropped" the baby.'[20]

The midwives' response *is* a wonderful joke, and a clever one too. See how skilfully they appeal to the pharaoh's racial prejudice by comparing the Hebrew women so unfavourably with his own Egyptian women! See how they trade on his sexism by coming so close to calling those same Hebrew women 'animals'! Yet the best part of the joke lies in how it is received. It is a transparent lie – and the pharaoh, being a man, and therefore never having witnessed the Hebrew women, or any other women for that matter, giving birth, believes it! There is no doubt that Shiphrah and Puah are to be counted among the clever female tricksters of the Bible. Genesis has furnished three of them before this in Rebekah, Rachel, and Tamar.[21]

Yet we would argue that Exodus 1.19 is not merely a joke, but a *midwives'* joke, precisely the sort of excuse such women might come up with. Now, if we are right, we might suppose that a sensitive, imaginative storyteller could identify sufficiently closely with these two women to put such words in their mouths. Yet would a man, living in a society where women in labour were attended only by women, be able to give us such a telling joke about such a subject as childbirth? We are left thinking this particular passage in Exodus 1 must have originated as a midwives' tale, that is a tale told not just about midwives but *by* midwives.[22] George Coats thinks it bears the marks of having once circulated as an independent unit.[23] As far as the larger narrative is concerned, there can be little doubt that the author was a man. It concerns itself to such an extent with the worlds of power politics, the army, and the cult, which were almost exclusively the domains of men. But it is probable that here he has made use of a story that originated among women, and which was primarily designed for a female audience. Certainly we can imagine how readily Israelite women would have enjoyed it, and how quick they would have been to grasp its humour.

We can also observe that for the first time we find ourselves handling a story in which we cannot detect a male bias. It is not written from a distinctively male standpoint. If there is any bias to be discovered, it would seem to be a female one. Though honours were showered upon Hagar in the desert, particularly in Genesis 16, we were left with the suspicion that it was because there was no man on the scene and she was the parent or parent-to-be of a one-parent family. Here there *is* a man on stage, and yet the women are undoubtedly the heroines of the piece. Their fear of God, their astonishing fearlessness before the pharaoh, and the sheer effrontery of their deception are clearly being held up for our admiration. They are exemplary characters, as Eve, Sarah, even Hagar, never were.

This last point is borne out by the concluding verses of the scene: 'So God dealt well with the midwives; and the people became many and grew exceedingly powerful. And because the midwives feared God, he made them households' (1.20–1). Shiphrah and Puah's reward spills over to the Israelite people. The oppression of the

Israelites began in the first place because, in the pharaoh's view, they were too 'many' and too 'powerful' (1.9). All his violence, all the cruelty of the Egyptian people, have got them nowhere. They are back where they began. As for the Israelites and the promises and purposes of God, they are still on course. It is quite clear in this second scene who God and the Israelites have to thank for that. God shows his gratitude by 'making households' for them.

The phrase is an unusual one, and in this context not entirely clear. It is interesting to note, however, that we find it again in 2 Samuel 7.11, where the prophet Nathan proclaims to king David: 'The Lord declares to you that the Lord will make you a house.' With Shiphrah and Puah we cannot be sure whether their reward is families of their own (surely an apt one for women who have been engaged so courageously in helping to provide families for others), or whether they now attain the status and privilege of having their own households among the Israelites. Whichever is the case, the storyteller has employed the same words to describe their reward as the narrator of 2 Samuel will use in describing the establishment of the Davidic dynasty!

If the phrase is to be understood in our second way, then it means that effectively Shiphrah and Puah become members of the Israelite people, and we should think of them as having been Egyptians. This brings us back to the question of their racial origins, and the two readings of their story that the uncertainty invites.

If we think of them as Israelites, then, as Cheryl Exum points out,[24] we can compare them to Moses. Like him, they act as saviours of their own people, and, as he will do eventually, they fearlessly confront the pharaoh and all he stands for. As Israelites they emerge as heroines who might encourage future generations of their people to stand fast in the face of oppression, and remain loyal to their calling. Their story can then be told among those who are themselves the victims of systematic cruelty and carefully calculated violence, and bring them some rare and precious laughter.

If, however, we suppose they are Egyptians, then they join the illustrious company of those foreign women and men in the Bible who are represented as showing conspicuous faith and obedience. They join the pharaoh's daughter and her attendants of Exodus 2; Reuel or Jethro of chapters 2, 4 and 18; Balaam of Numbers 22–4 (though not the Balaam of 22.22–35, where he does not emerge well from a comparison with his ass!); Rahab the Jericho prostitute of Joshua 2 and 6; Ruth from Moab, the ancestress of David; Jael, wife of Heber the Kenite, who appears in Judges 4 and is celebrated in the Song of Deborah in Judges 5; Uriah the Hittite of 2 Samuel 11; Naaman the Syrian of 2 Kings 5; the Syrophoenician woman of Mark 7; the centurion at Capernaum in Matthew 8 or Luke 7; and the other centurion at the foot of the cross in Mark 15, Matthew 27 and Luke 24.

If they are Egyptians, then they have a sense of awe before the God of an obscure, enslaved people, and serve his purposes, while mocking their own pharaoh, who was himself counted as divine. They share nothing of the paranoia of their own people, and none of their brutality. By their resolutely choosing the side of life and refusing to become dealers in death, they put into sharper relief the horror of the Egyptian pogroms. They sit in silent judgement upon their own people and their king.

Whether Egyptian or Hebrew, they teach the Israelites of the narrative not to be afraid. That is a lesson they will find very hard to learn, and even Moses will not come to it easily.

A son is born

(Exod. 1.22–2.10)

But the opening part of the story of the Israelites in Egypt is not finished yet. Storytellers frequently work in threes, and so far we have had only two moves from the pharaoh. Each has ended in failure. We can expect another twist, a yet further intensification of his attempts to destroy the Israelites as a people. The narrator does not keep us waiting. 'Then Pharaoh commanded all his people, "Every boy that is born to the Hebrews you shall throw into the Nile, but you shall let every daughter live"' (1.22). Abandoning the services of human midwives, the pharaoh turns for help to a divine one. The Nile was celebrated as a god by the Egyptians, and was undoubtedly one of their chief sources of life, their midwife, we might say. So another bringer of life is to be used, by royal command, as a dealer in death. As Cheryl Exum so chillingly remarks, 'Exposure was in ancient times a common means of disposing of unwanted children.'[25] This time the pharaoh will make sure the plan succeeds. He issues the command to 'all his people', to those who have already been caught up in his fear, and have co-operated so readily in his persecution of the Israelites. As before, he is intent on killing only the male babies.

And that is Moses' cue. 'Now a man from the house of Levi went and married a Levite woman. The woman conceived and bore a son . . .' (2.1–2a). There is nothing unusual about the language here. The man takes the initiative, marries the woman of his choice, she conceives and bears a child. That is how marriage and procreation are described over and over again in Old Testament narratives. What is unusual, what is terrifying, is the timing of this particular son's birth. What should be an occasion for such joy is turned by the dark designs of the pharaoh into a nightmare.

We have returned with these opening words of Exodus 2 to a male-dominated world, where men take women to be their wives, and where particular note is taken of a birth of a *son* – we will soon learn that this male baby already has a sister, but we have heard nothing about her birth, nor will we be told anything about it in retrospect. And yet the little story that is just beginning will from now on be concerned entirely with women, except for the baby – but then he will not have anything to do beyond lying there, doing a little crying, and growing up.

This time none of the women are named. We will learn later, in the genealogy of chapter 6, that the child's mother is called Jochebed (and his father Amram – see 6.20), and eventually, when the drama of the escape from Egypt is over, that his sister's name is Miriam (15.20).²⁶ In our exploration of the passage we will respect its silences and leave them unnamed.

'The woman conceived and bore a son; and she saw him, that he was good, and hid him three months' (2.2). Exodus 1, near its beginning, picked up the language of the Genesis 1 creation poem. Now this second chapter does the same. 'And God saw the light, that it was good' (Gen. 1.4), here becomes, 'and she saw him, that he was good'. Just as the narrator earlier encouraged us to compare the birth of the Israelite people to the birth of the world, so now he wishes us to make a similar link between creation and the birth of Moses. In the New Testament Matthew will draw a line from creation to Jesus by beginning his Gospel with the words, 'The book of the *genesis* of Jesus Christ', and Luke will make the connection even clearer by tracing Jesus' descent back to Adam and thence to the Creator himself (see Luke 3.38).

Not content with referring us back to the acts of creation, the narrator of Exodus 2 also reminds us of the Flood: 'When she could hide him no longer she got an *ark*²⁷ of papyrus for him, and plastered it with bitumen and pitch; she put the child in it and placed it among the reeds on the bank of the river' (2.3). So the child is set afloat on 'the waters of chaos', as Noah and his family were. He is hidden carefully among the reeds on the edge of what should be the river of life, but which has become, by the pharaoh's decree, the appointed river of death. Just as in Genesis 6 we heard of the elaborate preparation of Noah's ark, so now we learn the details of the materials and construction of the ark for Moses.

All this is designed to focus our minds on the child. The narrator has not provided any annunciation scene, as he did for Ishmael, and the birth of the boy is not miraculous, as was Isaac's. Yet, by his references to creation and the Flood, he is indicating the momentous character of the events. He is, in effect, making the extraordinary claims that with the birth of Moses a new era in the history of the world has dawned, and that through him, as through Noah, God will bring about a dramatic act of salvation, and rescue his purposes from the dark waters of violence.

With Shiphrah and Puah's story we were able to wonder whether it might have originated as a story told by a woman for women to hear. Such speculations are not possible here. This passage is primarily about Moses. It is his infancy narrative, and can be compared with the Matthean or Lucan infancy narratives about Jesus. Nevertheless, within its bounds women take all the initiatives, and are responsible for all the action and all the talking.

It is typical of the story that his *mother* should come up with the plan of the little ark of papyrus and put it into effect. The child's father does not come into it at all. Indeed beyond the first verse he is not mentioned anywhere in the story. He has gone and married a wife and enabled her to conceive a son. Beyond that the narrator is not interested in him.

It is not entirely clear, however, why Moses' mother should put him in the ark. When Hagar escapes to the desert with Ishmael, we fully understand why she abandons him to the shade of a bush. In Moses' case we know his mother cannot conceal him any longer, and we can indeed applaud her for being able to keep him a secret from the Egyptians for so long. Yet in consigning him to the waters of the Nile she is aping what her Egyptian enemies have been commanded to do. Perhaps that is precisely the point. Her desperate act is also another clever ruse. She does not wait for the Egyptians to find her child. She does their dirty work for them. She leaves him to the waters of the Nile. If summoned before the pharaoh, as Shiphrah and Puah were, she could argue that she has complied with his order already. She would not tell him, of course, about the basket, so carefully waterproofed and hidden! It seems she also belongs to the company of biblical female tricksters.

Care is taken not just to make the basket watertight and to conceal it, but also to guard it: 'His sister stood at a distance, to see what would happen to him' (2.4). This is the first we have heard of her. How old she is, we cannot be sure. Many of our versions call her a 'girl' in verse 8, but the Hebrew term employed there suggests a sexually mature young woman. It is, for example, the same word as Isaiah uses in his famous saying, 'a young woman is with child and shall bear a son' (Isa. 7.14). Certainly events will prove she is old enough to act on her own initiative when necessary, and will reveal that she can be very clever and resourceful. For the moment all she can do, and we the readers of the story with her, is wait to see what happens.

For a long time now scholars have drawn parallels between this story and others which tell of how great heroes were exposed at birth, were rescued, and eventually came to great power. The Greek story of Oedipus comes quickly to mind, but more significant is the Babylonian legend about Sargon of Akkad, who was also set by his mother in a basket of rushes, sealed with bitumen, and put into a river.[28] But Sargon appears to be abandoned by his mother, as Oedipus is by his father. Moses, however, is not abandoned. This is not a story of the exposure of an infant in the sense that he is rejected by his parents and consigned to a premature death. The preparations of his mother and sister are acts of desperation, but they are also acts of love. They are the best they can do for the child in the pharaoh's cruel circumstances, and they continue to give him the care that is possible.

There is no certainty their ploy will work. Here we must make a conscious effort, if need be, to read this story as if we do not know what happens next. Then the risk the women are taking, and the danger in which the child finds himself, despite all their preparations, will become at once apparent. Alas, the story has been romanticized by writers and painters alike, and much of its suspense, danger and excitement has been drained out of it. In the process the courage of all the women involved has been devalued.

So, there is no certainty their ploy will work. We, the readers of the story, have been reminded by the narrator's careful choice of language of the creation and the Flood, and have thus been able to pick up hints that all may be well. But we enjoy an advantage over the child's mother and sister. They can only wait and see.

The worst happens: 'The daughter of Pharaoh came down to bathe at the Nile, while her attendants walked beside the river. She spotted the ark among the reeds, and she sent her maid, took it, opened it, and saw him, the child – a crying boy!' (2.5–6a). The Hebrew is written with superb economy and skill. With just a handful of words it describes the various stages of the discovery, conjures up the suspense of it, and conveys the surprise that greets the princess when finally she opens the lid of the basket.

But her surprise is not as great as ours, so long as we persist in reading the text as if for the first time, when we hear of her reaction. She is, after all, the daughter of the pharaoh. She is the daughter of the author of the policy of genocide. All the Egyptians we have heard about so far in the book of Exodus have been willing parties to the persecution. We have heard nothing to make us think this princess and her maids will be any different. Indeed, with them coming from the palace, we can surely expect them to be particularly decisive and ruthless in their disposal of the child. Unless, of course, they think he is Egyptian. But the princess does not. She immediately recognizes him as one of the Hebrew children.

But before her words of recognition are spoken, the narrator inserts what in the Hebrew are just two more. They are the ones that contain the surprise, and on them the whole story turns: 'and she took pity on him' (2.6b). The word for 'took pity' does not occur anywhere else in Exodus, yet it can hardly fail to remind us of God's response to the suffering and cries of his people: 'The Israelites groaned under their slavery, and cried out. Out of the slavery their cry for help rose up to God. God heard their groaning, and God remembered his covenant with Abraham, Isaac, and Jacob. God looked upon the Israelites, and God knew' (2.23b–4). Twice we have seen God intervene to rescue Sarah from a pharaoh and from the king of Gerar. We have seen him come to Hagar's aid in the desert, and save her and Ishmael from death. We have heard how he stayed Abraham's hand at the last moment, and delivered Isaac from sacrifice on the mountain in the land of Moriah. The central theme of the first half of the book of Exodus is his being stirred into acts of salvation by the plight of his people, whether in Egypt or the wilderness of Sinai. Here on the bank of the Nile, he needs no intervention. He can rely instead on the resourcefulness of Moses' mother and sister, and on the compassion of an enemy princess.

In two respects God's response to his people is less remarkable than the princess's reaction to finding Moses. We were unnerved and surprised by God's siding with Sarah and Abraham in Genesis 21, but partly because it was so untypical of him. God spends so much of his time and energy in the Old Testament fighting oppression and delivering the oppressed, or calling for their deliverance. It is not too much to say he has a passion for such work. In that regard, then, we cannot be surprised when he meets

Moses in the blaze of a burning bush and reveals his plans to bring his people out of Egypt into the land of promise. However, we *can* be surprised, on the basis of what Exodus has told us so far, when the pharaoh's own daughter meets Moses with immediate compassion.

Second, the narrator reminds us, when he first tells us of God's becoming aware of the suffering of his people in 2.23–4, that he is under obligation to help them. He gave their ancestors promises, promises of land, independence, prosperity, blessing. He promised he would be with them and keep them wherever they went. He made a covenant with them, which bound him together with them for ever, and which amounted to a solemn assurance that his promises would be fulfilled. Pharaoh's daughter is under no obligation to rescue Moses. Quite the reverse. As one of her father's people, she is under obligation to see that the child is killed.

Up to this point the crisis for the child and his family has been deepening. The story has been sliding into ever greater danger, and getting ever closer to death. Now, with the princess's compassion, it turns upwards towards life and security. In its new mood it even has time for a joke:

'This must be one of the Hebrews' children,' she said. Then his sister said to Pharaoh's daughter, 'Shall I go and get you a nurse from the Hebrew women to nurse the child for you?' Pharaoh's daughter said to her, 'Yes.' So the young woman went and called the child's mother. Pharaoh's daughter said to her, 'Take this child and nurse it for me, and I will give you your wages.' So the woman took the child and nursed it. (2.6b–9)

This is as good as the midwives' excuse to the pharaoh!

By accepting the invitation to provide the child with a wet-nurse, the princess accepts responsibility for him and so adopts him into the royal family as her son. She will soon confirm her action by giving him his name. Whether or not she would have taken such a drastic step without the child's sister prompting her, we cannot tell. See how clever the sister is in her choice of words! She presents her plan as though she is doing the princess a favour! Yet still we do not know what the princess would have done without her. All we do know is that the sister plays a key role in turning her immediate feelings for the child into action, in turning compassion into deliverance.

Her adopting the child amounts to treachery. Let us be quite clear about that. Too often this story, and this point in it in particular, is overlaid by a sentimentality that prevents us from appreciating what the princess is doing. She is defying the pharaoh, as Shiphrah and Puah did. Unlike them, she is defying her own father, but still she does it with the same impudence that they showed. Not content with saving this Hebrew child from drowning, she brings him into the palace as her own son, and there brings him up right under the tyrant's nose, and keeps him there for years!

Yet she *is* an Egyptian. For all her astonishing pity and her great courage, she still belongs to the enemy. The storyteller cannot help making gentle fun of her. She is tricked by the child's sister (yet another trickster!) into hiring – into *hiring!* – the child's own mother as his wet nurse. Now she has two Hebrews in the palace, and is *paying* one of them to be there, giving her wages to nurse her own child!

And she is not found out. 'When the child grew up, she [i.e., his mother] brought him to Pharaoh's daughter, and she took him as her son. She named him Moses, "because," she said, "I drew him out of the water"' (2.10). The deceit has held. The princess's slave-women, who found the child with her, have not talked. They too have played their part in his deliverance, and thereby in the salvation of the Israelite people and the fulfilment of the promises of God. The story has so little to say about them. There is very little they actually do, and they have nothing to say. Yet without their taking part in the conspiracy, without their maintaining their loyalty to their mistress in the face of the demands of their king, all would have been lost. They are heroines also, but scarcely a note of their song has been sung.

The name the princess gives the child has its own sweet irony. It is a genuine Egyptian name, but it sounds like a Hebrew verb meaning 'to draw out'. As the princess herself explains, Moses is named Moses because he is 'drawn out' of the water. However, if we wish to be precise, then the word 'Moses' sounds as though it means not one who is drawn out, but one who draws out.[29] It is not that the princess has made an understandable mistake in her Hebrew – after all, she is an Egyptian – nor that the storyteller has got in a muddle. The narrators of the Old Testament tend not to be so pedantic as we can be over matters such as this, and the meaning and derivation of names was not approached in the scientific manner of the modern etymologist. Rather, what the princess does, all unwitting, is give the child a name that is prophetic. He will indeed be instrumental in drawing his people out of Egypt. She cannot know it, but the name she chooses underlines her treachery, and gives us a hint of its consequences.

This story of the women's rescue of Moses marks the last appearance of the pharaoh's plans for genocide. Moses will soon be fleeing the country, and the narrator follows him into the land of Midian. While he is there the pharaoh dies. His successor continues the oppression, but takes up where the first pharaoh and his people left off in the middle of chapter 1, when the Israelites were being put to building the supply cities. Now the people are no longer given straw with which to make their bricks. They have to collect that first, but without decreasing their output (see 5.6–9). This, of course, is cruel enough, but it represents a large step backwards from the 'solutions' to the Israelite problem proposed in the second part of chapter 1.

Quite why the genocide plan should be abandoned is left unclear. It is possible to argue that the story of Shiphrah and Puah, where the plan is first introduced, is told primarily to provide the background for the birth of Moses.[30] One can then go on to suggest that once Moses is safely delivered, the genocide plan has served its purpose as far as the larger narrative is concerned, and so is put aside. That may well be so, but it remains the case that on each of the two occasions we do hear of it, it is frustrated by the courage and resourcefulness of women. Shiphrah and Puah would seem to trick the pharaoh into thinking his first ploy of getting them to kill the male babies at birth is unworkable. They would seem on this occasion to have wielded considerable political power. It is harder for us to think that the women of 2.1–10 can have altered the plans to throw the babies into the Nile through their covert deliverance of just one of them. Nevertheless, they have saved the one who, from the point of view of the narrative, matters most. They have saved the one God will use as the deliverer of his people. For the purposes of the plot of the story, they have effectively seen the genocide plan off, and ensured it will not be heard of again. Within the not entirely plausible world of the story, they, like Shiphrah and Puah before them, are the ones who exercise power in Egypt.

Zipporah: 'merely one nubile daughter out of seven'

(Exod. 2.15b–22)

Zipporah, the final subject of our investigations in this chapter, does not come into her own until late in Exodus 4, but we must still look briefly at the passage in the second half of Exodus 2 where she makes her first entrance.

The scene is set in the land of Midian, by which is probably meant the area of the Negeb desert to the south of Canaan.[31] Moses is there because in Egypt he killed an Egyptian he saw beating one of his fellow Hebrews, and the pharaoh got to hear of it and was out for his blood. In Midian he finds himself beside a well. Such places have in Genesis already proved happy hunting grounds for men in search of wives (see 24.10–27 and 29.1–12). This one, also, will fulfil its promise.

At first it seems it will vastly exceed its promise. Moses is met at the well not just by one marriageable woman, but by seven! They are the daughters of Reuel, or Jethro, 'the priest of Midian'. Seven is a number which in the Old Testament often suggests completeness. Whether he has any sons, we are not told, but certainly Reuel's quiver of daughters is full!

They have come to the well to water his flocks. They perform the doubtless arduous task of drawing the water and filling the troughs, when some very unpleasant shepherds appear on the scene and drive them away. At that point Moses, who has, it would seem, been sitting idly by, watching the women toiling away, intervenes. He came to the rescue of the Hebrew being beaten by the Egyptian. So now he comes single-handedly to the aid of the defenceless women. He drives off the shepherds (at least that is the most obvious way to understand the text), and draws some more water – it seems he has not forced the shepherds to leave before their animals have finished the water drawn by the women – and refills the troughs. He does so in double quick time, for despite the delay caused by the gang of shepherds, the women get back home earlier than usual. Their animals, too, seem to have drunk the water drawn by Moses much more quickly than normal!

Reuel is surprised to see them back so soon, and learns about the 'Egyptian' who helped them. After that things develop with considerable rapidity.

He said to his daughters, 'So where is he? Why did you leave the man? Invite him to break bread.' Moses agreed to settle down with the man, and he gave Moses his daughter Zipporah in marriage. She bore a son, and he named him Gershom; for he said, 'I have been an alien residing in a foreign land.' (2.20–2)

This is decidedly not a woman's story. The tale of Shiphrah and Puah could be described as that, and women dominated the story of Moses' birth and rescue, and were its heroines. Though still dealing with a folk-tale whose details are a mixture of the plausible and the implausible, and which, like the midwives' story, contains clear elements of humour, we have come as far away from those earlier passages as Midian is from Egypt.

We have here several stereotypes that are clearly the product of a male mind. The women are weak and cannot defend themselves. They need to be rescued by a man. They are silly and impetuous and forget to show their deliverer the respect and the gratitude due to him. They go rushing back to their father with their flocks at a run to tell him the news, leaving poor Moses back at the well, hungry, with nowhere to go. Reuel has to remind them of their responsibilities. Furthermore, when Moses settles down with the family, it seems Reuel gives him Zipporah as a thank-you present for the help he gave her and her sisters. When her child is born, it is Moses, not she, who names him, and the name he gives him is not Midianite, but a pun on two Hebrew words, whose literal meaning is 'an alien there'. What Zipporah thinks about it all, we do not know. In fact, what *Moses* thinks about the match, we are not told either. The opportunities the storyteller has for creating a love story to match the one about Rachel and Jacob in Genesis 29 are not taken. As George Coats has demonstrated, he is more interested in establishing the relationship between Reuel/Jethro and Moses than in exploring that between Moses and Zipporah.[32] Robert Alter's comment is also important: 'Any presentation that would give more weight to Zipporah than merely one nubile daughter out of seven would throw the episode off balance, for her independent character and her relationship with Moses will play no significant role in the subsequent narrative.'[33] Exactly. Zipporah is 'merely one nubile daughter out of seven'. The male control of the passage and its detail is kept very tight, and the larger narrative, whose interest will lie almost entirely with the public sphere and the business of men, will spare her only the space of three verses for her to show what she is made of.

Before we come to that little passage, however, there remains one more point to be made about the scene in Midian, and, surprisingly, it is one we might regard as being in the women's favour. Their rescue from the shepherds foreshadows the deliverance of the Israelites from the Egyptians, in which, of course, Moses will again play a major part. The parallel is obvious enough, but becomes even clearer when we recall that 'shepherd' was commonly used in the ancient Near East as a royal title, and appears as such in the Old Testament.[34] So the real shepherds by

the well in Midian remind us of the particularly unpleasant
'shepherd' king who awaits Moses back in Egypt. Furthermore,
when they rush home to their father, the women tell him, 'An
Egyptian man rescued us from the hand of the shepherds' (2.19).
The Hebrew verb they use for 'rescued' is one that Jethro will use
himself once the Israelites have escaped and got across the Sea of
Reeds. When Moses meets him and gives him the news, he will
declare: 'Blessed be the Lord, who has *rescued* you from the
Egyptians and from Pharaoh' (18.10). If, therefore, in our scene
beside the well, the shepherds play the part of the pharaoh, and
Moses plays himself and God, then clearly the women play the
people of Israel. Their significance turns out to be greater than we
might have guessed, and a passage which seems at first sight to do
them so little justice, ends up paying them a great honour.

Yet another woman saves the day

(Exod. 4.24–6)

The passage we are about to examine is one of the strangest and
most obscure in the entire Bible. It describes an incident that takes
place as Moses and Zipporah and Gershom are on their way from
Midian to Egypt. Moses has received from God his great commission to bring Israel out of Egypt. With considerable difficulty he
has accepted it. He has gone to Jethro (as he is now called), and
asked his permission to go back. His father-in-law, with a grace
the pharaoh will never show, has told him to 'Go in peace' (4.18:
the verb 'go' is singular: Jethro does not, in the text, bid farewell
to his daughter or grandson). Finally, just before their departure,
God has given Moses a most terrible threat to carry with him. He
has predicted that the pharaoh will stubbornly resist any demand
to release the Israelites, and he has told him that when the time
comes, he is to play his trump card: 'Then you shall say to
Pharaoh, "Thus says the Lord: Israel is my firstborn son. I said to
you, 'Let my son go that he may worship me.' But you refused to
let him go; now I will kill your firstborn son"' (4.22–3). Ominous
enough, to be sure. Yet nothing can prepare us for what happens
next. God apparently goes berserk.

> On the way, at a place where they spent the night, the Lord
> met him and tried to kill him. But Zipporah took a flint and
> cut off her son's foreskin, and touched his feet with it, and

said, 'Truly you are a blood-bridegroom to me!' So he let him alone. At that time she said 'blood-bridegroom' in reference to circumcision. (4.24–6)[35]

The only other biblical passage like this occurs in Genesis 32.22–32, where Jacob is attacked by God as he is crossing the river Jabbok at night. Behind both stories lie dark tales of spirits or demons who attack travellers by night and try to kill them.[36] Yet in the Genesis passage the storyteller has taken such rough, primitive material, and fashioned it into something remarkably sophisticated and profound. Here in Exodus the narrator has done hardly any shaping at all. The story is left an ugly, bewildering fragment, of which it is very hard to make any sense. Indeed, some commentators have such difficulty with it that they wonder whether the author of the larger narrative, who inherited the tale and included it in his work, fully understood it himself.[37]

The passage poses a large number of questions which cannot be answered with any certainty: Why does God suddenly mount this attack? Who is he attacking, Moses, or Gershom, the son? How does Zipporah immediately know what to do? What exactly *does* she do? Whose 'feet' does she touch (the NRSV and some other versions tell us it was Moses', but the Hebrew simply has '*his* feet')? What are we to understand by 'feet'? Are we to take the word literally, or remember that it is frequently used in the Old Testament as a euphemism for the genitals? Who is Zipporah calling a 'blood-bridegroom', and what does that extremely obscure phrase mean? What does all this have to do with the history of the rite of circumcision, and with the way it was practised in ancient Israel?

It is not for us to tackle these questions, some of which are in any case unanswerable. Gratefully, we will leave them to the commentators.[38] All we will do is make some observations or ask some further questions about what the passage makes clear about Zipporah.

First, it is plain she performs a circumcision. This is remarkable in itself. The Old Testament has surprisingly little to say about circumcision, but in its two most detailed treatments of the subject it is men who administer the rite, Abraham in Genesis 17 and Joshua in Joshua 5. Zipporah is the only woman recorded in the Bible to have performed it. She does so, we should notice, with the proper implement. When God instructs Joshua to circumcise the Israelite males after they have crossed the Jordan and entered Canaan, he tells him to make flint knives (see Josh. 5.2).

Athalya Brenner compares Zipporah to a male witch-doctor or holy man.[39] In her view it is Moses who is under attack, and Zipporah manages to save him by offering the 'god-demon'[40] a part of his body instead of the whole. By that token, her action belongs to a realm of magic which was a familiar part of the ancient world, and which still remains in force in some contemporary societies, although it has left relatively few marks upon the documents of the Old Testament.

More significant, perhaps, is Claus Westermann's remark: 'At an early stage circumcision was, in many places, understood as a kind of sacrifice in which the shedding of blood was important.'[41] Twice the word blood occurs in our passage. Nowhere else in the Old Testament is circumcision explicitly associated with the shedding of blood. Such observations would seem to lie behind the fascinating suggestion which Drorah O'Donnell Setel makes in *The Women's Bible Commentary*, that Zipporah may, like her father, have had the status of a priest.[42] In the end, alas, we have to leave her question hanging in the air, for the passage remains too obscure, but we can emphasize that, despite its apparent spontaneity, Zipporah's act is clearly of a ritual kind; that it conforms to established rules, such as the one prescribing the use of a flint knife; and that, with the emphasis on the shedding of blood, it appears to have been understood as a type of sacrifice. To be able to say that much is extraordinary. For, as Drorah Setel tells us,[43] we possess no other evidence from anywhere in the ancient Near East that women performed acts of blood sacrifice.

Second, it is plain that Zipporah averts a great danger. We cannot be entirely sure who is attacked, but we can be quite certain that without Zipporah's resourcefulness, without her knowing exactly what to do, her lack of panic when they are ambushed by this God, and her steady hand in performing the delicate operation on her son, then either Moses or Gershom would have been killed. If it is Moses who is threatened, and the larger context and the immediate one do suggest that much more easily,[44] then Zipporah's prompt action could hardly be more significant, for then she saves the one who will play the central role in God's deliverance of his people, and who has already been commissioned to do so. If it is Moses, then Zipporah can be compared to God himself as he appears in Genesis 22 on the mountain in the land of Moriah. For there, we will recall, his intervention at the critical moment saved from death the one on whom so much depended for the furthering of his purposes and for the fulfilment of his promises to his people. In that story God himself was responsible for the danger Isaac found himself in, just as here he is the one who poses or embodies the threat to the travellers.

No just deserts

(Exod. 18.1–9; 15.1–21)

Zipporah has emerged from our discussion of this tiny, dark passage as possibly one of the most significant women in the Bible. How tragic then that she should be virtually written out of the story when she makes her third and final appearance in the narrative. In Exodus 18.2 we learn that at some point Moses sent her with their (by then) two sons back to Jethro to escape the horrors of Egypt. The crossing of the Sea is over, and now, as the Israelites approach Sinai, Jethro gets to hear of what has taken place and travels to meet Moses, and bring Zipporah and their sons back to him. The passage continues with this: 'He sent word to Moses, "I, your father-in-law Jethro, am coming to you, with your wife and her two sons." Moses went out to meet his father-in-law; he bowed down and kissed him; each asked after the other's welfare, and they went into the tent' (18.6–7). As we remarked when looking at the story of Moses and Zipporah's first meeting, the narrator was more interested in the relationship between him and Reuel, as he was then called, than in any love he might feel for Zipporah or she for him. Yet, in chapter 2, though she did not emerge from the page as an individual, with feelings and words of her own, Zipporah did, together with her sisters, play a major role in the action and the speech. Here the narrator and her husband and father proceed as if she were not there. They have other things on their minds, such as the giving of due praise to God for his deliverance of his people, the offering of sacrifices, and the sorting out of the legal system. All that they regard as men's work, and neither Zipporah nor her sons have any part to play. There is not even time to speak of Moses embracing them, or kissing them and asking them how they are. Zipporah is given no chance to weep tears of joy and enquire about the plagues and the crossing of the Sea and how her husband has been bearing up under the strain. She is given no chance to do anything, she who once circumcised her son, and most probably saved her husband from death, and rescued the promises of God from destruction.

Her fate is not so different from that of Moses' sister. If indeed the sister who played such a vital role in his rescue from the Nile is the Miriam of later passages, then she, too, does not receive her just deserts. Immediately after the crossing of the Sea, the narrator inserts a long song of triumph, and introduces it with the words, 'Then Moses and the Israelites sang this song to the Lord' (15.1). After it is finished we read:

> Then the prophet Miriam, Aaron's sister, took a tambourine in her hand; and all the women went out after her with tambourines and with dancing. And Miriam sang to them:
>
> > 'Sing to the Lord, for he has
> > triumphed gloriously;
> > horse and rider he has thrown into the sea.' (15.20–1)

The very first word of her song is slightly different from the one that begins the one Moses and the people have already sung: 'I will sing' (one word in the Hebrew) becomes 'Sing'. Otherwise Miriam's song is a precise quotation of the opening lines of the earlier poem. The conclusion to be drawn from that seems quite clear. Miriam was the composer of the larger song, but a later hand has ascribed it to her brother. The Song of Miriam has been turned into The Song of Moses, and Miriam has become in the process a musician who can do no more than pick up her brother's words and sing them as a refrain. She deserves, instead, to be reinstated along with Deborah, the composer of the war song in Judges 5, as one of the important minor poets of the Old Testament.[45]

A question of initiative

There is one last question we wish to consider before we move on to Hannah, and that concerns the matter of initiative. When we introduced Shiphrah and Puah, we remarked on how few people are given names in the first half of the Book of Exodus. Now we have come towards the end of our discussion, it is time to emphasize how few initiatives the human figures of those same chapters are allowed to take, and briefly to examine, or re-examine, the initiatives that are taken, to see what consequences they yield. (We speak of the *human* figures only. God, of course, is at the centre of the drama, plays by far the most significant part, and, apart from those occasions when he responds to Moses' pleas for some of the plagues to cease, he acts entirely on his own initiative.

His part in things would fill a chapter of a book by itself, and must remain outside the bounds of our own discussions.)

The first pharaoh of the oppression is represented throughout as acting on his own initiative, but those initiatives get him and his people nowhere. They run clean counter to the declared purposes of God, of course, but they are frustrated, on the surface of the text at least, not as a result of his intervention, but in the first instance by forces left unidentified, in the second by Shiphrah and Puah, and in the third by Moses' mother and sister and by the king's own daughter and her female slaves. In the end all this pharaoh can do is give orders, and eventually die, leaving behind him a legacy of an Egyptian people brutalized by fear, racial hatred and persistent violence.

The second pharaoh has a much larger part to play, and is a much more complex figure. He is, indeed, three figures in one. The least obvious one, because it tends to be hidden beneath the other two, is that of the tyrant, the cruel dictator, who enjoys his own brutality, who only reacts to suffering when he is himself party to it, and who, through his senseless clinging to power, brings his land, his people, their livestock, and finally his army to utter ruin. He becomes estranged from the religious establishment, when his wise men and magicians can bear the onslaught of the plagues no longer, and increasingly isolated from his political advisers. In all this he reveals his true colours. He is, as they say, his own man. But he has only the power to destroy.

The second figure within the body of this pharaoh is the negotiator, the one who tries to keep control over events by making carefully judged concessions in the face of the persistent demands of Moses and Aaron, and who goes a remarkably long way towards coming to terms with reality, particularly the reality of the God he is up against. 'Who is the Lord, that I should heed him . . .?' is his opening shot (5.2). After the frogs of the second plague have got into his own palace, into his bedroom and into his bed, he pleads with Moses and Aaron, 'Pray to the Lord . . .' (8.8). From there he moves on to, 'This time I have sinned; the Lord is in the right' (9.27; see also 10.16), and his last words to Moses conclude with, 'And bring a blessing on me too!' (12.32). Here also we see him speaking for himself, we see part at least of his mind, even if the reality he has glimpsed turns out to be too much for him to bear, and even if he is not the master of himself that he would like to suppose.

For the third figure contained in this pharaoh, and the one that dominates the other two, and controls the events of the story, is that of God's puppet, jerking to his tune, dancing his grotesque, almost interminable dance of death. Even his insane obduracy is not his own, for at every turn God 'hardens his heart'.[46] This pharaoh is God's plaything. He does not know his own powerlessness, and will never know it, until, with the rest of his army, he is lying drowned on the shore of the Sea of Reeds.

Two pharaohs are balanced in the narrative by two brothers. Aaron, though he is, according to 6.20, the elder of the two, and though much is promised of him, takes not a single initiative in the entire narrative. He simply does what his God or his brother tell him. He is quite overshadowed by Moses.

Yet, once the plagues begin, even Moses has surprisingly little to do and hardly any initiative to take. The plagues are God's doing, not his. The text makes that abundantly clear. He negotiates with the pharaoh for the Israelites' release on God's instructions. Even when he calls upon God to bring a plague to an end, as he does with the frogs, the flies, the hail, and the locusts, and has God doing his bidding, he is responding to the anguished pleas of the pharaoh. Only when his people are trapped between the Sea of Reeds and the pursuing Egyptian army, and he tries to banish their fear, does he speak entirely for himself, without the prompting of another: 'Do not be afraid, stand firm, and see the deliverance that the Lord will accomplish for you today' (14.13). If in these chapters we look for a Moses who acts on his own initiative, then we must look back to the early stages, when he is starting out on his career. We must recall his murder of the Egyptian bully, his attempt to stop two of his fellow Hebrews fighting, his drawing water for Reuel's daughters, his five protests to the commission God gives him at the Burning Bush, and finally his passionate prayer of protest,[47] when the pharaoh has given the screw of oppression another turn, and the Israelite supervisors have brought to Moses their bitter and hopeless anger. 'O Lord, why have you mistreated this people? Why did you ever send me? Since I first came to Pharaoh to speak in your name, he has mistreated this people, and you have done nothing at all to deliver your people' (5.22–3). But where do all these initiatives get him, and what effect do they have on the plot?

The magnificent plain speaking of his prayer leads immediately to God's second great speech to him, in which he assures him that he will come to his people's rescue, and after that the plagues, the means of that deliverance, or at least its prelude, get under way.

But of the rest, we do not have such positive things to say. The murder of the Egyptian results first in suspicion on the part of one of the two Hebrews he catches fighting: 'Who made you a ruler and judge over us? Do you mean to kill me as you killed the Egyptian?' (2.14). That is all the gratitude he gets for intervening in their quarrel. The longer term results of the murder are a little work for the Egyptian secret police, a death threat from the pharaoh, and for Moses himself fear and flight to Midian. It achieves nothing but one Egyptian corpse in the sand, momentary relief presumably for the unfortunate Hebrew being beaten at the time – though we notice the text does not point that out – and Moses' removal from the main action. His intervention at the well in Midian saves the backs of the women and satisfies the thirst of their animals and gets him a wife and son, as well as an exemplary father-in-law. Such things are not to be sneezed at, but God has more things up his sleeve for him than a happy family. As Charles Isbell says, 'Thrashing some country shepherds [if that is what he does] . . . is one thing, but the *real* bully is still safely far away, still belching forth orders of death, still enslaving the "brothers" with whom Moses had once felt such solidarity.'[48]

God remembers his people back in Egypt. Moses does not. He returns there, not because memories come flooding back and old loyalties prove their strength, but because God searches him out at the Burning Bush and drags him back by the ear. He declares his credentials, tells Moses of what he has seen and heard in Egypt, talks eloquently and repeatedly of deliverance, predicts ultimate success, and promises Moses the star role in the proceedings. And five times, as we have mentioned already, Moses protests. His protests, of course, get him nowhere. All they do is make God lose patience with him and send him packing.

Of the minor male characters in these chapters, Reuel or Jethro is most worthy of consideration. He provides Moses with a refuge, a wife, and a job, and later in chapter 4 he gives him his blessing when he asks for permission to return to Egypt. His first cluster of initiatives might be said to retard the plot, since they encourage Moses to settle down in what for God and the Israelites is the wrong place. But the second, with that 'Go in peace' so readily given, sets things once more on course.

Of all the initiatives taken by human beings in Exodus 1–14, it is those of the women, however, that display the greatest courage, invite our keenest admiration, and have the most powerful influence on events. But for the midwives, the women involved in Moses' rescue, and Zipporah, the larger story might conceivably have come to a dead stop. Shiphrah and Puah and the women of 2.1–10 together succeed in defeating the policy of genocide, and save

Moses from drowning. Zipporah averts some rather more obscure danger, but can probably be said to save Moses from death, just as he is on the brink of putting God's purposes of redemption into effect. By the terms of the plot, without these women the forces of evil might have triumphed. Most certainly, without them the subsequent story would have been very different, and its God might have had to begin a search for another Moses, if not another people.

5

Hannah: How the Feeble Gird on Strength!

(1 Samuel 1.1–2.10; 2.18–21)

The Books of Samuel are primarily concerned with the lives of three men, Samuel, Saul, and David. It is possible to say that they are really to do with just one man, with David, for Samuel comes to prepare the way for him, while the account of the reign of Saul very soon becomes the story of David's own rise to power. David appears on the stage of the narrative in 1 Samuel 16, and after that is part of the action, or not far from it, until 2 Samuel has run its course.

The First Book of Samuel deals with the establishment of monarchy among the tribes of Israel, and the Second charts the final stages in David's rise to power, and the course of his reign in Jerusalem. Both books, then, focus on Israel's public life, on struggles for political and military power. Their concern is with worlds in which men were dominant. Yet still Jo Ann Hackett can justifiably describe them as 'a gold mine for readers interested in women in ancient Israel'.[1] Some of the Bible's most lively, most compelling stories about women are to be found in their pages. Our last two chapters will draw on their material.

The story of Bathsheba is not told until David is on the throne in Jerusalem. Upon it his larger story will pivot. It will mark the turning-point in his long career, the place where his rise becomes his decline. Hannah, on the other hand, appears right at the start of it all, when David is but a twinkle in the narrator's eye. Her story provides the beginning of this great chapter in Israel's story, just as Eve's began the whole work, and Shiphrah and Puah and the women of Exodus 2 presided over the accounts of Israel's beginnings as a people in Egypt, and of the emergence of Moses as their deliverer. They, the women of the beginning of Exodus, helped set in train a series of events which would eventually take Israel out of Egypt, to their encounter with God at Sinai, and then on into the Promised Land. Hannah will begin a tale which will lead Israel into the ambiguities of monarchy, into the division of the tribes into the kingdoms of Israel and Judah, and, in the end, to the catastrophes of invasions by Assyria and Babylon, of collapse, destruction, and deportations.

Stories of barren women

(1 Sam. 1.1–2)

When Hannah makes her brief appearance in the narrative, however, the Assyrians and the Babylonians are nowhere to be seen. Her story begins with catastrophe, well enough. But it is not the noisy affair with which the books of Kings will end. It is not to do with the destruction of a city and its temple, the capture and blinding of its king, and the taking of its people into exile. Hers is the small, quiet catastrophe of infertility.

> There was a certain man of Ramathaim, a Zuphite from the hill country of Ephraim, whose name was Elkanah son of Jeroham son of Elihu son of Tohu son of Zuph, an Ephraimite. He had two wives; the name of the one was Hannah, and the name of the other Peninnah. Peninnah had children, but Hannah had no children. (1 Sam. 1.1–2)

At first it would seem this is not to be Hannah's story, but Elkanah's. Not only does the narrator begin with him, but he takes the trouble to trace his ancestry back to his great-great-grandfather. When figures are introduced into Old Testament narrative, it is the usual practice to name only their parents (often just their fathers), and occasionally their paternal grandfathers.[2] Once Samuel is born, and we can look back to these verses from his vantage point, we can see that the extra details of his father's ancestry are given to mark his, the son's, importance. For the moment it must seem they put Elkanah himself on a high pedestal.

Moreover, the two women are introduced to us not as individuals in their own right, but as Elkanah's wives. We learn nothing of their ancestries, nor the places from which they come. All we are told is their names, and that one of them has children and the other has not. The story is not yet their story. It is not yet being told from their point of view. Nevertheless, the mention of their names suggests the significance they might attain to as the narrative unfolds, and the mention of their children, or, in Hannah's case, the lack of them, hints to us that it will centre round the question of offspring. More than that, it suggests it will concern itself primarily with Hannah, and with the matter of whether or not she will have a son. For we have encountered barren women before.

One of them, Sarah, has already been the subject of our discussions. In Genesis she is followed by Rebekah (see Gen. 25.21), and by Rachel (Gen. 29.31), and then, in the book of Judges, by the unnamed wife of Manoah (Judg. 13.2). These four are all figures of some importance, and each of them eventually gives birth to a son who is to play a major role in the narrative. Sarah gives birth to Isaac, Rebekah to Jacob (as well as Esau), Rachel to Joseph (and Benjamin), Manoah's wife to Samson. The stories of Sarah and Manoah's wife, and a large part of Rachel's, are dominated by the question of their having or not having a son. Only in Rebekah's case is the problem of barrenness quickly solved (see again Gen. 25.21).

Furthermore, the stories of Sarah and Rachel suggest there will be conflict between Hannah and Peninnah. Each of those two earlier women finds herself in competition with a second and fertile wife. Sarah gives Hagar to Abraham as a wife, and then lives to regret it. When Rachel marries Jacob, he is already married to Leah, and she has six sons and a daughter before Rachel herself bears Joseph. Not surprisingly, Rachel envies Leah her fertility, and when that temporarily disappears they get into an argument over some aphrodisiacs (Gen. 30.1–2, 14–16).

We can expect Hannah's part to be more important than Peninnah's, and not just because she is Elkanah's first wife. Leah's six sons give their names to six of the tribes of Israel, and she as a result receives a good deal of attention from the narrator, and has her own poignancy as a fertile but unloved wife. Nevertheless, she lives in Rachel's shadow, just as Hagar, for all the honours heaped upon her, lives in Sarah's. In each of those two stories it is the barren wife who counts, the one who seems so unlikely to produce any children at all who bears the son we have all been waiting for.

Already, then, if we bear in mind those earlier stories, the narrator of 1 Samuel has aroused certain expectations in our minds: that Hannah's role will be more important than Peninnah's; that conflict of some kind will arise between them; that Hannah will eventually have a son; that that son will be of great significance for the next part of the story. Sarah and Manoah's wife would also lead us to think that once the favoured son is born and weaned, Hannah will play little part in the narrative. He will take over, while she, like the mother of Moses also, will quickly disappear. For those three women from Genesis, Exodus and Judges have already reminded us that the larger narrative is primarily concerned not with mothers, but with sons. Women have their scenes to play, and sometimes they are dramatic and highly important. But they provide mere interludes in a drama that tells of God and men.

Already we can guess the bare bones of the plot of Hannah's story. But we cannot yet know what flesh the narrator will put on them. A pattern or patterns can be found running through the Old Testament's stories of barren women, but each one retains its own distinctive character, to the extent that differences outweigh similarities. The stories of Sarah, Rebekah, Rachel, and the wife of Manoah do not tell us what exactly, in Hannah's case, will happen next.

Hannah's isolation

(1 Sam. 1.3–9)

The Hebrew text of the first few chapters of 1 Samuel has more than its fair share of obscurities. At various points it would seem to have got damaged in the process of transmission, so that we have to turn to the ancient translations, such as the Septuagint, or to the Qumran scrolls, or to modern scholarly conjecture, in attempts to reconstruct the original text.[3] At the start of Hannah's story, the narrator has added to our difficulties by the way he has composed it. He soon begins to tell us of a particular occasion, but first he must set the scene. There is nothing unusual in that, of course, but unfortunately he barely begins the story proper before he goes back to building the set, and he does not finish doing that for another three verses. To make matters worse, his methods are relatively clear in the Hebrew,[4] but tend to be much obscured in our English versions. We need, therefore, to set out first the material that provides the background, beyond the two verses we have already dealt with, and discuss that, before we go on to the particular episode with which we will be concerned.

Now this man used to go up year by year from his town to worship and to sacrifice to the Lord of hosts at Shiloh, where

the two sons of Eli, Hophni and Phinehas, were priests of the
Lord . . . he would give portions to his wife Peninnah and to
all her sons and daughters; and to Hannah he gave a – – – –
portion [the Hebrew is extremely obscure at that point],
because he loved Hannah, although the Lord had closed her
womb. Moreover, her rival used to taunt her, yes, taunt her,
to irritate her, because the Lord had closed her womb. Year
after year he [i.e., Elkanah] did this, whenever she went up to
the house of the Lord, and she [i.e., Peninnah] used to taunt
her. (1.3–7, omitting the start of v. 4 and the end of v. 7)

It was about fifteen miles from Ramathaim, or Ramah, as it is
usually called (see 1.19), to Shiloh. Whether the story is referring
to one of the great pilgrim festivals, or whether the family are in
the habit of making private pilgrimages of their own is not clear.
It makes little difference either way. Even if Shiloh is crowded with
other worshippers, the focus of the narrative remains on this single,
small group. It allows us to venture behind their scene, into the
privacy of their devotion, their feasting and their celebration. Yet,
in their case 'celebration' is not an apt word to choose, for it
obscures what the storyteller is doing here, and hides Hannah's
pain.

The storyteller puts all the emphasis he can on Hannah's plight.
Once he gets us to Shiloh he presents us with the picture of the
whole family gathered to share in the meat of the animal they have
sacrificed. Such an occasion would not normally have been a
solemn one. Israelite religious observance, as the Psalms reveal,
was a vigorous, sometimes rumbustious affair, and pilgrimages
provided for most people some of the few occasions in the year
when they could eat meat in any quantity and drink wine freely.
We will see later in Hannah's story that the high priest of the
sanctuary mistakes her for having drunk too much. The storyteller
tries to add to the sense of well-being with a note about Elkanah's
love for Hannah, and his inclusion of her in the feast, despite the
fact that the God to whom the animal has been sacrificed has not
blessed her with children.

Unfortunately it is now impossible for us to be certain how
Elkanah demonstrates his love for her. The Hebrew, when it comes
to talk of her portion of the meal, makes no sense as it stands. If
we try to amend it, we come up with various suggestions: that
Hannah is given the best part of the animal; that she is given a
double portion (that is the reading adopted by some of our
versions, including the NRSV); that she has a single one which is

equivalent in size to the total amount given to Peninnah and her children; that she has one, normal-sized portion, in contrast to the many given to her rival and her children, but is loved by Elkanah more than Peninnah (this interpretation is suggested by the Greek of the Septuagint).[5]

In the end it matters little which reading we choose. Enough is clear in the text for us to detect the direction in which the storyteller is leading us, and to perceive what is going on in this little family circle. The first sour note is introduced by the mention of Hannah's barrenness, and the explanation of it. The ancient Israelites regarded their God as the giver or withholder of children. On that count the talk of him having closed Hannah's womb should not surprise us. Nor should we be surprised that the yearly sacrifice is a time when Hannah's inability to have children is felt particularly keenly. (In our own society Christmas lunches are often occasions when underlying tensions within families break to the surface!) Hannah is faced by Peninnah and her *children*. She has to share a feast with a God who has persistently denied her children of her own. She has to travel to his sanctuary to do him honour, and to help cement the ties between him and the family to which she belongs. Peninnah, for her part, is faced by Elkanah's special love for Hannah.

So very little is said about Peninnah in this story. Yet, even if we do not follow the Septuagint's version of verse 5, the text strongly suggests Elkanah loved Hannah *more* than her. The parallel which can be drawn between our passage and the stories of Rachel and Leah would itself encourage that interpretation, for as we have mentioned already, Leah is the more fertile of the two, but is the one not loved by Jacob. There is no mention of any love of Elkanah for Peninnah. He shows her no special attention, as perhaps he shows Hannah in verse 5, and as he certainly does in verse 8. In verse 4 the narrator speaks of 'his wife Peninnah'. In verse 5 he simply calls Hannah by her name, and twice at that. On the second occasion the NRSV has 'because he loved *her*', but the Hebrew gives her name not her pronoun, and indeed we could well translate it the way Kyle McCarter does in his commentary, 'for Hannah was the one he loved'.[6] That translation aside, by not using her title of wife, but only her name, the storyteller reinforces the notion that Hannah's relationship with Elkanah is more intimate than the one Peninnah enjoys.

Though it is not stated explicitly, as it is in the Rachel–Leah stories, it would seem quite clear, therefore, that again we have a barren wife who is loved, and a fertile one who is not. Earlier we described the conflict between Sarah and Hagar as virtually inevitable. So it is now between Hannah and Peninnah.

Three times in verses 6 and 7 the storyteller uses the word 'taunt' to describe Peninnah's treatment of Hannah, as we have indicated in our translation. Only two of them are clear from our usual English versions. In the NRSV, for example, the second is hidden behind the words 'most severely'. The Hebrew of the beginning of verse 6 is better reflected in our still rather loose translation, 'Her rival used to taunt her, yes, taunt her . . .' And then the word for 'taunted her' brings the narrator's set-building to a close towards the end of verse 7.

The substance of the reproach is given in the final words of verse 6, 'because the Lord had closed her womb'. But we should notice that we hear this from the narrator's mouth, not from Peninnah's. The storyteller does Peninnah scant justice. The conflict between the two women is aptly described by Robert Alter as 'so eminently the stuff of dialogue'.[7] Yet there is no dialogue here. Peninnah is nowhere allowed to speak for herself. This is Hannah's story, not hers. Already the storyteller has made that plain. He has not told us the names of any of Peninnah's children. We will never learn them. Her children, by their presence at Shiloh, underline Hannah's inability to have a child of her own. Beyond that they are of no importance. Ever since the start of verse 6, the story has been written from Hannah's point of view. It began as Elkanah's story, and spoke of him going up to Shiloh. Now in verse 7 it is Hannah who goes up (though Elkanah is still with her), and in verse 8 Elkanah is referred to as 'her husband'. At no point is it Peninnah's story. The narrator does not even tell us in so many words that Elkanah does not love her. We have to work it out for ourselves. Nowhere is her pain brought to the surface, as Leah's is so movingly in Genesis 29.31–5 and again in 30.14–20. Instead it is buried in the terms of her unquoted taunt. After verse 7 we will hear no more of her. She will have done her job. She will have rubbed her annual dose of salt into Hannah's wounds, and succeeded at last in driving her away from the feasting. Like Sarah before her, who treated Hagar with such cruelty, she will be given no chance to redeem herself.

Yet, as it turns out, she will achieve something of huge importance. Through her cruelty she will drive Hannah to make a desperate vow to God that will, when finally it is fulfilled, bring Samuel, Hannah's long-awaited son, to Shiloh as the servant of God. That vow, the one that she, Peninnah, has provoked, will determine Samuel's career and make him what he is. Peninnah may not have the last laugh of these chapters, but she makes for their first great irony.

We have now completed our exploration of the scene the storyteller has set for the drama, and come to the particular episode he wishes to describe. 'One day when Elkanah was sacrificing . . . Hannah began to weep and would not eat. Her husband Elkanah said to her, "Hannah, why are you crying? Why are you not eating? Why are you so upset? Am I not better for you to have than ten sons?"' (1.4a and 7b–8). Hannah cannot take it any more. Faced with the contempt of the pregnant Hagar, Sarah turned her furious disappointment and bitterness upon her rival, until the woman could bear it no longer and fled into the desert. Hannah does not vent her feelings upon Peninnah. Instead she turns in upon herself. She isolates herself from the feast, and for the moment hides herself in her grief.

Elkanah tries to bring her out of her hiding-place. His words have come in for considerable praise from some of the commentators. Robert Alter speaks of his 'touching effort to console his beloved wife',[8] and H. W. Hertzberg of his 'exceptionally loving words of consolation'.[9] Jo Ann Hackett is not so sure. She readily acknowledges that his 'is hardly the response of a patriarch who can see value in women only as childbearers[10] and implies the possibility of a relationship in which love was more important than childbearing'. But she goes on to point out that Elkanah is himself not childless: 'Since he had already filled his need for a family to remember and honour him . . . his lack of understanding for Hannah's unhappiness begins to look less sentimental and more naive or even insensitive.'[11] We ourselves would wish to be less tentative than that. Elkanah's questions are very strange. The Old Testament narratives, and none more so than this one in 1 Samuel, bear eloquent witness to the pain caused to women by persistent childlessness. It is impossible to say that that pain was only understood by women, for the narrators who draw our attention to it were almost certainly male. Elkanah himself shows by his final question that he knows the cause of Hannah's distress. Beyond that, however, he seems to know nothing. The understanding he conveys in that enquiry is outweighed by its crass insensitivity, and its words lend a note of reproach or accusation to his first three questions. To anyone in Hannah's position it must seem almost cruel. Elkanah cannot make up for her lack of children by his own love for her. He cannot through his own tenderness or passion satisfy her longing for a child, nor give her the status within the family, the standing in Peninnah's eyes in particular, or the position in the community at large that such a child would bring. His suggestion that his love could compensate for all that is arrogant. It reveals he thinks he should be regarded as the centre of her world. Hannah is already isolated from Peninnah and her children. Now it would seem she is isolated from her husband also. His words betray no real intimacy. It is hardly surprising that she does not respond, except to leave the family circle as soon as the meal is over. Unable to get any help or true sympathy from her husband, she turns to the one who *is* at the centre of things, who will surely understand her, and who can, if he so chooses, enable her to have a child. She turns to God.

The vow is made

(1 Sam. 1.10–11)

Hannah's vow represents her first speech in the narrative. It will break her silence not just for the time of its utterance, but for the rest of her story. After this we will find her much more vocal, indeed she will have far more to say than anyone else.

It is introduced by a reminder of her anguish and a further emphasizing of it:

She was deeply distressed and prayed to the Lord, and wept bitterly. She made this vow: 'O Lord of hosts, if only you will see, if only you will see the misery of your servant, and remember me, and not forget your servant, but will grant your servant offspring,[12] then I shall set him before you all the days of his life. Wine or strong drink he shall not drink,[13] and no razor shall touch his head.' (1.10–11)

Effectively Hannah is promising to dedicate the son she is praying for as a nazirite (the word nazirite may have belonged to the original text here; the NRSV inserts it). The terms of the nazirite vow, which normally men or women took for themselves, are laid out in Numbers 6.1–21. Nazirites were consecrated or set apart for God's service, and signalled their overriding loyalty to him by such things as abstaining from alcohol or not cutting their hair. In the story of Manoah's wife, when God promises her she will conceive and bear a son, he declares that that child too will be a nazirite (see Judg. 13.4ff.). Here the initiative is left with Hannah. What God commands in Judges 13, she herself vows at Shiloh.

This is the first time in the Old Testament that a barren woman prays to God for a child. Sarah understandably appears to think an appeal to God senseless. She substitutes Hagar's womb for prayer, and later, behind the door of the tent, laughs at the idea that she will have a child. Rachel turns not to her God, but to her husband and demands, 'Give me children, or I shall die!' (Gen. 30.1). That is plain speaking, well enough, but Jacob reminds her where she should have taken it. 'Am I in the place of God . . .?' he asks (Gen. 30.2). Manoah's wife has no time for prayer, for God anticipates any pleading she might make and assures her of the birth of a son before she can say anything (Judg. 13.3ff.). In Rebekah's case there *is* prayer to God, but, significantly, it is Isaac who offers it on her behalf (Gen. 25.21). In Judges 13, though God first appears to and speaks with Manoah's wife, the prayer that is recorded is Manoah's, not hers. She says nothing to God. She only runs to her husband to tell him what he has said (see Judg. 13.6 and 10). Hannah, however, does not need Elkanah to pray for her. *She* prays, and in doing so becomes the first woman, indeed the *only* woman, in the entire Bible to utter a formal, spoken prayer, and have her prayer quoted in the text for us to read. Eve, Sarah, and Hagar converse with God, and Rebekah (Gen. 25.22) 'enquires' of him; Miriam, Deborah, and Mary the mother of Jesus all sing songs to God (Hannah herself will have her own song to sing to him in 1 Sam. 2). And in the stories of the Apocrypha there are several substantial prayers put in the mouths of women characters.[14] Yet in the narratives of the Old and New Testaments Hannah's prayer is unique – and no other woman pays God such a vow as hers, either. Recorded prayers ascribed to men are fairly common in biblical narrative,[15] and so it is surely both astonishing and disconcerting that Hannah's prayer should be so unusual. As Celia Thomson remarked to me, it illustrates 'how hidden is the story of women's relationship with God in the Old Testament [she could have said the Bible] and how deep we have to dig for it'.

The Hebrew of the prayer is very simple, and devoid of sophisticated rhetorical devices. Robert Alter suggests that the storyteller has deliberately written it in such a style, and comments, not without condescension, 'All in all, it is just the sort of prayer that a simple, sincere country wife, desperate in her barrenness, would utter.'[16] Yet it is not so artless as it seems.

For a start, it picks up the language Genesis uses when the unloved Leah responds to the birth of her first child by saying, 'the Lord has seen my misery' (Gen. 29.32), and more accurately, and more significantly, echoes the wording of the Burning Bush passage in Exodus, where God says, 'I have seen, have seen the misery of my people' (Exod. 3.7). Just as elsewhere in Exodus, in the episode at the well in Midian, Reuel's daughters are compared to the Israelites in Egypt,[17] so now Hannah's misery is also being compared with theirs, and, by implication, the son she prays for, who indeed will be born, is to be something of a new Moses.

Furthermore, her readiness to hand over such a long-awaited child to God is an important reminder of Abraham's being prepared to sacrifice Isaac in the land of Moriah (Gen. 22). John Mauchline rewards her generosity with the comment, 'No greater self-denial was possible.'[18] Yet, beneath the surface of the text, there may be some subtle bargaining going on! Jo Ann Hackett compares Hannah's dedication of her firstborn son to the practice in ancient Israel of offering the firstfruits of harvests or domestic animals to God, in the hope that he might bless the worshippers with fertile fields or flocks. As Hackett goes on to say, if we read Hannah's vow in this light, then she declares her readiness to offer up her firstborn son in hope of receiving more children in return.[19] If that is the case, then she does not hope in vain, as we shall see.

God is interrupted

(1 Sam. 1.12–17)

Hannah's unique prayer receives no immediate answer from God. We might expect him to give her an assurance that she will conceive and bear the son she longs for, and to promise a bright future for the child. If the story were to proceed along those lines, then we would be able to compare it to that of Hagar's first meeting with God in the desert, and to the other annunciation stories of the Bible. But there is no annunciation here. Though Hannah offers him such a remarkable vow, and though later she will sing him a triumphant hymn of praise, God nowhere addresses her. In Sarah's case God's silence was part of her tragedy. With Hannah, however, it is somewhat different. For in the matter of her vow, at least, God does not get the chance to respond. He is interrupted by Eli, the high priest of the sanctuary of Shiloh. It is Eli who 'answers' Hannah's vow, and his first reaction is very far removed from the answer she wants.

Skilfully, the narrator has introduced us to Eli before Hannah opens her mouth, and has told us he is sitting on his seat beside the door of the temple. When Hannah prays, therefore, we know, even if she does not, that Eli is present. Where exactly Hannah prays is not made clear, but it is near enough for Eli to see her lips moving. She prays silently. Only she, God, and we, the readers of the story, know what she is saying. Eli thinks she is drunk. 'How long are you going to stay drunk? Shake off the effects of your wine!' (1.14). We might well think his words peculiarly offensive. When, however, we recall the evidence this story provides, and this very part of it, too, for pilgrims in ancient Israel indulging in heavy drinking as part of their festivities, then at least his response becomes more readily understandable. Nevertheless, this is the second time Hannah's distress has been observed by a man who does not understand it. Elkanah thinks he understands it, and at least recognizes it for what it is, and tries to show her some kindness, even if his way of doing it is so inept. Eli, too, supposes he knows what is going on, but he does not see the anguish, and pulling himself up to the full height of his authority, displays no kindness at all. Whether he would have spoken to a man in the same way, we cannot know. All we learn, a little later in the narrative, is that he turns a blind eye to the greed, corruption, and blasphemy of his sons (see 2.29 – it needs to be read against the background of 2.12–17 – and 3.13). From those verses we can see he takes more seriously the apparently drunken (yet silent!) behaviour of a woman than he does some of the heinous crimes of his sons (he does at least remonstrate with them over their sexual abuse of some women on the staff of the sanctuary – 2.22–5).

To Elkanah's questions Hannah made no reply. But now, with the making of her vow to God, she has found her voice.

> 'No, my lord, I am a woman deeply troubled; I have drunk neither wine nor strong drink, but I have been pouring out my soul before the Lord. Do not regard your servant as a worthless woman, for I have been speaking all this time out of my great anxiety and because I have been greatly taunted.' (1.15–16)

Her reference to 'wine and strong drink' recalls the terms of Eli's accusation, but more accurately those of the nazirite vow which she has just made on behalf of her unborn and as yet unconceived son.[20] Her explanation that she has been 'taunted' looks back to verses 6 and 7, where the same term was used three times of Peninnah's treatment of her. Most interestingly of all, perhaps, her protesting that she is not 'a worthless woman' looks forward to 2.12 and the narrator's description of Eli's sons as 'worthless men' (the NRSV gives 'scoundrels' there, but the phrase in the Hebrew is the same). Thus, by the terms employed in the narrative, Hannah not only rebukes Eli (*most* politely!) for treating her like dirt, but dissociates herself from the behaviour of the high priest's own sons, and, indeed, since he will get tarred with the same brush, from the excesses of Eli himself. When we reach the second part of chapter 2 and then look back to Hannah's reply, we can see that her great courtesy conceals a stinging accusation that undermines the authority of the one she is addressing.

Yet the obtuse Eli does not pick it up. Instead he pronounces his priestly blessing on the vow she has made! 'Go in peace; the God of Israel grant the petition you have made to him' (1.17). As Robert Alter has observed,[21] Eli does not know what Hannah has prayed for. In asking God to grant her petition, he is praying blind. Unwittingly he creates both irony and humour. Hannah, as we already know, has prayed for a son. That son, as we will soon find out, will be placed by her as a cuckoo in Eli's nest. In a famous scene God will appear to Samuel at night and pronounce the end of the high priest and his family and all their works (3.2–14). Though Eli will do something there to redeem himself and to gain our sympathy, here Hannah has made him seem a fool. He has mistaken her distress for inebriation, he has not spotted her veiled accusation, and now he makes a contribution to the fulfilment of a vow which will help bring about his downfall. The high priest of the ancient sanctuary of Shiloh has effectively been duped by a 'simple country wife' (to use Alter's language). The power of her grief and the sincerity of her prayer have undermined that great authority of his, to which she pays such lip-service. Their dialogue anticipates the terms of the triumph song that she will sing once Samuel is born, weaned, and firmly ensconced at Shiloh:

> 'The bows of the mighty are broken,
> while the feeble gird on strength.' (2.4)

Already this story has begun to take on the character of a revolutionary piece.

Hannah's restoration

(1 Sam. 1.18–20)

Yet, as if the passage has not already given us sufficient irony, Eli's blessing upon her vow does the trick. Although it shows no real understanding of her, it reaches out to her in her isolation, draws her back into the family circle, dispels her grief, restores her appetite, and sets in train the events that will lead to her final restoration. With a touch of her forelock in the words, 'Let your servant find favour in your sight' (1.18), she takes her leave of Eli, goes back to her husband, and eats with him once more, and, if we understand the difficult Hebrew aright, no longer wears the disconsolate expression she had when last she left his presence. The story has turned. So far its curve has taken us deeper and deeper into Hannah's anguish and isolation. From now on its course will rise steeply upwards towards her great celebration of her triumph.

The pace quickens. The narrator took some time to set the scene at the start of chapter 1, and then slowed right down as he gave us Hannah's vow, and reported her dialogue with Eli. Having introduced the problem of her barrenness, he now moves quickly to its resolution.

> They rose early in the morning and worshipped before the Lord; then they went back to their house at Ramah. Elkanah knew his wife Hannah, and the Lord remembered her. In due time Hannah conceived and bore a son. She named him Samuel, for she said, 'I have asked him of the Lord.' (1.19–20)

The form of the verbs in the first sentence are important. Near the beginning of chapter 1 the narrator spoke of Elkanah going up every year to Shiloh (1.3); four verses later, when he had made it Hannah's story rather than Elkanah's, he referred to her making her pilgrimage there. This is the first time he has used verbs of them in the third person plural, the first time he has referred to them as 'they'. Hannah's returning to eat 'with her husband' (1.18) prepared the way, but now they are acting together. Their relationship, which before, as we have seen, was not based on as deep a love and understanding as some commentators have suggested, is now restored. It is appropriate that the first thing we should hear about after their return home is their love-making. Using the usual euphemism, the narrator speaks of Elkanah 'knowing' Hannah.

Inevitably, though only Hannah knows how important is this particular act of intercourse, the storyteller has Elkanah take the initiative. The husband 'knows' the wife. It is always that way round in the Old Testament. The wife never 'knows' the husband. Yet the narrator contributes to the restoration of Hannah's dignity by calling her Elkanah's 'wife'. When we were discussing the relative positions of Hannah and Peninnah in his scene-setting of chapter 1, we suggested that his referring to Peninnah as 'Elkanah's wife' while using Hannah's name was a signal of the greater intimacy that Hannah enjoyed with her husband. Now, in the new context, the title 'wife' indicates a return to her proper status, and looks forward to her exercising that function of wives, so important in the Old Testament, namely the bearing of children. '. . . and the Lord remembered her.' The same expression was used in Genesis 30.22 of the curing of Rachel's barrenness. These words, only two in the Hebrew, mark God's response to her vow. They are disappointingly few, but they are enough. Conception follows, and then the bearing of a son. Again and again in the narratives of the Old Testament we find storytellers reporting momentous events in as few words and as straightforwardly as they can manage. There is no hint of sensationalism here, nor is any sentiment expressed, or judgement passed, or comment made. All is understated. Only later, when the child is weaned and left at Shiloh, will we hear of Hannah's joy. For the time being we will have to be content with her naming the child, and with the particular name she gives him. This is still her story, and will remain so until her song is over, and so it is to be expected, as well as appropriate, that she should name the boy herself. After all, beside ourselves, the readers of the story, only she knows the substance of her vow, only she sees the child as an answer to prayer. That is, in effect, what she calls him, 'an answer to prayer'. The name Samuel is connected in this story with the Hebrew word, *sa'al*, to ask. That word was used twice by Eli in verse 17 (who thereby was unwittingly prophesying the boy's birth), and it will be used four times in verses 27 and 28, and once in 2.20.[22]

The act of dedication

(1 Sam. 1.21–8)

The son is born, but the vow has yet to be paid. Hannah waits until Samuel is weaned. Hertzberg comments: 'It is understandable that the woman draws out the time until she must give up her child as long as possible.'[23] That is surely a misreading of the text. It is true Hannah has to explain herself to Elkanah when he returns to Shiloh on his next annual visit and she declines to go with him, but we can find no reluctance on her part to pay her God what she owes him. Instead, she tells her husband of her plans and repeats the terms of the vow she has made: 'As soon as the child is weaned,

I will bring him, that he may appear in the presence of the Lord, and remain there forever; I will offer him as a nazirite for all time' (1.22). This is the first time, as far as we know, that Elkanah learns of Hannah's dedication of his son. Surprisingly, he shows no surprise, but readily gives Hannah his blessing: 'Do what seems best to you, wait until you have weaned him. May the Lord establish what you have said' (1.23).[24] Some commentators draw our attention to a passage in Numbers that speaks of a husband's right to confirm or to nullify any vow made by his wife (Num. 30.6–15).[25] By the terms of that passage a woman could not take ultimate responsibility for any vow she made, presumably because she might have to rely on her husband's property to pay it. For the second time in this story, then, a man lends his authority to what Hannah has promised to God. But we will have noticed that Hannah has not asked Elkanah to confirm her vow. She does not actually tell him that she has made a vow at all. She presents her plan to dedicate Samuel as something already decided upon. Far from asserting Elkanah's authority as her husband, this passage sets it aside. His 'Do what seems best to you' is superfluous, a sop to convention, a weak attempt to preserve his dignity. When he prays that God might help Hannah carry out what she has promised, he is not giving her permission to go ahead, but merely recognizing what it will cost her to do so.

At this point Elkanah bows out of the story. It is possible the original text made mention of him in 1.24;[26] it is also possible that he is among those in 1.25 who perform the sacrifice at Samuel's dedication; the Hebrew text includes him in 2.11, though there he does not fit the context, and it would seem better to follow the Septuagint and make Hannah the subject of the first verb in that sentence;[27] he will, certainly, make a last appearance along with his wife in 2.20. But from now on he will have nothing to say, and nothing to do (he does not take any action in 2.20). Except for a few words of blessing from Eli in 2.20, all speech in the rest of Hannah's story will be put in her mouth, all the initiatives taken will be hers, all that is done, apart from the performance of Samuel's sacrifice (in which she as a woman could not take part), will be done by her.

We are reminded of the beginning of the Book of Exodus and the extent to which the narrator there allowed the events surrounding the birth and infancy of Moses to be dominated by women. With regard to those chapters Drorah O'Donnell Setel remarks: 'Within what appears to be an exclusively female sphere of birth and child-rearing, women act without male authority.'[28] That comment does not apply precisely in Hannah's case, for Eli and Elkanah, for all that their authority is played down or even undermined, both add their blessings to what she plans to do. It may help, nevertheless, to explain why women are quite so prominent in these birth and infancy narratives, although we should remember that it was perfectly possible for biblical writers to compose such stories as these and give much more significant roles to men. Manoah plays as large a part as his wife in the story of Samson's birth in Judges 13 (and he is the one who has a name there), and Joseph is a much more conspicuous figure than Mary in Matthew's stories of the birth of Jesus, while that evangelist's account of the visit of the magi mentions Mary only once and is otherwise peopled entirely with men. Even Luke, who gives such a large and fine part to Mary to play, and a relatively small one to Joseph, makes Zechariah more prominent than Elizabeth in the stories surrounding the birth of John the Baptist. In the end, with the possible exception of the 'midwife's tale' in Exodus 1, we cannot be sure why the birth stories of Moses and Samuel should be dominated by women to the extent they are. All we can do is observe this feature of them, and try to give it the recognition it deserves.

So, returning to the text of 1 Samuel 1, we discover that once she has weaned Samuel, it is Hannah who takes him to Shiloh, together with a prime bull and a quantity of flour and wine to offer with him, and that after the bull is sacrificed, and the child is brought to Eli, it is she who speaks and reminds him of the previous time they met.

> 'Please, my lord! As surely as you live, my lord, I am the woman who was standing here in your presence, praying to the Lord. For this child I prayed, and the Lord granted me the petition that I made to him. Therefore I have dedicated him to the Lord. For as long as he lives, he is dedicated to the Lord.' (1.26–8)

The Hebrew contains a play on words which it is impossible to reproduce in English. The word *sa'al*, which Hannah gave as the explanation for the name Samuel in 1.20, occurs twice in the clause we have translated 'the petition that I made to him', and even, in an unusual use of it, lies behind the twice repeated 'dedicated'.[29]

Hannah's courtesy is, if anything, more exaggerated here. Only once did she call Eli 'my lord' in her first encounter with him, and her speech then contained no 'please' or 'pardon me', though there was a clear subservience in her parting shot. Her manner of speaking is also more halting than before. And yet she has much greater authority now, and a considerably higher status. Now she can tell Eli what it was she was praying for when he took her for a drunkard. It is she, now, who has come to Shiloh, on her own pilgrimage, expressly to perform her own vow. It is she who has come with such fine offerings for sacrifice, and, remarkably, with her own child to dedicate to the service of God. When Mary presents Jesus to God in the temple in Jerusalem, she takes him home with her after the ceremony. Hannah will return to Ramah without Samuel. We have already compared her dedication of her son to Abraham's readiness to consign Isaac to God in the blood and fire of sacrifice. We might also recall Moses' mother, and her bringing him to the pharaoh's daughter, once he was weaned, so that she could take him as her son (Exod. 1.10). Beyond that, Hannah's offering of Samuel is without parallel in biblical literature. (Samson's being a nazirite from birth means only that he must obey certain rules; it does not separate him from his family.)

It is hard to respond adequately to such an act as Hannah's, and Eli does not try. This time he does not answer her. Only Hannah herself can speak to what she has done. After noting that she left Samuel with Eli, the narrator takes us straight into her song. For the second time she pours out her soul to God.

Triumph!

(1 Sam. 2.1–10)

The song that Mary sings in Luke's Gospel, after the angel Gabriel has announced to her that she will have a child, the poem that Christians call the *Magnificat*, is formed from a string of Old Testament quotations, many of them taken, as we would expect, from the Psalms. But it has long been recognized that it owes more to Hannah's song than to any other poem. It takes its shape and something of its tone from her poem, as well as some of its detail, and, of course, it has a similar narrative context. Hannah, and Hagar, whose annunciation scene in Genesis 16 was, as we saw earlier, the model Luke used for Gabriel's appearance, are the madonnas of the Old Testament, the two women from whose shadows the mother of Jesus emerges.

We are liable, if we are not careful, to misread or mishear both the *Magnificat* and Hannah's song. It is particularly hard for us to see the Mary of the Gospels beneath the many layers of doctrine and piety smothering her, and almost as difficult for us to appreciate the tone of her song through the myriad of beautiful, but so often deferential and polite musical settings it has been given. Hannah, of course, does not occupy the place in Christian piety that Mary does, and has not been buried so deep. Nevertheless, that same piety still encourages us to romanticize her, to make her *nice* – after all, she is presented in her story as an exemplary figure – and to turn her song into something that would not ruffle any feathers, and which could be sung with confidence in the best circles.

But if that is what we expect her song to be, then we are in for a shock. It is a vigorous shout of triumph, enough to make Peninnah and Eli and their like tremble. There is nothing ladylike about it!

Indeed, it does not look like the song of a woman in Hannah's position at all. At one point it uses the imagery of war. It speaks of the shattering of enemies, and closes with a prayer for the king. That final reference is significant, of course. In Hannah's day there was no monarchy. Though the idea was mooted and indeed for a brief period tried out in the narrative of the Book of Judges (see Judg. 8.22–3, where Gideon rejects a call to become king, and 9.1–6, which describes how Abimelech seizes kingly power), we have not heard of any monarchy among the tribes of Israel since, and will not hear of it again until 1 Samuel 8, where Samuel will roundly condemn any plans for it. Saul will not be anointed king (by Samuel!) before 1 Samuel 10, and monarchy will not become firmly established in Israel until 2 Samuel 7, and David is secure in Jerusalem and has received divine promise of a dynasty. Hannah's song cannot date from before the period of the monarchy, and it must be compared with those other songs in the book of Psalms which were originally composed for royal occasions, and which celebrate the power of the king under the overall sovereignty of God. The precise occasion for which it was composed we cannot know. Kyle McCarter suggests it was written to celebrate the birth of an heir to the throne;[30] Walter Brueggemann thinks it may have been sung after a victory in war.[31] Whichever the case, or even if neither of those notions is correct, it would seem clear that the song, for all its revolutionary talk, comes from the heart of Israel's later national life, and from the centre of its monarchical establishment. Hannah sings *a king's song*! Indeed, she may sing the king's part! How exactly the sacred songs of Israel were performed we do not know, but her song is most readily understood if the king, or some cultic official on his behalf, is envisaged as singing at least the first verse. Those lines seem to express the king's sentiments, and no one else's.

The narrator, then, in anticipation of the Davidic kings, has dressed this 'simple country wife' in the robes of a queen. In putting this royal psalm in her mouth he has transformed her, and he has transformed the words she sings also. No longer do they speak of the nation's enemies and their downfall; no longer do they describe the Israelites' triumph over powers mightier and more pretentious than they; no more do they talk of Israel's and her king's rise to power and the end of their disgrace. Now their talk is of Hannah, of *her* enemies, of what God has done for *her*, and the end of *her* disgrace. Now it is *her* triumph that it celebrates. On her lips, despite its declared support for the establishment at the end, it becomes indeed 'a song of high revolt'.[32]

> 'My heart exults in the Lord!
> My horn is lifted high by my God!
> My mouth is stretched wide against my enemies.
> For I rejoice in my deliverance!' (2.1)

This is how the song begins. The imagery is earthy and vivid, typical of that used in the Psalms and in the poetry of the Old Testament as a whole. The raised horn evokes the picture of 'an animal carrying its head high, and proudly conscious of its strength'.[33] As Kyle McCarter remarks,[34] referring to other passages where this image is employed, the horn is a conspicuous part of an animal, and the one in the herd with the largest horns is likely to be the leader, the 'king' (we do have to use the male term here) among them. So Hannah is celebrating not only her triumph, but its conspicuousness. Her barrenness is gone, and Samuel is there for all to see as the proof of her fertility.

The image of the wide open mouth would also seem to bear two connotations. If we examine its use in places such as Psalm 35.21 – read together with verse 25 – and Isaiah 57.4, then we are made to think of a person mocking their enemies, sticking their tongue out at them (the Isaiah verse asks, 'Whom are you mocking?/ Against whom do you open your mouth wide/ and stick out your tongue?'), and also of an animal stretching its mouth to consume its prey.

This is not the talk of the polite tea party! The question becomes urgent as to who Hannah's enemies are. Only the song's context

can answer that question for us, but first we must examine its next
few lines to see if they give any more precise clues. We will stop
at the point where most obviously they speak of Hannah's own
story.

> 'There is no Holy One like the Lord,
>   there is no rock like our God![35]
> Talk no more so haughtily, haughtily!
> Let no more arrogance come from your mouth!
> For the Lord is a God who knows,
>   and by him are actions weighed.
>
> 'The bows of the mighty are broken,
>   while the feeble gird on strength.
> The sated have hired themselves out for bread,
>   while the hungry are fat with spoil.
> The barren woman has borne seven,
>   while the one with many children has become sterile.'[36] (2.2–5)

Alice Laffey, at the end of a brief discussion of the song, identifies
Hannah's enemies as 'powerlessness, barrenness and inferiority'.[37]
But the language of Hebrew poetry is more concrete than
that. Hannah is talking about people, not abstractions. Walter
Brueggemann is nearer the mark when he writes: 'The tone of the
lyric bespeaks a well-established . . . resentment against those who
have been too well off for too long, who now are consigned
precisely to the loss of what they most valued.'[38] And Alice Laffey
herself hits the mark, or one of them, when, just a little earlier,
she refers to Peninnah.[39] We would add Eli.

So Hannah raises her head high above the rival who once taunted
her, and the high priest who took her for a drunkard. She pokes
her musical tongue out at them, and will have them for breakfast.
She condemns the things they said to her as arrogance. She rejoices
that Peninnah's child-bearing days are over, or soon will be, and
that Eli will soon be toppled from his prestigious position, and will
no longer be able to treat the worshippers at Shiloh with such
disdain. They stand condemned, because God knows – because he
knows what Hannah has had to endure from Peninnah all the years
they have been coming to Shiloh, and he knows what kind of priest
Eli is behind his fine authority. They will fall, because, as Hannah
has hinted already, he is a God of justice, and because, as she
now moves on to say, he has the power to turn things upside
down:

'It is the Lord who kills and brings to life,
    who sends down to Sheol and raises up.
It is the Lord who makes poor and makes rich;
    who brings low, and yes, exalts!' (2.6–7)

So much for Hannah's courtesy in her speeches to Eli! So much
for her inability to face Peninnah's taunts! In this vigorous poetry
she is getting her own back on the pair of them, and is enjoying it
hugely. Eli will indeed fall. We can read about that in the next
three chapters of the narrative. As for Peninnah . . . We have
remarked already that she does not appear after 1.7. After this song
she will be given no more chance to defend or redeem herself than
she was in chapter 1. Of her fate we know nothing. All we do know
is that she must now live in a household with a co-wife who is not
only the one who is loved, but is now fertile and able to give her
husband children, and who is relishing her new status and the
chance to hit back. Her prospects at Ramah are as bleak as Hagar's
were with Sarah.

For four verses the clauses of Hannah's poem have been
neatly balanced, and a series of contrasts has been given. Now,
prompted by that '. . . yes, exalts!', Hannah reflects for a few more
lines on her own extraordinary experience of conceiving and
bearing Samuel, while, mercifully, forgetting everyone else except
God.

'He raises the poor from the dust,
    he lifts the needy from the dung heap,
To give them a place among princes,
    and grant them the seat of honour.' (2.8a–b)

Before she had a child it was like living on the refuse dump outside
the town, the place where those in utter misery and destitution go
(see Job 2.8 and Lam. 4.5). In her grief she could not eat. Now it
is as if she is a heroine at some fine banqueting table, eating, we
can imagine, to her heart's content!

In its last section Hannah's song broadens its scope, and places
her experiences within the general patterns of God's activity. In a
few lines she recalls his creation of the world, the exercise of his
justice, his loyalty to his people and his destruction of their
enemies. Only by putting her triumph on such a huge canvas as
that can she make plain its nature and its true significance. We
might think she gets carried away here, but her language is no more
extravagant than that of the one who expresses her or his own

release from suffering in Psalm 22 (see vv. 25–31, and notice how
the imagery progresses). Hannah declares:

> 'For the pillars of the earth are the Lord's,
>   and on them has he set the world.
> He guards the steps of his faithful ones,
>   while the wicked fall silent in darkness.
> For not by might does one prevail.
> The Lord! his adversaries are broken!
> The Exalted One thunders in heaven.
> The Lord judges the ends of the earth.
> He gives strength to his king,
>   and lifts high the horn of his anointed.' (2.8c–10)

Hannah's thoughts return to enemies and their fall from grace, and
the very last words of the song, with their image of the uplifted
horn, take us right back to the beginning, when she was telling of
her own exaltation. Thus, having said she feels like a princess,
eating at a royal table, she ends up going one step further and
compares herself to a king! Such is the joy, the defiance, the
impossible triumph of this 'simple country wife'!

We should not think of her singing this song to herself. We have
much to learn about how individuals prayed in the sanctuaries of
ancient Israel, though we do know that a poem like Psalm 22,
which seems at first such an intensely personal and private prayer,
was in fact sung 'in the midst of the congregation' (see v. 23 and
the verses following). We cannot be sure, as we have said already,
whether Hannah, Peninnah and Elkanah's pilgrimages were family
affairs, or whether they were part of larger national gatherings. If
they were made at the time of some great festival, then we are
free to imagine Hannah singing her song 'in the midst of the
congregation'. If they went up for private family celebrations, then
presumably they were not the only family to do so. There is
nothing in the text to suggest their custom was unusual, and we
should not think of them as the only worshippers at Shiloh,
although, for obvious dramatic purposes, the narrator has written
his story as if they were. At the very least we should imagine
Elkanah, Eli, Peninnah and the children being present to hear
Hannah sing and to join in her prayer. We do not know whether
Peninnah and Eli caught its nuances, but Hannah does more in
this song of hers than pour out her soul to her God: she hurls her
victory in her 'enemies'' faces.

More children

(1 Sam. 2.18–21)

The narrator has not yet done with Hannah. After giving us some details of the corruption at Shiloh and the blasphemous greed of Eli's sons, he picks up for the last time the theme of the annual pilgrimages of Hannah and her husband.

> Samuel was ministering before the Lord, a boy wearing a linen ephod. His mother used to make for him a little robe and take it to him year by year, when she went up with her husband to offer the yearly sacrifice. Then Eli would bless Elkanah and his wife, and say, 'May the Lord repay you with children by this woman in place of the gift that she dedicated to the Lord.' Then they would return home. And the Lord visited Hannah, and she conceived and bore three sons and two daughters, while the boy Samuel grew up in the presence of the Lord. (2.18–21)

One of the remarkable features of these two chapters of 1 Samuel has been the degree to which the story has been told from Hannah's point of view. With the exception of the midwives' tale in Exodus 1, we are not used to dealing with texts told in such a way. Even the passage about the women in the first half of Exodus 2 was primarily about Moses – it is not called 'the story of Moses in the bulrushes' for nothing, nor is it insignificant that none of the women there are named. It is not as if Hannah has the stage to herself at any point, without male company. Even when she is praying silently to herself, Eli is there watching her. It is true, of course, that the narrator has in his mind purposes and events larger than the curing of a woman's barrenness and the expression of her joy. She plays a small part and it is soon done. Her son Samuel, by contrast, will be at the centre of things in chapter 3, from chapter 7 to chapter 16 (with the exception of chapter 14), again in chapter 19, and will even, through the good offices of the medium at Endor, make a posthumous appearance in chapter 28. Hannah's story forms *his* birth and infancy narrative. Yet it remains *her* story, and not just because we have chosen to approach it from her angle, but because that is how the narrator has carefully written it.

He maintains his stance right to the end. Though he frames the final episode with references to Samuel, and though the second of those means that we have left Hannah behind (and Elkanah, for that matter), and the focus is now clearly on her son, still, in her last scene, he again puts her centre stage. It is her continuing care for Samuel, not Elkanah's, not Eli's, that we hear of. *She* makes the robe to go over his priestly ephod. *She* takes it to him every year. *She* goes up to Shiloh, with *her* husband. The pattern is broken only when Eli comes into view. As we have seen, he cannot be relied upon for his sensitivity towards women. It is now 'Elkanah and *his* wife', and, though he acknowledges that Samuel is at Shiloh as a result of Hannah's generosity, Eli prays that *Elkanah* might have the reward of more children 'by this woman'. Though, ostensibly, he blesses Hannah also, the prayer he utters is addressed to Elkanah alone – its 'you' is singular, and even in translation it is plain that Hannah is excluded. We are reminded of Abraham in Gerar receiving gifts from Abimelech that are really Sarah's. But at least then it was Sarah who was addressed by the king (Gen. 20.16), and at least we were able to have Claus Westermann explain to us that 'He hands the money . . . to Abraham because by the rules governing such a society the wife cannot acquire it.'[40] The conventions of Israelite society did encourage Eli to speak of future children as a reward for the husband (see, for example, Psalm 127), yet he could still have prayed that both Elkanah and Hannah might be rewarded with more children, or even, in the circumstances, since the vow was Hannah's and hers alone, have spoken without reference to Elkanah at all. After all, we hear nothing of the husbands of the midwives in Exodus 1, when they are rewarded by God with families or households.

At least God, though he hears Eli's prayer, takes no notice of how it is addressed. He visits *Hannah*.[41] She has five more children, and Elkanah is not even mentioned. So much for Eli's respect for convention!

Thus Hannah ends up with six children. Seven was the ideal. Seven signified completeness. Hannah is left one short. Yet as the narrative moves on beyond her, her song is left still ringing in our ears. It is for that, not for a missing daughter or son, that she will be remembered, and for its fearsomely triumphant lines. Mary will provide her own memorial to her when she sings her *Magnificat*.

6

Bathsheba: From Rape Victim to Queen Mother

(2 Samuel 11–12; 1 Kings 1–2)

There were no corridors of power in Eden. God had no palace there, and the woman, though the victim of a snake's duplicity, did not have to deal with any dark bureaucracies. Sarah twice found herself in a king's harem, but the tent was her usual domain, and it was not great and powerful men who made for her tragedy, but a rival wife, two children, a husband whose carelessness of her sometimes beggared our belief, and a God who did not communicate with her and kept her on the margins of his promises. Hagar seemed for a short time like a princess, alone in a desert with her God, but her normal realm, like Sarah's, was small and domestic, until in the vastness of the wilderness she discovered how to live away from men of power altogether. With Shiphrah and Puah, however, we encountered two women who were at ease in a throne room, and knew, indeed, how to make a fool of a king. And in the next chapter of Exodus we met with a woman who did not visit palaces, but lived in one. Sarah had the name of 'Princess'; Hagar, with the honours heaped upon her by God, invited comparison with one; the pharaoh's daughter *was* one. With Hannah we moved away from monarchs and their courts, though we still found her having to deal with Eli, high priest of Shiloh and judge of Israel, and finally heard her singing a king's song at the top of her none too delicate voice.

Bathsheba takes us into the innermost recesses of a king's palace, and keeps us there. In her company we will witness events of shocking brutality. We will see a king committing sexual acts of a kind that would, if they were contemporary, keep the British tabloid press going for weeks. We will see that same king arranging the murder of one of the troops closest to him. We will see rape, unthinking exploitation of women, palace intrigue, and in the end two kings getting rid of those who get in their way. All that we hear about will belong to that great history the Israelites told of themselves, that story that stretches from creation to Babylon and takes in the books from Genesis to Kings. More remarkably still, all of it will belong to the stories of the two most renowned kings Israel ever had, David and Solomon. Its candour will be astonishing, and, if we have absorbed the propaganda about those kings that is offered in later sections of the Bible and in our traditions, hard to come to terms with.

For a few verses of Exodus 1 we found ourselves handling what was possibly, perhaps probably, a woman's story. In 1 Samuel 1–2 we noted the extent to which the story was told from Hannah's point of view, and how it came to be dominated by her actions and her speech. Bathsheba, however, is quite another matter. She has six scenes, and appears briefly at the end of two more, but all of them have chiefly to do with men, either with David and her husband Uriah, or the prophet Nathan, or David's son Adonijah, or the son born to her and David, Solomon. What is more, it is very difficult for us to be sure in those passages what kind of woman we are dealing with.

Solomon does not show us his character until the end of Bathsheba's last scene, but then it, or part of it at least, is plain for us all to see. Uriah, Adonijah, and Nathan are lively figures from the start. As for David, his is one of the most striking portraits of a king to have come down to us from the ancient world. But we will find it hard to know what to make of Bathsheba. In her first scene in particular she will remain so far back in the shadows of the narrative that at first it will be hard to make her out at all. We will have to reserve our judgement upon her part in that passage until we reach Nathan's parable in 2 Samuel 12. Then we will become certain, or as certain as we can be, about how the narrator sees her. In her other five main scenes in the first two chapters of 1 Kings, she will step much further out into the open, and will have a good deal to say, but even then she will remain an ambiguous figure, and we will have to search the words and shapes of the narrative very carefully to achieve any clarity. It will be fascinating work, or should be, for we will be studying some of the most sophisticated and carefully crafted narratives in all Scripture.

David's rise to power

(1 Sam. 16 – 2 Sam. 10)

Before the narrator sets the scene for Bathsheba's first entrance, we must briefly set the scene for David. Bathsheba does not appear until 2 Samuel 11.2. That is a very long way into the story of David. He is anointed king by Samuel back in 1 Samuel 16, and has his first triumph in 1 Samuel 17, when the Philistine giant, Goliath, comes crashing down to his sling-stone. Samuel's anointing of him is an act of treachery, for Saul is occupying Israel's throne at the time. It represents a *coup d'état*. Such things are usually resolved one way or another with considerable swiftness. Rival armies are raised, palaces are stormed, and amid great slaughter either the pretender comes to power, or the established king remains to continue his reign and mop up the insurgents. Certainly things cannot be left as they are. For Israel has two men anointed king, and that is one too many.

At first David's rise to power is astonishingly rapid. Though his anointing is done on the quiet at Bethlehem, with no great celebrations, his slaughter of Goliath leads immediately to Saul taking him on as a member of his palace staff, and to the king's son, Jonathan, becoming his close friend. It also turns him overnight into a popular hero. Jealous of that popularity, Saul takes what we might think the fatal step of appointing him a commander in his army, where he achieves instant and repeated success and widespread acclaim. Thus Saul, who knows nothing of the episode at Bethlehem, has brought him to the centre of his power amid cheering crowds, has enabled him to gain support in his own family, and has put troops in his hand. And all by half-way through 1 Samuel 18. By the end of that chapter he has also given him the hand in marriage of his daughter, Michal. For David, all is going to plan, and, most important of all, the plan is God's. We are assured several times by the narrator that David is God's man, and that Saul is rejected. We have known since his secret anointing that David will come to power. Since that moment it has been just a question of time. When we reach the end of 1 Samuel 18, we are surely convinced that that time will come in the very next chapter.

In truth David does not occupy Saul's throne until another fourteen chapters have finished their course. He spends that time on the run, as a bandit, a runner of a protection racket, and as a mercenary in the service of one of the kings of Israel's enemies, the Philistines. It is not an edifying tale, nor is it meant to be. He is not presented as a fine moral figure. He is presented as a nobody – even his own father does not think of presenting him to Samuel as a possible candidate for anointing in 1 Samuel 16 – who comes from nowhere to challenge, humiliate, and ultimately to defeat the establishment. He is presented as God's man who cannot put a foot wrong, caught up in a struggle for power with a king who was once God's man, but who now cannot put a foot right.[1] As Walter Brueggemann has so powerfully suggested,[2] this part of David's story is one designed for those who find themselves on the margins, who long for God to take their side, who wait for a hero to emerge who will lead them in their struggle, and who are not going to be over-critical of him when he does.

By the time Bathsheba comes on the scene, however, the story has changed radically. Saul is dead, killed in battle with the Philistines. David has been anointed again, this time in public, this time not as God's secret pretender to the throne, but as the acclaimed occupier of it, at least in the territory of Judah. One of Saul's sons, Ishbaal, has reigned for a time over the rest of his father's land, but he too is dead, together with the other members of Saul's family who might have posed a threat to David's sovereignty. Only Mephibosheth, Saul's grandson, remains, but he, as the narrator is careful to tell us, is a cripple. By the time Bathsheba appears, David has finally achieved his destined place as the ruler of all Israel; he has shrewdly moved his capital from Hebron, where he was first anointed as king of Judah, to Jerusalem; he has seen off the Philistines, who have so dogged the fortunes of the Israelites since early in their time in the promised land; most important of all, he has received through the prophet Nathan a divine assurance that he will found a dynasty in Israel that will last for ever. He is no longer the one who challenges the establishment. He *is* the establishment.

In the chapter immediately preceding Bathsheba's first scene, he reaches the position where he does not need always to fight his own battles any more. He can send his general Joab to fight the Ammonites and their mercenaries for him. Yet his own strength as a soldier and leader of troops has not declined. Faced by a renewed threat from the Aramean kingdoms, he again leads the Israelites into battle, and again inflicts a crushing defeat upon the enemy. Thus when Bathsheba appears he is at the very height of his powers. She, through no power of her own, except her ability to conceive, will change all that, and begin his sad, long and most troubled decline.

Scene 1: A victim in the shadows

(2 Sam. 11.1–5)

Bathsheba's first scene is short and remarkably unadorned and sparse in its presentation. We have noticed already the use of understatement by the storytellers of the Old Testament, their technique of using a few plain words to describe momentous events, their willingness to give us mere skeletons of speech and leave our imaginations to clothe them with flesh. The first five verses of 2 Samuel 11 provide one of the most striking examples of their art in the entire Hebrew Bible.

> Now in the spring of the year, the time when kings go out to battle, David sent Joab with his officers and all Israel with him; they ravaged the Ammonites, and besieged Rabbah. But David remained in Jerusalem. It happened, late one afternoon, when David rose from his bed and went for a stroll on the roof of the king's house, that he saw from the roof a woman bathing. Now the woman was very beautiful to look at. He sent and enquired after the woman, and said,[3] 'Isn't this Bathsheba, daughter of Eliam, the wife of Uriah the Hittite?' So David sent messengers and he took her, and she came to him and he lay with her. (Now she was purifying herself after her period.) Then she returned to her house. And the woman conceived and sent and informed David. She said, 'I am pregnant.' (2 Sam 11.1–5)

At no point does the narrator tell us what to think. Judgement will be passed at the very end of the chapter, and that will be followed by Nathan's famous parable that will shed much light on the passage. However, some of the ambiguities will never be resolved. That, of course, is not a weakness of the writing. Quite the reverse. One of the reasons why this passage and those that immediately follow it are so powerful is that they arouse our imaginations so quickly and then tease them and play with them so adroitly. Those who wish to control texts like these, and arrive at a clear, definitive reading will be disappointed. Those who wish instead to enjoy them, and to allow themselves to be led a merry, or in this case a most sombre, dance, will discover the delight and the terror they have to offer.

The first question the passage poses is how we are to interpret David's staying behind in Jerusalem. As we have already mentioned, he has sent Joab to do his fighting for him before now (10.7). We suggested then that his doing so was a measure of his power and security on the throne. Later, in a passage that looks back to his wars with the Philistines, his men will charge him not to lead them into battle any more. 'You must not put out the lamp of Israel,' they will say (21.17); he is their light, their hope, and he must not put his own safety at risk. Yet, back in 1 Samuel 18.16, when Saul first put him in charge of troops, we saw the risks a king might take when he stayed at home: 'All Israel and Judah loved David; for it was he who marched out and came in leading them.' David has, as yet, no pretender to his throne, but still that verse from near the beginning of his story makes us uneasy. It is after all, as the passage reminds us, the season when kings go to war,[4] and this particular king is staying behind.

We may not be entirely clear how to judge David's staying in Jerusalem, but we can be more certain about the impact of his doing so on the story. Joab, the officers closest to David, and 'all Israel' (in time of war 'all Israel' means the soldiers fighting in the army; that women and children also belonged to Israel is not recognized in such a context) are some forty miles away at Rabbah (on the site of the modern Amman). David is not, of course, entirely on his own. He has servants about him to care for his needs and run his errands for him, as Bathsheba's scene itself acknowledges, and as the subsequent passage will make even clearer. Yet they remain shadowy, anonymous figures. He has, too, his harem, his wives and his concubines, though they are not even mentioned; it is as if they are not there. They do not come to his mind when, as seems to be the case, he is overcome with sexual desire. They are cast aside by this narrative, and no one pays them the slightest heed. We only know of their presence from other passages, such as 1 Samuel 18.27; 25.42–3; 2 Samuel 3.2–5; 12.8; 16.21–2. David may not be on his own, but he *seems* to be on his own, with no one in the palace to occupy him and nothing to do but go for a stroll after a siesta. While the mice are away, this particular cat will play.

Just as the details of the narrative convey a sense of David's isolation, so they suggest Bathsheba's vulnerability, once she is inside the palace. Who is there who might protect her from the designs of the king? We are made to feel there is no one. In fact, her vulnerability emerges from the text before she gets there. The king can see her bathing. He is in a position to invade her privacy. Her nakedness is exposed. Unknowingly, even before she is summoned to the king's presence, she is thus humiliated and put to shame. The palace roof puts him above her (archaeology confirms that, but the passage itself will later talk repeatedly of 'going down' to where Bathsheba lived; 11.8, 9, 11, 13). As J. P. Fokkelman remarks, the story here puts him 'in the position of a despot who is able to survey and choose as he pleases'.[5]

All David sees is Bathsheba's body, and all he recognizes is its beauty. Her beauty proves to be her downfall, just as it was so nearly Sarah's in both Egypt and Gerar (see Gen. 12. 10ff.; 20). The narrator does not tell us in so many words of David's lust. He does not need to. It is enough that all he speaks of, beyond the details of Bathsheba's father and husband, is her physical form. It is enough that that is sufficient to spur David into action, and to drive him to immediate sexual intercourse with her, despite his knowing he is committing adultery with the wife of one of his own officers. It is enough that David wants nothing from her but the pleasure of her body.

Unless, of course, Bathsheba means to invite his attention, and becomes not his victim but his co-conspirator. Alice Laffey would condemn such a suggestion as 'male chauvinist',[6] and we are fully aware that it risks such quick condemnation. But it needs examining for a number of reasons: first, we cannot presume that the text portrays Bathsheba in a way that we ourselves find congenial – it *may* contain what we would call 'male chauvinism', and if it does, we must not be shy of saying so; second, as we have made quite clear already, it is particularly difficult to see Bathsheba's character here, drawn as she is with so few lines – any interpretation which claims to be supported by the text, and this one does, must therefore be taken seriously; and third, our suggestion is far from original, but has been made by several commentators and on occasion has been argued at great length.

Some commentators assume Bathsheba was bathing on the roof of her house.[7] If we imagine she was, then it is possible for us to suppose that she was being deliberately provocative in exposing herself in a place that she knew was overlooked by the palace. So H. W. Hertzberg speaks of a possible element of 'feminine flirtation'.[8] With much greater care and at much greater length, Randall Bailey argues that Bathsheba is 'a prime mover', 'a willing and equal partner to the events which transpire', and that she and David strike a deal, whereby he gains close ties with an important aristocratic family, and she marries into the palace to be assured that the son born to her and the king will succeed to the throne.[9] Thus, claims Bailey, 'the David-Bathsheba narrative is better read as a tale of political deal-making and intrigue than one of mere lust having run awry'.[10]

Bailey supports his reading by noting a number of features of the text. When Bathsheba is introduced to us, her father's name is mentioned, and before the note about her marital status – this, Bailey says, suggests that David is primarily interested in her political connections and in contracting a political alliance. David's actions are neatly paralleled by Bathsheba's – in verse 3 David 'sends', 'enquires', 'says', while in verse 5 Bathsheba 'sends', 'informs', 'says'. In the crucial verse 4, the place where sexual intercourse takes place between them, David 'sends', 'takes', 'lies with', while Bathsheba 'comes', 'has been purifying herself', 'returns'. Those balances in the use of the verbs, Bailey argues, indicate that Bathsheba is as much in control of the action as David is, that she is an 'equal partner to the events which transpire'. He places particular emphasis on her 'coming' to the palace, and on her 'sending' to inform David of her having conceived. She 'comes', she is not brought, and in 'sending' a messenger or messengers to David she is doing precisely what he did himself earlier in the action, and joins 'a highly select number of powerful and/or devious women' who are represented as the subject of this particular verb in the books from Joshua to Kings.[11]

To those not familiar with the intricacies of Old Testament scholarship such arguments might seem forced and pernickety. But we have already discovered in our earlier chapters that whether a character in a biblical story is the subject or object of the verbs that are used can be very significant when it comes to assessing their portrayal in the narrative. We have also seen that we can learn much from the use of particular verbs that are echoed in other passages. Furthermore, it can be shown over and over again that the storytellers of the Old Testament delighted in creating the kind of patterns and balances in their writing that Bailey detects in verses 3 and 5 and within verse 4, and that such things are important for our appreciation not only of their artistry, but of the meanings they are attempting to convey. There is nothing wrong with the kind of arguments that Bailey produces. We need, however, to discover whether his conclusions stand up to close scrutiny. Our whole understanding of Bathsheba in this scene will be affected by our decision.

First, let us go back to the idea that Bathsheba was bathing on the flat roof of her house, a notion that Bailey himself does not employ. We need here to avoid assumptions, particularly ones that might stem from the so pervasive stereotype of the wicked and dangerous temptress. We readily saw the necessity to cast aside that particular stereotype when we were considering the portrayal of the woman in the Garden of Eden. We must beware of it here also.

We must be quite clear that the storyteller does not tell us where Bathsheba was bathing. All we know is that David, with the advantage of the height of his palace roof, could see her. We do not know she was on her own roof. She may have been in a courtyard, or David may even have been able to see her through a window. We cannot tell. If we wish to know whether she was being deliberately provocative or flirtatious, we cannot do so yet, but must look for clues in the rest of the scene.

We might think that the balance of verbs between verses 3 and 5 and within verse 4 provide them. In truth, however, the balance is more artificial than real, more a question of outward form than inner meaning. For see what verbs are balanced with what! Within the dramatic verse 4, the verse on which the whole scene turns, David does the sending, the taking, the 'love'-making, Bathsheba does the coming and going, and, in a parenthesis, the ritual purifying. David's verbs speak his power, and tell, surely, of his abuse of that and of Bathsheba herself. There is a terrible abruptness and stark quality to his actions. There is no time for speech or conversation, no time for care, and certainly none for love, no time even for the kind of courtly etiquette that we will hear of in some of Bathsheba's scenes in 1 Kings. In particular, David is the subject of the two verbs at the centre of it all, the verbs that matter more than any of the others. He 'takes her'; he 'lies with her'. *He* takes *her*. *He* lies with *her*. That is how the storyteller puts it. In doing so he tells us all we need to know.

Bathsheba's verbs in verse 4, by way of contrast, merely describe the setting for those actions of David, and their immediate prelude and aftermath. The reference to her purifying herself after her period does a number of things: it tells us that when she conceives David must be the father, and there can be no question of Uriah having fathered the child before he went off on campaign; it suggests it is possible for her to conceive, and so emphasizes the dangers for her of any illicit sexual union, and underscores that vulnerability of hers that we have already commented upon; it speaks of her purity, her cleanness, and, in this sordid context subtly suggests that that goes more than skin deep;[12] it signals her piety and thus ties her more closely to her husband, Uriah, who in the subsequent passage will show a dogged determination to obey the terms of God's torah in the face of a king who rides roughshod all over them. As for Bathsheba's coming and going, they hardly speak of her power, for what else can she do?

Summoned by the king, she must obey. Whether she has any notion of his purpose, we are not told. After he has abused her, all she can do is go home. If there is a terrible abruptness and starkness to David's actions, then there is an equally terrible pathos and loneliness to Bathsheba's.

The initiatives she takes in verse 5, which so clearly ape those taken by David in verse 3, also need not be interpreted in the way Bailey does. Indeed, given what we have just said about verse 4, they demand to be understood in other ways. It is here, in this verse, that the narrator most clearly allows Bathsheba some dignity of her own, and puts some power in her hands. Whether she refuses to go to the palace herself out of fear or disgust, again we cannot know. But she is now playing the king's game. She is doing what David did. She is sending him a message. She is answering his show of power with hers. He asserted his power over her by raping her. She asserts her power over him by conveying to him the words 'I am pregnant'. They are few enough in the English. In the original Hebrew they are even fewer. There are only two of them, and their impact could hardly be more dramatic. To David they are devastating. He will never be the same again. On them the plot of his whole story, from 1 Samuel 16 to 1 Kings 2, turns. They are not the triumphant cry of a woman who knows she bears the probable heir to the throne. They are the plain speaking of a woman who has been raped and discarded, and who wishes most courageously to make clear to her rapist the consequences of his act.

The mention of her father at her initial introduction is certainly interesting. It is almost certainly an indication that she comes from an influential and aristocratic family.[13] As Bailey has reminded us,[14] there are other stories of David being attracted to women of high social status (see 1 Sam. 18.20–9; 25.1–42). Nevertheless, it tells us nothing about the part she plays in the affair, and it cannot count against the suggestions in the rest of the passage of lust and rape. Indeed, for an audience belonging to a hierarchical society, such as prevailed in ancient Israel from the time of the monarchy onwards, it could only serve to emphasize the enormity of David's crime.

Murder, disgrace, and a touch of defiance

(2 Sam. 11.6–27a)

Yet, despite all we have said and argued, some doubt must still remain in our minds. The telling of that scene is so very economical.

So little lies on its surface, that we cannot help wondering whether we have not dug up what we wanted or expected to find. Fortunately the narrator comes to our aid. He tells a parable, or rather he has the prophet Nathan tell one, and in its lines he provides not just Nathan's but his own comment on what has transpired.

He does not tell it immediately, however. First he relates the story of David's murder of Uriah, Bathsheba's husband. He does it all with exceptional brilliance, but to us, interested as we are first and foremost in Bathsheba, the results are unnerving. For he takes much longer over Uriah's murder than he did over Bathsheba's rape, twenty verses instead of five (11.6–25). His account of it is full of life and colour. There is dialogue between Uriah and David, between David and Joab, and between David and Joab's messenger. Uriah may only have one speech to make, but it is a fine one and serves to put David to shame. Though we are left not knowing enough about Uriah, though we are uncertain at the end of it all whether he has ever suspected anything of what the king has been doing to him or has done to his wife, nevertheless he emerges as a well-rounded figure, who readily commands our sympathy. Indeed, since the narrator tells us he is of Hittite blood, he clearly belongs to that select band of foreigners we referred to in chapter 4[15] who are conspicuous in their obedience towards the God of Israel, and who so often show up the disobedience of one or more of the Israelites who surround them in their narratives. He belongs to the company of Shiphrah and Puah, if they were Egyptians, of the daughter of the pharaoh and her attendants in Exodus 2, of Jethro, Balaam, Rahab, Ruth, Jael, Naaman, and the Syrophoenician woman and the two centurions in the Gospels. In short, Uriah is a hero. The narrator has not yet told us enough about Bathsheba for us even to have the option of thinking her a heroine.

All this might well lead us to suppose not only that the narrator is much more interested in Uriah than he is in Bathsheba, but also that he takes his murder much more seriously than her rape. Such impressions are only reinforced by the way he closes the scene in 11:26–7a: 'When the wife of Uriah heard that her husband was dead, she made lamentations for her lord. When the period of mourning was over, David sent and gathered her to his house, and she became his wife, and bore him a son.' We are back to the bald speech with which the chapter began. Bathsheba has not been mentioned during all David's intricate manoeuvering to get Uriah saddled with the paternity of the child in her womb, and to see him killed. Throughout that section the scene has been set either in the palace, or at the siege of Rabbah. At no point has it shifted to Bathsheba and Uriah's house, and allowed Bathsheba to appear on stage. Only now that it is all over does it do so, and enable us to hear her grief. We do not know whether she heard of Uriah's coming to Jerusalem, of David's attempts to get him to go home and sleep with her, of her husband's return to Rabbah, or the contents of the letter he took with him from the king that sealed his fate. Whether she ever learns the truth, we do not know. Uncomfortably, we recall Sarah's tragic exclusion from the story of Abraham's binding of Isaac.

At least Bathsheba does reappear in this narrative. At least she does get to hear of her husband's death and is permitted some grief. After the episode in the land of Moriah, we will remember, the narrator of Genesis only mentioned Sarah to tell us the length of her life, the place of her death, and the comic attempts of Abraham to purchase a place for her burial.

Moreover, sparse though the writing is, here in 2 Samuel the narrator adds more, much more, to Bathsheba's pain (or, if we agree with Bailey, to her delight), and with a single touch of the utmost subtlety suggests a toughness in her we have not seen before.

First, he makes it sufficiently clear that she does not hear about Uriah from David himself. The king does not attempt to redeem himself by paying her that courtesy. Either he sends a messenger again, or else the news is passed on to her by someone hidden entirely from our sight.

Second, the narrator describes how this man who once raped her, the man who has murdered her husband, now sends for her a second time, harvests her (the verb employed here is normally used of gathering in a harvest or mustering an army[16]), and makes her his wife and puts her in his bed once more. If we still think that Bailey's reading of her first scene is correct, then this is a moment of triumph for Bathsheba, the moment she and David have been working towards. If we think him wrong, then we must find this the most terrible climax of her humiliation, and of the king's ruthlessness and brutality.

Yet still the narrator tells us so little. Yet still, perhaps, he tells us enough. Of David, he informs us that he 'gathers' Bathsheba in as soon as the formalities of mourning are done. The king, it seems, has no regrets, shares no grief. All he wants is Bathsheba in his bed, and being king, he gets what he wants. Bathsheba herself, however, grieves for 'her lord'. The wording the narrator has chosen is significant. He uses a strong verb to express her wailing and lamentation, much more heavily freighted with emotion than the one he uses in the next verse of the rites of mourning.[17] And he has Bathsheba crying for 'her lord'. We may not like it that she so clearly expresses her subservience to Uriah, but in its context the term has a distinct defiance about it, and gives us a hint of the strength she will show at the beginning of the books of Kings. For if Uriah is her 'lord', then David is not. The king may take her with most cruel haste into his harem, but she is not his, not yet at least. The narrator, who thus does her more justice than immediately meets our eye, also persists in calling her 'the wife of Uriah' in the next scene with Nathan (see 12.9–10), and at the start of the one after that, when the child conceived in the rape dies (see 12.15). Not until David comes to console her for the loss of her child will she be called 'David's wife' (12.24).

The parable

(2 Sam. 11.27b–12.7a)

Now we have reached, or very nearly reached, the parable which, in our view, will settle the matter of the nature of Bathsheba's involvement in the events of chapter 11. There are just two half-verses before it begins. 'But the thing which David had done was wrong in the eyes of the Lord. So the Lord sent Nathan to David' (11.27b–12.1a). Bathsheba's 'I am pregnant' fell like a stone into what for David had been the calm waters of his success. Now the narrator chucks in a rock. Uriah spoke of the sacred ark in his speech to David in 11.11, but otherwise there has been no mention of God in the whole episode. Now there is. It is made with the extreme brevity we have become familiar with, but its impact is all the more powerful for that. David has behaved as if he is above the law, and not subject to the demands of God. He has behaved as though he has absolute mastery over events and over those around him. With the seven words of the Hebrew of 11.27b the narrator reminds us that he is wrong, and 'sends' Nathan (more sending) to remind him.

What it is that has so displeased God is not yet plain. Is it the rape of Bathsheba, or the murder of Uriah, or both? The parable will tell us. One thing, however, does seem clear already, though its significance will again need the light of the parable upon it. David is here condemned by God, but Bathsheba is not. The most natural way to interpret that is to suppose that Bathsheba has indeed been the innocent party all along, and David's victim, not his co-conspirator. Yet we have already had cause to observe how indistinct for the most part are the lines of communication between God and women in the Old Testament, and how he is usually represented as dealing only with men. Is that sufficient to explain the one-sidedness of his condemnation here? Does only the man, who is after all his chosen king, count as far as God is concerned? Does he simply ignore Bathsheba and her part in the affair? We shall see.

> [Nathan] came to David, and said to him, 'There were two men in a certain city, the one rich and the other poor. The rich man had very many flocks and herds; but the poor man had nothing but one little ewe lamb, which he had bought. He brought it up, and it grew up with him and his children; it used to eat of his morsel and drink from his cup and lie in his bosom. It was like a daughter to him. Now there came a traveller to the rich man, but he spared taking an animal from his own flock or herd to prepare for the wayfarer who had come to him. Instead he took the poor man's ewe lamb, and prepared that for the man who had come to him.' (12.1b–4)

Nathan the prophet does not put his speech in the form of an oracle or solemn pronouncement from God. Very soon he will deliver two such oracles, and twice the words 'Thus says the Lord' will go ringing round the palace. For now he plays the trickster, and pretends to present a legal case to David and invite his judgement. The king falls into the trap, and in passing judgement on 'the rich man' passes judgement on himself. The beginning of Nathan's response provides one of the most dramatic moments in Scripture.

> Then David's anger was greatly kindled against the man. He said to Nathan, 'As the Lord lives, the man who has done this deserves to die! He shall restore the lamb fourfold, because he did this thing, and because he had no compassion!' Nathan said to David, 'You are the man!' (12.5–7a)

Some have complained that Nathan's parable does not fit chapter 11 closely enough.[18] It is quite true that it does not appear to reflect on the bulk of it. It does not comment on the murder of Uriah, for example. Yet, as David Gunn has remarked, 'it is absolutely plain that it encapsulates the essence of David's dealing with Bathsheba'.[19]

Its focus comes as a surprise. The balance of chapter 11, which,

as we have remarked, devotes so much more space and colour to
Uriah's murder, would lead us to expect the parable to concentrate
on that. Instead it neglects it entirely. The 'little ewe lamb' is so
much at the centre of Nathan's story that one commentator prefers
to call the piece a fable rather than a parable,[20] and the lamb is,
of course, Bathsheba. It seems that the attention of the God of this
narrative is focused exclusively on the rape and on David taking
her away from Uriah into his already well-stocked (if that description can be forgiven) harem. That is what has aroused his anger
and driven him to come out of the shadows of the narrative and
send a prophet. Uriah, the figure behind the 'poor man', appears
not as the murdered soldier, but as the husband robbed of his wife.

We said 'of course' the lamb was Bathsheba. We do not have to
make any presumptions. Nor is our judgement based merely on
the general shape of the parable, or on the way in which its plot
so obviously takes us through what she has suffered. Some of the
details of the writing quite plainly confirm it. The clues are given
in verse 3, in the ways in which the poor man's lamb is described.

The lamb is clearly not regarded as a mere item of livestock by
the man. She[21] is even more to him than a pet. As George Coats
has pointed out, the reference to her growing up with him 'carries
such personal, human connotations'.[22] The Hebrew verb employed
is the same, for example, as that used of the growing up of Isaac
in Genesis 21.8, or that of Ishmael in Genesis 21.20, or Moses in
Exodus 2.10–11. The phrase 'lying in his bosom' also occurs in
another Old Testament passage of a small child sleeping with its
mother (see 1 Kings 3.20[23]). As Nathan himself explains, the lamb
was 'like a daughter' to the man.

Or does he really mean 'like a *wife*'? The Hebrew word for
daughter is 'bath'. Is there the beginnings of a play on words here?
Are we meant to catch an echo of Bathsheba's name? It would seem
so, for, not surprisingly, 'lying in someone's bosom' is also used in
the Old Testament to describe sexual relations. We will meet the
phrase in that sense just five verses later, in 12.8, and again in 1
Kings 1.2. It also occurs with sexual connotations in Micah 7.5.
Nathan could hardly have said the lamb was like a wife to the man,
because then he would have ruined his story by giving it overtones
of bestiality! Yet surely he is referring to the marriage bed of
Bathsheba and Uriah. If we suspect he is, then our suspicions are
confirmed by his talk of the lamb eating the man's food and
drinking from his cup. For as David Gunn points out, such
language is often used in the Old Testament in sexual imagery.[24]
The love poetry of the Song of Songs has plenty of talk of eating

and drinking that is heavy with sexual innuendo (see, for example, Song of Sol. 2.3–5; 4.10–5.1; 7.8–9).

The parable, then, is primarily about Bathsheba, and about David's taking her away from Uriah when he had plenty of wives and concubines to satisfy his passion. It does, admittedly, still reflect male values. It tends to make us feel more sorry for 'the poor man', Uriah, than for his 'lamb', Bathsheba. It provides echoes, the only ones we have, of Uriah's love for Bathsheba, but cannot, because of the image of the lamb, speak adequately of any love of Bathsheba for Uriah. Nevertheless, Uriah's devotion to her and passion for her is carefully and movingly suggested, in a way that allows us to appreciate another dimension to her suffering. For now we begin to know what their relationship was like. With the subtlety of his great art, the storyteller here gently runs our finger along the knife of the pain of this woman, who has been raped, has lost her husband, and then has scarcely had time to mourn his death before being sent for by the man who abused her to become his wife. As yet we have been given no sign that David loves her at all. Quite the reverse. His treatment of her is compared to murder, for the lamb in the story is slaughtered.

Now there can be no doubt left. The lamb in Nathan's parable is an innocent victim. Nothing could be clearer. And that means Bathsheba in chapter 11 was also an innocent victim. Unless, of course, both Nathan and God have seriously misjudged the events!

The aftermath of the parable

(2 Sam. 12.7b–24)

Nathan follows the parable and his 'You are the man!' with two oracles of judgement. No longer does he speak as a trickster, but openly as a prophet, formally declaring the mind of God through sayings introduced by those sonorous words, 'Thus says the Lord'. The oracles elicit a confession from David, and then a final pronouncement of judgement by the prophet. That judgement is carried out almost immediately, but we witness David making a desperate attempt to avert it, and then see his reactions when he fails and it is carried out. Then, and only then, does Bathsheba reappear, but it is only for a single verse, and a further twelve chapters will go by before we hear of her again. We need to examine briefly the passages leading up to her reappearance, and then, of course, that verse itself.

We expressed our surprise that the parable concentrated on the rape of Bathsheba and did not touch on the murder of Uriah. The oracles of judgement go a little way towards redressing the balance. When so much space has been devoted to David's ultimately successful attempts to get rid of Uriah, we could hardly expect Nathan to leave the king's presence without pronouncing upon them. Nevertheless, when we take the two oracles together, and also look at Nathan's final judgement, we see that the greater emphasis still lies on the rape.

The first oracle, in 12.7b–10, begins with God rehearsing what he has done for David in the past. He lists his anointing him king, his rescuing him from Saul, his giving him Saul's daughter and his wives – 'I gave you your master's daughter and made his wives lie down in your bosom' (12.8)[25] – and his further gift of the house of Israel and Judah. In the context, the most interesting item here is the one about David's wives. Never mind that we have not heard before of David taking over Saul's harem (though we have heard of his marrying his daughter, Michal – see 1 Sam. 18.20–7). The very mention of David's wives, and the language this God employs, mean that the terms of the parable and its lamb lying in the poor man's bosom, and the taking of Bathsheba, are brought at once to mind. The focus is still on the rape. There is nothing in God's list to remind us of Uriah, and when God goes on to say, 'if that had been too little, I would have added much more', we naturally understand this to mean yet more wives. Gwilym Jones' somewhat cold remark conveys the sense if not, perhaps, the feeling of the text: 'Coveting Bathsheba was therefore unnecessary.'[26]

In verses 9–10 the oracle turns to the recent past, and here, for the first time since Nathan's entrance, we have mention of Uriah's murder. Twice God condemns it. Yet the taking of Bathsheba is also twice condemned, and the oracle closes with the words, 'for you have treated me with contempt, and have taken the wife of Uriah the Hittite to be your wife'. The oracle begins and ends with her, not with her husband. It is clear where the emphasis still lies.

It is sustained in the second oracle in verses 11–12, which is concerned exclusively with the crime against Bathsheba, and the punishment to fit it, and makes no reference to Uriah's murder at all. Nathan's final words in verse 14 share its focus and pronounce most terrible judgement on one of the consequences of the rape, the child to whom Bathsheba has given birth. David's confession, which immediately precedes them, is powerful in its simplicity, its plain speaking, and its brevity. In those respects its mere two words in the Hebrew balance the two earlier Hebrew words of

Bathsheba's 'I am pregnant': 'I have sinned against the Lord' (12.13). To this Nathan responds: 'Yes, but the Lord has transferred your sin.[27] You will not die, but because you have so utterly scorned the Lord, the child who has been born to you shall most surely die.' The child is to be another innocent victim. He will be the scapegoat that will bear David's sin away. His final illness and death will, by a prophet's divine decree, be an act of vicarious suffering that will ensure the life of the king.

But what of Bathsheba? Nathan the prophet and God have paid her much heed. Their minds have been chiefly on her, and to her plight they have continually returned. David's treatment of her has shaken them more deeply than his murder of Uriah. In effect they have declared the rape worse than murder. If we thought from the balance of chapter 11 and the character of the writing that the narrator regarded the attempted manipulation of Uriah and his death as much the more serious of David's crimes, then this chapter 12 has put us right. Yet the child who will die for the life of the king is Bathsheba's child also. As far as we know he is her firstborn. Neither Nathan nor God acknowledge that. In the death sentence they pronounce, they do not consider the loss and pain she will endure. And just in case we might try to defend them by suggesting Bathsheba would wish an end to a child born of rape, we will soon hear of her grief. In the end both the prophet and God, having paid her such close attention, forget her.

The narrator himself almost does the same. As soon as Nathan has left the palace, the child falls ill, and the spotlight then falls on David as he pleads with God for him not to die, and after that, once death has come, as he perplexes his servants by not mourning for the child (12.15b–23). Only at the very end of the crisis is Bathsheba mentioned: 'Then David consoled his wife Bathsheba . . .' (12.24a). That is all we will hear of her feelings for her child, the only acknowledgement that she is, or was, his mother. It is the first and the only time she is called David's wife. It is the only suggestion we are given anywhere in her story that David might have any love for her. When in 12.5–6 he pronounced judgement on himself, he condemned 'the rich man' of the parable for having no compassion. Now, after he has been faced with the truth of what he has done, and after he has confessed his sin, he turns to Bathsheba, and, it seems, shows her some pity. For the first time he pays her some attention without abusing her.

Or does he? The whole verse reads like this: 'Then David consoled his wife Bathsheba, and went to her and lay with her; and she bore a son. She[28] called him Solomon. The Lord loved him.'

'In the circumstances her chief comfort would lie in having another child,' says John Mauchline,[29] and H. W. Hertzberg comments, 'When a mother has lost a child in the East today [Hertzberg was writing in the mid-1950s] she is usually told, "May God support your husband"; with great realism this refers to the begetting of a new child in place of the one who has been lost.'[30] However, those who have lost a child themselves, even through stillbirth or miscarriage, let alone after the child has lived for some time, know very well, and those who have not can readily appreciate, that no 'new' child can provide such compensation, or take the former child's place. If David himself supposes that one can, and if we read that supposition into his having intercourse with Bathsheba so soon and fathering another child, then he shows no more sensitivity towards his wife than Elkanah did towards Hannah when he suggested his love made up for her not having any children (1 Sam. 1.8). Though the wording and actions are not the same, David's behaviour here reminds us all too uncomfortably of the conclusion to the events of chapter 11, when with indecent haste he sent for Bathsheba and made her his wife. The initiative, the power, lay with him then. So they do here. *He* goes to *her*, *he* lies with *her*. She cannot help herself in bearing another son. What she thinks of it all, whether there is any love to be found here or not, we cannot tell. At least, if we believe the margin of the Hebrew text, and those commentators who think it gives the original reading,[31] *she* gives her son his name. It is a name of great renown. It is 'Solomon'. When eventually Bathsheba reappears in the story, she will not be called David's wife, but Solomon's mother. Then she will receive her identity, her significance, her status, not from any husband – not from the first one, who loved her; nor from the second, who raped her – but from her son. It will prove to be nearly the most that any woman in the court at Jerusalem could hope for.[32]

Further disintegration

(2 Sam. 13–24)

The birth of Solomon is followed almost immediately by a story of another rape. Here there is no question about what is going on. It is one of the most vivid pieces of writing in the Old Testament. Tamar, David's daughter, is raped by his eldest son and her half-brother Amnon (2 Sam. 13). Absalom, David's third son and

Tamar's full brother, avenges her by having Amnon killed, and that leads indirectly to civil war, with Absalom attempting to seize his father's throne, and all but succeeding, before he is himself killed by Joab in the aftermath of a battle. David's return to Jerusalem at the end of the war is accompanied by a bitter dispute between the people of the two parts of his kingdom, Israel and Judah, and this leads to a second, though mercifully much shorter, period of civil war. 2 Samuel ends with a few chapters (21–4) that provide a series of appendices. They include a long psalm in which David sings heartily of his triumphs and vigorously protests his righteousness. It comes from another world, the world of the establishment that was interested in canonizing the founder of the dynasty, and is shockingly out of place after all the events that have transpired. Nevertheless, it reminds us, as David Gunn has pointed out,[33] of Hannah's song in 1 Samuel 2, and so in one sense brings the course of the Books of Samuel full circle.

It is a sorry tale, with only a few flashes of light in the darkness. There is no mention at any point of Bathsheba or of any of David's other wives, though twice we hear of his concubines. At the height of the war with Absalom, David flees from Jerusalem with his whole household, except for ten concubines whom he leaves behind 'to look after the house' (15.16). In the circumstances, that is an impossible and dangerous task. When Absalom enters Jerusalem and is proclaimed king by his followers, the first thing he is encouraged to do is to take over what there is of the king's harem, to show that now he possesses his father's virility and authority. He only needs to be encouraged once, and after they have pitched a tent for him on the palace roof, the same roof that led to Bathsheba's undoing, he goes in and enjoys his spoil (16.20–2). Later, when the war is over and David reoccupies his palace, he places the same concubines in a prison, presumably because they did not succeed in the task he gave them, and because they wear the taint of his son's intercourse with them. There they remain, 'shut up until the day of their death, living as if in widowhood' (20.3). David Gunn's comment on these two fearful episodes is worth quoting at length:

> Unable to keep in order his own house (family), unprepared to guard his own house (city and nation) [David] leaves ('forsakes', 15.16) the women he has taken for his pleasure. They are expected to do what he will not do – with a rapacious Absalom descending upon the palace! But now deeming them tainted by Absalom's intercourse, he will do what patriarchal

honour and political wisdom dictate. He 'takes' them and
'gives' them . . . a prison cell, 'the house of keeping'! Thus
these women are condemned by a man's sin to be shut out of
society. Their fate at the hands of Absalom and David
compounds that of Tamar at the hands of Amnon and David
(who offers her no help or consolation). They are both
members and victims of David's house.[34]

To his mention of Tamar we would add ours of Bathsheba. She
too is both member and victim of David's house, and so far has
found little if anything but abuse there. With David's psalm in 2
Samuel 22 the Books of Samuel come full circle. With Bathsheba's
story our own book has also returned to the beginning, not just to
the treatment suffered by Hagar at the hands of Sarah and
Abraham, or to that endured time and again by Sarah at the hands
of Abraham, but to the abuse heaped upon the woman in the
Garden by generations of commentators and theologians, whose
efforts have made her as hard to discover in the text of Genesis as
Bathsheba has been here in 2 Samuel.

But Bathsheba's story is not yet ended.

Scene 2: Palace intrigue I – Bathsheba and Nathan

(1 Kings 1.1–14)

'Now king David was old and advanced in years . . .' That is how
the Books of Kings begin. In less than one and a half chapters he
will be dead. Bathsheba has three important scenes to play before
he dies, and two more soon after he is gone. There will be no
mention of her own death. The deaths of kings get recorded here,
not those of queens and queen mothers.[35]

The story of David's decline has been a long one. The remarkable candour with which it has been told is sustained in the account
of his last days. He is presented to us in its opening verses as an
old man who cannot get warm, however many bed-clothes his
servants put on him. They suggest a plan to him that will involve
the exploitation of yet another woman in his court and in his bed.
They suggest the country be scoured for a young virgin, a very
beautiful young virgin, who can act as his nurse, and who can 'lie
in his bosom' – there is that phrase again – and give him some heat.
David's courtiers are not merely concerned about saving him from
hypothermia. The heat they are talking about includes sexual heat,

as they reveal by their talk of the woman sharing his bed. They mean to provide him with another concubine. But they are doing more than trying to give him some sexual pleasure. They are testing his virility, and, almost certainly, his fitness to rule.[36] Psalm 72 clearly indicates the connection the Israelite mind made between the well-being of the king and the fertility of the land. Strange though such a connection might seem to us, it was commonly asserted in the ancient Near East.[37] By its token an impotent king spelled an infertile land. David's servants are not just trying to cheer him up. They are putting him to a test that is of crucial importance for the life of the land and the prosperity of the people of his kingdom.

He fails. The young woman they find for him, Abishag (at least she is done the courtesy of having her name recorded), makes no difference. 'The king did not know her', we are told. The NRSV makes the sense plainer by translating, 'but the king did not know her sexually'. Quite. The suspicions of his servants were correct. He is impotent.

That means there is a crisis in the palace. It will not be necessary, as the rest of David's story will show, to dethrone him, but there is a need for one of his sons to become co-regent. Whoever is appointed will become sole ruler when David dies.

Things happen quickly: 'Now Adonijah son of Haggith exalted himself, saying, "I will be king"' (1.5). Adonijah is David's fourth son. Both Amnon and Absalom are dead, and his second son, Chileab, has not been heard of since he was first mentioned in a preliminary list of David's sons in 2 Samuel 3.3–5. Adonijah is presumably the eldest of those who have survived. Some scholars are quick to point out that with the monarchy and David's dynasty so young, it would not have been taken for granted that the eldest son would succeed to the throne.[38] But what they say would not have been presumed, Adonijah presumes, and in 2.15 he will claim that 'all Israel' presumes it also. In a royal family which has seen such appalling internal strife, a presumption of that kind is surely dangerous.

The terms the narrator uses to begin to describe Adonijah's actions, and the comments he introduces, only increase our sense of foreboding: 'he prepared for himself chariots and horsemen, and fifty men to run before him. His father had never displeased him by asking, "Why have you done so and so?" He was also a very handsome man. His mother had given birth to him after Absalom' (1.5b–6). Everything here, not just the man's name at the end, reminds us of Absalom and of his attempt to seize power from

David. In the prelude to his revolt we were told that Absalom was
the most handsome man in all Israel (2 Sam. 14.25). At the very
beginning of his bid for power we heard how he got himself a
chariot and horses and fifty men to run ahead of him (2 Sam. 15.1).
Before the start of what was to be Absalom's final battle, the only
instruction David gave his generals was to 'deal gently' with his
son (2 Samuel 18.5). When, against those instructions, he was
killed, the king was so overwhelmed with grief that his troops were
ashamed to celebrate their victory, and Joab had to remind him to
put the needs of his army and the state above his own personal
feelings (2 Sam. 18.33–19.7). Much earlier, David's affections for
his first son, Amnon, had also prevented him from punishing him
for his rape of Tamar (2 Sam. 13.21). That had left Absalom a
bitter man, intent on taking revenge, and that in turn had led to
the rift between him and his father that widened into the chasm of
civil war (2 Sam. 13.22ff.). Adonijah is not the only son whom
David has over-indulged. With Amnon and Absalom the consequences were disastrous. Now that Adonijah is after the throne,
memories suggest he has made a most inauspicious beginning.
They will not deceive us.

Next we hear of a pro-Adonijah and an anti-Adonijah faction.
The second is made up of the priest Zadok, the soldier Benaiah,
David's bodyguard, of which Benaiah is the leader, the prophet
Nathan, and Shimei and Rei. The last two we will not hear of
again. It is not even certain from the Hebrew that Rei is a proper
name. Only one of the others, Nathan, will play a crucial role in
defeating Adonijah's bid for power.

Two names are missing from the list: Solomon and Bathsheba.
The omission of Solomon's is surprising. One might have expected
him to be among the first to challenge his brother's presumptions.
In fact, while he will waste little time in getting rid of him once
he himself is on the throne and his father is dead, he will not put
himself forward as a rival candidate for power, and for the time
being will remain a passive and colourless figure. The absence of
Bathsheba's name from the list is surprising for another reason.
She will be the one who will co-operate with Nathan in the plot to
get her son anointed king in Adonijah's place. The conspiracy will,
so far as we can see, belong to just the two of them, and Zadok
and Benaiah will only reappear to perform the coronation. The
narrator does not do justice to Bathsheba in leaving her out, unless
he means to indicate that she really bore little responsibility for
Solomon's coming to power, and was simply manipulated by the
anti-Adonijah faction, and by Nathan in particular.

How we are to assess Bathsheba's part in these events is the most important question we will have to consider in this section of our study of her. Again, we will find scholars divided in their opinions. Again, we will have to sift the text very carefully for any clues the storyteller might give us. He has provided us with one already, in omitting Bathsheba from his list. Unfortunately it is not clear how we should read it.

The details of the factions are followed by Adonijah calling a great feast just outside Jerusalem. Nathan and Bathsheba will later represent it to David as a coronation feast. Whether that is Adonijah's purpose is not certain, but the guest list is clear enough. He invites all his brothers, all the king's sons, except one, Solomon. He also invites 'all the royal officials of Judah', and leaves out Nathan and Benaiah. Still there is no mention of Bathsheba. Presumably this is men's work, though if that is what he thinks, Adonijah has made a serious miscalculation, for the narrative will show that no one possesses more influence over David than the queen. Perhaps he thinks his father is past being consulted. If so, Nathan and Bathsheba will prove him wrong in that too.

Plainly things are reaching a critical stage, and the anti-Adonijah faction must act fast. Nathan approaches Bathsheba, and the anti-Adonijah party quickly becomes the pro-Solomon party. The events that now unfold take place while Adonijah's festivities are going on. The technique of the narrator is especially sophisticated here.

> Then Nathan said to Bathsheba, Solomon's mother, 'Have you not heard that Adonijah son of Haggith has become king and our lord David does not know it? Now therefore, come, let me give you some advice. Save your life and the life of your son Solomon! Come, go to David the king and say to him, "Did not you yourself, my lord the king, swear to your servant, saying, 'Your son Solomon shall succeed me as king, and he it is who shall sit on my throne?' Why then is Adonijah king?" And then, while you are still there speaking with the king, I will come in after you and fill in what you have said.' (1.11–14)

The way Nathan plays on Bathsheba's feelings is plain for us all to see. Not only does he suggest Adonijah's actions have put her and her son in mortal danger – a reasonable enough supposition in the circumstances – he also reminds her that Adonijah is not her son, but the son of her rival wife Haggith. Adonijah was introduced to us in 1.5 as Haggith's son. Now we can see that the narrator had

Bathsheba in mind in that earlier part of the chapter after all. Outside 1 Kings 1–2 Haggith is mentioned only in the course of the list of David's sons in 2 Samuel 3.3–5. Adonijah there appears as her only son. We know nothing else about her, but no doubt Bathsheba does, and Nathan exploits that knowledge. Third, Nathan reminds Bathsheba of an oath that David swore to her that Solomon would be king. Thus, in a few words, Nathan plays with Bathsheba's affections and ambitions for her son, conjures up fears for her safety and Solomon's, assumes she is caught up in the rivalries of the harem and has ambitions to be queen mother instead of Haggith, and brings to the surface memories of a long-established pact between her and the king.

One thing is curious. This is the first we have heard of any oath of David's that Solomon would succeed him. We have known from Solomon's birth that he is the one beloved of God, and therefore the one who will surely one day come to power. But God's special favour and a king's oath are two different things. Has Nathan made it up? Is he playing the trickster again, as he did before with that parable of the rich man and the poor? Some think so.[39] If he is, then he is asking Bathsheba to tell a momentous lie that might put her in danger if David sees through it, and himself also, when he follows her for his own audience with the king. For we have to remember we do not yet know where David's sympathies lie. We cannot assume he is Solomon's man. We have heard nothing at all about his relationship with him. All we know is that he has been in the habit of being overly indulgent towards *Adonijah*.

What are we to make of Bathsheba here? As Gwilym Jones observes, estimates of her 'range from attributing to her an important part as an ambitious, capable, energetic, shrewd and powerful queen-mother to making her a colourless and even stupid woman who was a mere instrument in Nathan's hands'.[40] We will have to see what she does with Nathan's advice. She gives him no verbal response, but goes straight to the king.

Scene 3: The plot thickens – Bathsheba and David

(1 Kings 1.15–27)

So Bathsheba went to the king in his room. The king was very old; Abishag the Shunammite was looking after the king. Bathsheba bowed and did obeisance to the king, and the king said, 'What is the matter?' She said to him, 'My lord, you yourself swore to your servant by the Lord your God and said, "Solomon your son shall succeed me as king, and he it is who shall sit on my throne." But now, look, Adonijah has become king, and you, my lord the king, know nothing about it! He has sacrificed oxen, fatted cattle, and sheep in abundance, and has invited all the king's sons, the priest Abiathar, and Joab the commander of the army. But Solomon, your servant, he has not invited. But you, my lord the king – the eyes of all Israel are on you to tell them who shall sit on the throne of my lord the king after him. Otherwise, when my lord the king sleeps with his fathers, I and my son Solomon will find ourselves in the wrong.' (1.15–21)

This is the first time we have ever seen Bathsheba on stage saying anything. In 2 Samuel 11–12 she uttered just those two (in the Hebrew) words, 'I am pregnant', but we heard them from the lips of her messenger to David. She was not present to speak them for herself. Now we have a speech of some length, and of very considerable subtlety.

She is not in the easiest of situations. The king, presumably, is confined to his bed, and Abishag is there looking after him. Bathsheba must know why the young woman has been brought into the court. She herself is no longer young. When David's courtiers wished to test his potency, she was not considered for the task. Once she was taken by the king because of her beauty, but she cannot now compete with an Abishag, even if she wished to. She does not command the attention of the men of the court any more, and David's desire for her is long gone. Abishag is a reminder of all that.

Bathsheba and David do not, on the surface, meet as wife and husband. She bows to him, does him obeisance, calls him, 'my lord the king', and refers to herself as his 'servant'. She observes all the stiff etiquette of the court. Yet her status is clear, and she is making all the use of it she can. When Nathan comes into the king's room at the end of her speech, he will have to be announced, and will have to exhibit a greater degree of subservience by putting his face to the ground. When after that David pronounces judgement on the matter they have brought to him, he will send again for Bathsheba, and will address her alone. And, of course, why has Nathan approached her with his plan in the first place, if not because he realizes that she is the only one who has sufficient influence over the king? Bathsheba is not David's wife for nothing.

For all the authority she may possess, she is, according to

Gwilym Jones,[41] simply Nathan's accomplice. He has devised the plot, given her her part to play, and the words she is to speak. But for a mere accomplice she shows a remarkable degree of initiative and skill.

She begins by repeating the 'vow' that David once made to her. Thus far she is following Nathan's plan. Yet even at this juncture she puts her own stamp upon it. She turns Nathan's question, 'Did not you yourself, my lord the king, swear . . .?' into a statement of fact: 'My lord, you yourself swore . . .' What is more, she claims, as Nathan did not, that David took his oath in the name of the Lord his God. Thus she invests it with a far greater solemnity and power than Nathan gave it. She leaves no room for doubt about it in David's mind.

She does, however, still leave some room for it in ours. She does not clear up the question of whether this 'vow' is an invention or not. We will have noticed she did not challenge Nathan on the point. She did not say to him, 'What vow? I remember no vow.' But still we cannot be sure what to make of that. She may have acquiesced because she was used to doing what men told her to do without questioning them. But that is hardly the Bathsheba who emerges from the speech she makes here to David. She may have acquiesced because she immediately saw the cleverness of Nathan's ploy, thought that David would not see through it, and was sure it would work out to the advantage of herself and her son. Alternatively, she may have acquiesced because what Nathan said was true: David *had* made the vow. If indeed he had, then it would seem her part in the birth of the conspiracy is more significant than we might suppose from the narrative. For if Nathan knows of David's vow to Bathsheba, a vow which is not public knowledge, and which is not generally known in the court, who has told him? It cannot be David, for in his own speech to the king he will be careful to avoid giving the impression that he knows of any vow. It can only be Bathsheba. Has she then been plotting with him for some time? Is she the real instigator of the conspiracy to get her son on the throne? Is she another Rebekah?[42] When Nathan came to her with the news of the actions taken by Adonijah, was he merely impressing upon her that it was time to act? Is it Bathsheba who approaches David first, not just because she has more influence than Nathan, but because she is the prime mover in the plot? And is that why she is more forceful with David, turning Nathan's polite question into a statement of fact, and why it is she whom David will summon to hear who is to occupy his throne?

We cannot answer those questions, and we will never know the answer to them. That is one of the fascinations of this opening to the Books of Kings. There is evidence on both sides, more than we have indicated already. Why, if the vow was truly made, did David or Bathsheba not tell Solomon? Nathan knows of it, but the first chapter of Kings makes it plain that Solomon and the rest of his supporters do not. On the other hand, if it is a fabrication, would Bathsheba and Nathan really have been able to trick David's memory on such a very serious matter? The king may be frail, but his final charge to Solomon in chapter 2 will reveal he has his mental faculties intact, and show us that his memory is still frighteningly accurate. In the end we will emerge from this tantalizing narrative still wondering, and still not knowing quite what to make of Bathsheba.

Yet several things are perfectly plain from her speech: her inventiveness, her resourcefulness, her cleverness, her grasp of the subtleties of rhetoric and her persuasiveness, what Celia Thomson calls 'her surefootedness in the way she steps into David's mind'.[43] She does not act as Nathan's lackey. Far from it. He may have played on her feelings, but she now plays on David's with just as much skill and determination. She goes a very long way beyond the brief Nathan gave her to remind the king of his 'vow'. She tells him of Adonijah's feast, and creates the clear impression that it has been called to celebrate his coronation. She emphasizes that it is going on behind David's back. She increases his fears by telling him that Adonijah has gained significant support in the army and among the priests. She makes clear Solomon's loyalty, not just by dissociating him from the plot, but by calling him David's 'servant'. She drops dark hints of what is in store for her and her son if David does not act. She reminds him of the authority he still holds, not merely by continually calling him 'king', but by conjuring up the picture of 'all Israel' hanging on his decision. By that description, which patently goes beyond the truth, she gives him the sense that all is not yet lost: the conspirators are few, and there is still time to undo their work. In the course of it she picks up once more the terms of the 'vow' with which she began.

It is, as Robert Alter acknowledges, 'a brilliant speech'.[44] Less charitably, and much less accurately, Richard Nelson calls her 'the fearful co-conspirator', and contrasts her with Nathan, 'the crafty instigator'; he is 'the wily manipulator', she 'the frantic mother'.[45] His judgements, particularly the second one regarding Bathsheba, owe more to destructive stereotypes than to the details of this most subtle and sophisticated of biblical texts.

Good as his word, Nathan comes on the scene as Bathsheba is

finishing. After he has gone, she will need to be summoned back, so we must think of her as leaving as soon as her words are over. For the moment she receives no response from the king, but Nathan's interruption is, of course, all part of their plan. His speech is not quite as long as Bathsheba's, but shares her brilliance:

'My lord the king, did you yourself say, "Adonijah shall succeed me as king, and he it is who shall sit on my throne?" For today he has gone down and has sacrificed oxen, fatted cattle, and sheep in abundance, and has invited all the king's sons, the commander of the army, and the priest Abiathar. There they are eating and drinking before him, and saying, "Long live king Adonijah!" But as for me, your servant, Zadok the priest, Benaiah son of Jehoiada, or your servant Solomon, he has not invited us. Is my lord the king responsible for this being done? Have you failed to let your servant know who should sit on the throne of my lord the king after him?' (1.24–7)

Nathan repeats just enough, he omits just enough, he adds just enough. He omits mention of any vow, as he must, for whether it is real or a lie, he cannot show he knows of a pact made between the king and queen that the king has not told him about. Yet twice, at the start of his speech and again at the end, he uses its terms and thus keeps it uppermost in David's mind. Like Bathsheba, he refers to Adonijah's feast, but he also emphasizes that it is going on even as he speaks, and adds further colour to her earlier description and underlines the treachery of the occasion by reporting (or inventing) cries of 'Long live king Adonijah!' He adds to her list of those who have not been invited, so that David is aware he still has a powerful faction of his own to call upon. And he ends with a reproach that he knows very well the king will wish to deny, and which will further increase his fear and his anger – the suggestion that David has been acting on the sly is bound to rub salt into his wound, bound to remind him of the way Adonijah and his band are acting behind his own back.

Scene 4: The plot succeeds – Bathsheba and David

(1 Kings 1.28–31)

The effect of these two speeches on David, coming as they do hard on the heels of one another, is clearly meant to be irresistible.

David does not resist. He summons Bathsheba at once. Since Nathan has to be sent for once this second audience with the queen is over, we must imagine him leaving David's room, just as we had to think of Bathsheba leaving after her speech.

The manner of Bathsheba's entrance and of her exit is interesting. She enters with no reported ceremony. 'So she came before the king and stood before the king' (1.28b). That is all the text says. We must not think of her as making a pointed omission of the etiquette she followed before. That would be to insult the king, and, for a ha'p'orth o' tar, would risk spoiling the ship she and Nathan are sailing so expertly. The omission is the narrator's, not hers. Its impact upon us, the readers of the story, is to emphasize her authority and her new power. We do not see her bowing to the king and obeising herself, because in truth it is David who is now doing her (and Nathan's) bidding. Thus before he opens his mouth we know what he will say.

> The king swore, saying, 'As the Lord lives, who has redeemed my life from every adversity, as I swore to you by the Lord, the God of Israel, "Solomon your son shall succeed me as king, and he it is who shall sit on my throne in my place", so will I do this day.' (1.29–30)

This is the third time David has asked for Bathsheba. He 'sent and took her' when he raped her (2 Sam. 11.4); he 'sent and gathered her' when Uriah was dead and he seized his chance to make her his wife (2 Sam. 11.27). Now he 'summons' her, but this time there is no 'taking', no 'gathering', only speaking. This is the first and the last occasion on which we hear David speaking to his wife. He quotes and accepts the terms of the 'vow' presented to him, and agrees it must be put into effect immediately. Whether he has been duped, or simply had his memory jogged and been told how urgent things are, we still do not know. What is clear is the honour he does Bathsheba. The 'vow' described Solomon as *her* son. By leaving its terms as they are, David gives the impression he is settling the succession issue out of respect for her and the promise he made to her. When in the next few verses he gives instructions to Zadok, Nathan and Benaiah for Solomon's coronation, he will refer to Solomon as *his* son (see 1.33). But while Bathsheba is in the room, it is her son who will come to power. No wonder, then, that as she leaves his presence she bows with her face to the ground, does obeisance to her king, and cries, 'May my lord the king, David, live for ever!' Her exaggerated courtesy, the same as was properly shown by Nathan at his entrance in verse 23, expresses her gratitude as eloquently as her words. Yet for the first (and last) time she dares to call her husband by his name. The courtesy of her obeisance hides her power. The manner of her speech reveals it. For the first time, perhaps, because we cannot be sure his consoling her after the death of their first child was welcome, he has given her something she wants. In return she calls him David. At long last she has proved a match for the king.

Scene 5: Palace intrigue II – Bathsheba and Adonijah

(1 Kings 2.13–18)

The rest of 1 Kings 1 tells in dramatic terms of the coronation of Solomon outside the walls of the city. Adonijah and his supporters, still in the middle of their own feast, hear the noise of the celebrations, and as they are wondering aloud what it is going on, a messenger arrives to give them the news in all its alarming detail. Their feast is thus brought to an abrupt end, and Adonijah flees to take sanctuary at the altar of God's shrine, and begs for his brother's mercy. For the time being that is granted, on the condition that he does not put a foot wrong. Given the track record of the members of this particular family, we cannot expect that pardon to be in force for very long.

1 Kings 2 brings us beside David's deathbed, and to his final charge to the son who has been anointed as his successor. That begins with fine pious words about obeying God, but soon slips into the largely sordid business of the settling of old scores. With the loose ends of his reign now tied up, David dies and is buried. Soon he will be canonized as Israel's greatest king, as the one who embodied the ideals of kingship. All future kings will be measured against him, and almost invariably will be found wanting. Such are the larger ironies of this story which Israel told about herself.

In all this we have had no further mention of Bathsheba. But no sooner is her son the sole ruler than we see her again, not at first, as we might expect, with him, but with the disgraced Adonijah.

Then Adonijah son of Haggith came to Bathsheba, Solomon's mother. She said, 'Do you come peaceably?' 'Peaceably,' he said. Then he said, 'I have a matter to discuss with you.' She said, 'Go on.' He said, 'You know yourself that the kingship was mine, and that all Israel was firmly expecting me to become king; but the kingship has turned about and become my brother's, for it was his from the Lord. Now I have one request to make of you; do not refuse me.' She said, 'Go on.' He said, 'Please, speak to Solomon the king – he will not refuse you – and ask him to give me Abishag the Shunammite as a wife.' Bathsheba said, 'Very well; I will speak on your behalf to the king.' (2.13–18)

This is another small masterpiece of writing. No adjectives are employed, no comment is made, no colour or explanation is added by the narrator. Apart from a string of she said/he said's (Hebrew narrative style is perfectly comfortable with such a thing), there is only direct speech, and not a great deal of that. Yet the storyteller conveys perfectly Adonijah's tentativeness and anxiety. His speech is halting and awkward. In the end he blurts out what he has come to say, but in getting there he says more than perhaps he meant to, certainly much more than is good for him. By contrast, Bathsheba remains calm, uses the minimum of words, and keeps her feelings strictly to herself. And again the storyteller tantalizes and leaves us wondering.

What is Adonijah up to? What does he really want? Some say he is after the throne, that his request for Abishag is a devious attempt to get control of Solomon's harem, and to gain access to Solomon's kingly power through the back door.[46] They remind us of the marriages David made for his own political advancement, and in particular of Absalom's taking over David's harem at the height of his revolt. Others argue that Adonijah could only be so brazen and unsubtle, and Bathsheba could only support such a claim, if they were imbeciles, and that what Adonijah wants is Abishag and no more.[47] The narrator has not given us Adonijah's motives. He has left us some freedom to speculate and disagree, and the clues he has hidden in the larger narrative and in the passage itself point in different directions. It is important we examine them, for they will bear upon our assessment of what Bathsheba herself is up to in going to Solomon so readily to press Adonijah's suit.

This is only the third time we have heard of Adonijah in the entire story of David and his sons. The first was a mere mention of him in the list of David's sons in 2 Samuel 3.2–5. The second was the episode we have already considered in 1 Kings 1. From that we have learned two things of significance: his impetuousness and his desire for power. What he wants is the throne, and in trying to get it he does not stop to think what others' reactions to his bid might be. When we look again at his dialogue with Bathsheba, we see that his desire for power has not diminished. 'You know yourself that the kingship was mine, and that all Israel was firmly expecting me to become king', is how he begins. That is his preamble to his request for Abishag. It is hard for us to avoid interpreting his desire for her as a cover for his desire for the kingdom, and if it is hard for us, then surely it is equally difficult for Bathsheba. Certainly it will be impossible for Solomon. He will immediately jump to such a conclusion.

On the other hand, Adonijah does acknowledge to Bathsheba that the throne is Solomon's because of God's wishes. If we think he is being sincere in that, then his reference to the kingship is no more than an awkward expression of his disappointment, and his request for Abishag betrays no more than his lust. In that case, Solomon's reaction is paranoid. David's story has provided, after all, not only political marriages and the taking over of a harem, but also tales of lust and impetuosity, the tales of David and Bathsheba and of Amnon and Tamar.

If we cannot be clear about Adonijah, we cannot be certain about Bathsheba either. What is *she* playing at? How does *she* understand Adonijah's request? We will have to come back to those questions when we examine her last scene and her approach to Solomon. For the moment, we can observe how much her authority has grown. We noticed the power she had in the court in 1 Kings 1. That is even greater now. As Solomon's mother, she commands an attention and has an influence that she never had as David's wife, even at the end. Adonijah comes to her. This is the first time anyone has done that. With David, she was the one being sent for, or the one who had to go to him. Even Nathan was not recorded as seeking an audience with her when they hatched the plot to get her son on the throne. That scene was simply introduced with the words, 'Then Nathan said to Bathsheba'. Second, there is true dialogue between them, and it is Bathsheba who initiates it. She has never had that privilege before. In 1 Kings 1 she delivered her speech to David, and then later he made his to her and provoked her loyal response. But there was not the interchange between them, the toing and froing of speech we see here. Third, Adonijah puts himself at her mercy. No one has done that before. Nathan asked for her co-operation, and assumed she had more influence over David than anyone else at court, at least in the matter of Solomon's succession. Now Adonijah openly acknowledges that he depends on her and that Solomon will not refuse her. She has come a very long way since that late afternoon when David spied her bathing.

Abishag, of course, has come nowhere. She has no more power than she had with David. She still has no say in things, and the narrator still has not brought her out of the shadows. We still know nothing about her, except that she is still a pawn in men's games, in Adonijah's and the narrator's.

And she would seem now to be a pawn in a woman's game also, for Bathsheba takes Adonijah's request straight to her son.

Scene 6: The plot crumbles – Bathsheba and Solomon

(1 Kings 2.19–24)

> So Bathsheba went to king Solomon, to speak to him on behalf of Adonijah. The king rose to meet her and did obeisance to her; then he sat on his throne and set a throne for the queen mother, and she sat on his right hand. Then she said, 'I have one small request to make of you. Do not refuse me.' And the king said to her, 'Make your request, my mother; for I will not refuse you.' She said, 'Let Abishag the Shunammite be given to your brother Adonijah as a wife.' (2.19–21)

The contrast between her entrance in her third scene, when she went to speak with David, and this one could not be more obvious. Then she did obeisance to the king, now he does obeisance to her. David, it would seem, left her standing for the duration of each of her audiences with him. Solomon at once seats her on her own throne, and in the place of honour at his right hand (see Ps. 110.1). But is this the moment of her triumph or her folly? Adonijah said Solomon would not refuse her. Solomon himself assures her of that. Yet that is exactly what he does.

> King Solomon answered and said to his mother, 'What are you doing asking for Abishag the Shunammite for Adonijah? Ask for the kingship for him! He is my older brother, after all! Ask it for him and for the priest Abiathar and for Joab son of Zeruiah!' Then king Solomon swore an oath by the Lord: 'So may God do to me and more, for Adonijah has devised this thing at the cost of his life! Now, as the Lord lives, who has established me and placed me on the throne of my father David, and who has made me a house as he promised, today Adonijah shall be put to death!' (2.22–4)

That marks the end of the audience. The next sentence records the killing of Adonijah, and after that we hear of the banishment of Abiathar the priest, the murder of Joab beside the altar of God, and then of the events leading up to Solomon's killing of Shimei, the last person left over from David's reign who might pose a threat to his power, and whom his father had ordered him to deal with. Thus Solomon comes in as David went out. We will not have mention of Bathsheba again, at least not in the Old Testament.

It would seem her short-lived triumph has been shattered by the ruthlessness and fear of her son. Or has it? Might she have got exactly what she came for? In 1 Kings 1 she played a key role in depriving Adonijah of the throne. It seems very strange that she should now fight his corner for him. Then she was keen to do all she could to protect the interests of her own son, and make sure he came to power. It is decidedly odd that she should now take willing part in a ploy that might smell so strongly of treachery, and which to Solomon's nostrils stinks of it. Burke Long suspects that Solomon's immediate reaction to the request for Abishag indicates further that Bathsheba may have anticipated the outcome all along: if the king can see through Adonijah's request so easily, or thinks he can, then surely Bathsheba must have the same suspicions, and must know very well what her son will do.[48]

We may think her a woman whose life is wholly one of being manipulated by men and of doing their bidding. We may possibly think her rather silly and impetuous herself, quite oblivious to the possible nuances of Adonijah's request, with no thought for how Solomon might react, but with a simple desire to please Adonijah. That, however, is not at all the woman who has emerged from the plot with Nathan. There she proved herself clever and astute, and whether she or Nathan was the prime mover of their scheme, she certainly did not speak to David as Nathan's puppet. She spoke with an authority of her own, an authority recognized by her husband and subtly drawn by the narrator, and one which has received further emphasis in these scenes with Adonijah and Solomon.

Furthermore, we can claim that she again exhibits considerable rhetorical skill in her audience with Solomon. She leads up to the request for Abishag by saying how small a thing it is. If she does suspect how *large* a thing it might be, and anticipates her son seeing it as such, then her making light of it is skilfully calculated to increase his anger when the request is made. When she comes to the request itself, she adds no further preamble. She could hardly give it the introduction Adonijah gave it, and refer to his disappointment at not getting the throne. To do so would put her in danger of a charge of treachery, of acting in league with a usurper. So she does not attempt to wrap it up at all, but leaves it bare in all its starkness and ugliness. In her scene with David, she showed herself most inventive, ready to add to the brief Nathan had given her, and knowing exactly the right amount to say. We suspect that her skill has not left her. We suspect she means not to support Adonijah, but finally to destroy him. She has got him out of the way once. Now, we think, she tries to do so again, for good. Her plan works. Adonijah is hastily murdered, his friends are disposed of, and Solomon, her son, is now safe and secure on the throne she (with a little help from her friends) gave him.

If we pick up the hints given us by this most subtle of writers, that is the most natural way to interpret her actions, the most plausible picture of her that we can paint on the basis of the few lines drawn in the text. We might, of course, be wrong. In the end we cannot be absolutely certain whether her final scene represents the height of her triumph, or a last return to her former tragedy.

A final footnote

(Matthew 1.6)

Bathsheba will feature once more in the Bible. Without her name, alas, and, interestingly enough, under her old title of 'the wife of Uriah' – and in the company of the Tamar of Genesis 38, Rahab the prostitute of Jericho, Ruth the Moabite, and Mary – she will appear at the beginning of Matthew's Gospel, in the genealogy of Jesus of Nazareth. Thus we leave her in the courtly circle of another 'king of the Jews', another 'king of Israel' (Matt. 27.37, 42), who Matthew tells us 'is called Messiah' (1.16), and who, at several points in his Gospel, including its very first verse, appears as 'the son of David'.

Final Reflections

I cannot leave these remarkable stories behind without pausing to reflect and to gather some of my thoughts together. Others will have their own responses to make, but these, for what they are worth, are mine.

When I wrote my first book on Old Testament texts, *Lo and Behold!*, I learned a great deal in the process, but it informed and confirmed what I was already doing at the Theological College. When after that sabbatical and that period of writing I resumed my teaching duties once again, there was a sense in which I took up where I had left off. This time it has been different. Looking at these texts consistently from the points of view of their female characters has for me been exhilarating and liberating, but it has shaken me and disturbed me more than I could have anticipated. It has put me in touch with my own sexism, with destructive stereotypes about women, and about men also, deep rooted within me. Returning to College at the start of the academic year, I have found myself looking with fresh eyes at my courses, introducing new elements, teaching things in new ways, having my ears more attuned, I would hope, to the voices of the women among the students. In short, writing this book has, I believe, done me good!

I have learned things about myself, and I have learned things also, of course, about the Old Testament. Some would condemn it as thoroughly patriarchal. I have come to believe they are wrong. We have in these few chapters of ours discovered a story of a Garden that, for all its flaws, makes room for a celebration of woman, and for a brilliant and acutely sensitive summary of the plight of the women in the villages of early Israel; we have found an Egyptian slave-woman more highly honoured in some respects than almost any other figure in the Bible, with the obvious exception of Jesus of Nazareth; we have come across in Exodus 1 a story probably first composed and told by women, and other stories in the early chapters of that book that portray women as true heroines of their day, and do so without condescension; with

Hannah's story we have encountered material written almost certainly by a man, but presented so carefully from her point of view.

Furthermore, we have found women's stories occurring at key points in the larger narrative, and women's actions playing quite vital roles in the plot. The tale of the Garden, in which the woman is so prominent, comes at the very beginning of the Bible's great history of the relationship between God and human beings. The call of Abraham marks a new chapter in that history, a new initiative on God's part, a new era of promise, a new destiny for humankind. The part Sarah is allowed to play in the proceedings is at times tragically small. Too often the narrator keeps her behind the tent flaps, out of sight, and usually out of earshot also. Yet without her bringing Isaac to birth, without her bringing him safely through to his weaning feast and to the years beyond, the purposes and bright promises of God would have come to nothing. When in Exodus we reach the part of the story that records the emergence of the people of God as a distinct people, women are conspicuous by their presence in the text and by their significance. Without Shiphrah and Puah, without Moses' mother and sister, without the treacherously compassionate daughter of the pharaoh and her loyal female attendants, without quick-thinking and quick-acting Zipporah, God's purposes would again have been destroyed. Later still the narrative concerns itself primarily with the moves towards the establishment of monarchy in Israel. Steps are taken towards it in the Book of Judges, and one false start is made, but the new chapter only truly begins with the birth of Samuel, the king-maker. And his story starts with Hannah's, and her vow is instrumental in bringing him to a position of power and influence among the tribes. The story of the monarchy becomes for a surprisingly long time the story of one king, David. Bathsheba's first appearance finds him at the height of his power, and marks his fall from grace and the start of his prolonged and terrible decline, and her last scenes surround his death and ensure the coming to power of his successor, Solomon. Solomon, as we know from the moment of his birth, is the one loved by God; from the beginning he is the divinely chosen successor. Yet without Bathsheba, his half-brother Adonijah might have come to the throne in his stead, and without Bathsheba it is possible Adonijah would have managed to wrest power out of Solomon's hands when he had scarcely taken hold of it. Bathsheba, too, plays an indispensable part in the furtherance of the declared purposes of God.

Why then should God have so little to do with these women? Sarah is neglected or abused by Abraham. The narrator does her scant justice himself. Yet it is God's neglect of her which I find most disquieting of all. Despite the way those chapters of Genesis have been written, they still allow us the freedom to imagine Sarah's pain, to share the brief moment of her joy, and discover her tragedy. Enough is there to evoke our sympathies for her, and allow us to exercise them even when she is not on stage at all, as in the case of the story of Isaac's near-sacrifice in the land of Moriah. We can, through persisting in seeing things from her standpoint, begin to put those things to rights. I find it much harder to correct God's silence towards her.

Things are little better when we look at those other women with whom we have been concerned. The woman in the Garden may have played as prominent a part as the man in the story as a whole, and the storyteller may have gone out of his way to try to put them on a par with each other. When, however, we look at how much God has to do with the man, and how much he has to do with the woman, the disparity is striking. Though the women of Exodus 1–4 play such significant parts in the survival of God's people and his promises, though they prove so indispensable to God, they nowhere receive from him any commission to do what they do. No desert bush burns mysteriously for them. They hear no clear divine call. They are given no chance of demonstrating their obedience, just as Sarah before them is given no real opportunity to show herself a great woman of faith and win our praise. We have already commented on how little space Hannah's story devotes to God's responses to her. Indeed, for all the uniqueness of her prayer, for all the self-sacrifice her vow entails, for all the vigorous triumph of her song, we are left wondering at the end whether it has not been the prayers of the inept, insensitive, but male and priestly Eli which have actually stirred God into action! With Bathsheba things are rather different, for God remains remarkably hidden in the story of that part of David's reign with which she is concerned. His dealings with David himself are hardly touched upon, at least on the surface of the text, outside the episode of Nathan's parable and oracles. It is not so surprising, therefore, that outside that same episode we do not hear of God paying Bathsheba any heed. Only Hagar presents a conspicuous exception to the rule, but as we explained in her chapter, only in those scenes where no man is on stage and God has no man to deal with. And even Hagar receives no great commission from God. The only command he gives her is the terrible one to return to the harsh treatment of her mistress.

The Bible pays little heed to the religious life of women, and says very little about their distinctive relationships with God, and God's distinctive dealings with them. What are we to conclude from all this, and what are we to do with it? That is for me, as I come to the end of this study, the most urgent question. It is a question which I must answer for myself, and so I must slip back now into the 'I'-speech with which I began. Shall I conclude that God always gives his more important tasks to men? But that would be absurd. Shall I think he prefers dealing with men? But such a notion is so patently silly as to be close to blasphemy. Shall I believe that he calls men and not women to be the conspicuous bearers of his promises? But I for one have had more than enough of that belief in the Church, and wish to see no more of the great harm it does to those who hold to it, or of the greater harm it does to their victims. Or shall I conclude instead that it is time the silences of the Bible were filled, filled by the voices of women? Shall I rejoice that in our day the prayer of women and the distinctive spirituality of women are beginning to make such an impact? Shall I be determined not to talk quite so much, so that I can more easily hear and heed what women are saying? Shall I be prepared to lose some of the power and status that I enjoy as a male priest, in order that women might gain the power and status that are rightfully theirs? Shall I long and work for the record to be set straight?

The writing of this book might help me decide.

Notes

Introduction

1. Carol A. Newsom and Sharon H. Ringe (eds), *The Women's Bible Commentary* (Louisville, KY: Westminster/John Knox Press; London: SPCK, 1992).
2. See Renita J. Weems, 'Song of Songs', in Newsom and Ringe (eds), *The Women's Bible Commentary*, p. 157; Athalya Brenner, *The Israelite Woman: Social Role and Literary Type in Biblical Narrative* (Sheffield: JSOT Press, 1985), pp. 46–50.

1. Eve: A Woman Much Maligned

1. Among the more important studies for our purposes are: Phyllis Trible, *God and the Rhetoric of Sexuality* (Philadelphia: Fortress Press, 1978), ch. 4; Carol Meyers, *Discovering Eve: Ancient Israelite Women in Context* (Oxford: Oxford University Press, 1988), especially chs 4 and 5; David J. Clines, *What Does Eve Do to Help? And Other Readerly Questions to the Old Testament* (Sheffield: Sheffield Academic Press, 1990), ch. 1; Ilona N. Rashkow, *Upon the Dark Places: Anti-Semitism and Sexism in English Renaissance Biblical Translation* (Sheffield: Almond Press, 1990), ch. 3.
2. Trible, *God and the Rhetoric*, p. 76 – see also pp. 77 and 80 for a discussion of the translation.
3. Meyers, *Discovering Eve*, pp. 81–2.
4. Mary Phil Korsak, *At the Start . . . : Genesis Made New* (Louvain: Leuvense Schrijversaktie, 1992), p. 5.
5. See Rashkow, *Upon the Dark Places*, pp. 80–1.
6. Trible, *God and the Rhetoric*, p. 98.
7. Meyers, *Discovering Eve*, ch. 7, particularly p. 148.
8. For the translation of the phrase I am indebted to Rashkow, *Upon the Dark Places*, p. 82.
9. Trible, *God and the Rhetoric*, p. 90.
10. See Rashkow, *Upon the Dark Places*, pp. 82–3; also Trible, *God and the Rhetoric*, p. 90; Meyers, *Discovering Eve*, p. 85.
11. Clines, *What Does Eve Do to Help?*, p. 30 (see pp. 28–37 for his full discussion of the point).
12. Rashkow, *Upon the Dark Places*, p. 84, points out that the verb 'build' in the Old Testament always suggests a good deal of hard work.
13. This is all the more remarkable, given the nature of other creation stories in the ancient Near East. Claus Westermann, in *Genesis 1–11: A Commentary* (London: SPCK, 1984), p. 232, claims that, 'Genesis 2 is unique among the creation myths of the whole of the Ancient Near East in its appreciation of the meaning of woman, i.e., that human existence is a partnership of man and woman'.
14. See ibid., p. 85; Korsak, *At the Start . . .* , p. 7, also has 'sides' and 'side' in her translation.
15. ibid., p. 231.
16. See, for example, Gordon J. Wenham, *Genesis 1–15*, Word Biblical Commentary (Dallas: Word Publishing, 1987), p. 68; and for a very careful discussion of the point, Clines, *What Does Eve Do to Help?*, pp. 38–40.
17. See Westermann's painstaking treatment of this verse in *Genesis 1–11*, pp. 233–4.
18. Gerhard von Rad, *Genesis: A Commentary*, 2nd edn, Old Testament Library (London: SCM Press, 1963), p. 86.
19. Westermann, *Genesis 1–11*, pp. 239–40.
20. ibid., pp. 249–50.
21. Meyers, *Discovering Eve*, ch. 5, pp. 95–121.
22. ibid., pp. 102–3 and 105–6.

23. ibid., pp. 117–18.
24. ibid., pp. 114–17.
25. Rashkow's chapter on this story in *Upon the Dark Places*, pp. 75–96, reveals the enduring impact upon us of the English Renaissance translators.
26. See Westermann, *Genesis 1–11*, p. 290.
27. See ibid., p. 338.
28. It is usually the mother who names the child in the Old Testament, particularly in Genesis, though the second account of the birth of Seth, in Gen. 5.3, has Adam naming him.
29. Not long after the New Testament was written, the doctrine of the New Eve was developed, with Mary, the mother of Jesus, gaining the title. The link between Eve and Mary was made as early as the mid-second century by Justin Martyr. See Deborah Sawyer, 'Resurrecting Eve', in Paul Morris and Deborah Sawyer (eds), *A Walk in the Garden: Biblical, Iconographical and Literary Images of Eden* (Sheffield: Sheffield Academic Press, 1992), p. 281.

2. Sarah: A Woman Caught up in God's Promises

1. Sharon Pace Jeansonne gives them that title in *The Women of Genesis: From Sarah to Potiphar's Wife* (Minneapolis: Fortress Press, 1990), p. 2.
2. Most versions have something akin to the NRSV's 'so that you will be a blessing'. Our version is a straightforward translation of the Hebrew as it stands. For a discussion of the text and its translation, see David J. Clines, *What Does Eve Do to Help? And Other Readerly Questions to the Old Testament* (Sheffield: Sheffield Academic Press, 1990), pp. 55–6.
3. See Trevor Dennis, *Lo and Behold!: The Power of Old Testament Storytelling* (London: SPCK, 1991), ch. 2.
4. See Claus Westermann, *Genesis 12–36: A Commentary* (London: SPCK, 1986), pp. 162–4.
5. ibid., p. 164.
6. ibid.
7. John Calvin, not having access to the ancient Near Eastern background as we have, and judging Sarai and Abram by the ethics of his own day, condemned Sarai's offer as 'foolish and preposterous'; see his *Commentaries on Genesis*, 2 vols (Grand Rapids, MI: Wm B. Eerdmans, 1948), ad loc.
8. See Gen. 30.1–13; also 22.24 and 25.6.
9. *Commentaries on Genesis*, loc. cit. However, Calvin shows that he is not entirely unsympathetic towards Sarai, by appreciating her desire to acquire 'material rights and honours' and thereby a share in the blessings of God promised to her husband.
10. Gerhard von Rad, *Genesis: A Commentary*, 2nd edn, Old Testament Library (London: SCM Press, 1963), p. 186. The German original of the first edition came out in 1956.
11. Jeansonne, *The Women of Genesis*, p. 19.

12. See Francis Brown, S. R. Driver, C. A. Briggs (eds), *A Hebrew and English Lexicon* (Oxford: Oxford University Press, 1907), p. 329b.

13. See Robert Davidson, *Genesis 12–50*, The Cambridge Bible Commentary (Cambridge: Cambridge University Press, 1979), pp. 59–60. Alternatively, Mary Phil Korsak, *At the Start . . . : Genesis Made New* (Louvain: Leuvense Schrijversaktie, 1992), p. 54, translates Sarai as 'My Princess' (and Sarah as 'Princess').

14. The Jewish Masoretic scholars, who pointed the Hebrew text in the early centuries of our era, putting the dots and dashes below or above the Hebrew consonants to indicate the vowels (Hebrew does not have vowels of its own), pointed the word for 'My Lord' in a way usually reserved for when God is being clearly addressed. Thus they wished to indicate that Abraham saw through the disguise at the start, and in so doing removed much of the suspense and vitality from the story, not to mention its humour.

15. 'at lifetide' is Korsak's brilliant rendering (*At the Start . . .*, p. 58) of a Hebrew phrase which has caused the translators some problems. The more usual translation, 'in due course', is colourless by comparison, and not nearly so close to the Hebrew.

16. See the comment we made in chapter 1, pp. 31–2, with regard to the woman in the Garden.

17. The discrepancy was noticed by the rabbis, who commented: 'Abraham might have taken amiss what his wife had said about his advanced years, and so precious is the peace between husband and wife that even the Holy One, blessed be He, preserved it at the expense of truth'!; see Louis Ginzberg, *The Legends of the Jews*, vol. 1 (Philadelphia: Jewish Publication Society of America, 1909), pp. 244–5, quoted in Katheryn Pfisterer Darr, *Far More Precious than Jewels: Perspectives on Biblical Women* (Louisville, KY: Westminster/ John Knox Press, 1991), p. 103.

18. These are not the only occasions in the Old Testament when a foreigner teaches an Israelite, or an ancestor of the Israelites, a lesson and puts them to shame. See, for example, Jethro in Exod. 18 (compare his praising God with the complaints of the Israelites in the previous chapters); Naaman in 2 Kings 5 (compared with the greedy Gehazi); the pagan sailors in Jonah 1, or the Ninevites in Jonah 3 (as compared with Jonah himself).

19. See Gen. 11.31–12.3.

20. See von Rad, *Genesis*, p. 224.

21. See Westermann, *Genesis 12–36*, p. 327.

22. In Isaac's case, when his birth is first predicted, it is said that Abraham will give him his name: see 17.19.

23. See Exod. 4.25.

24. For that we have to refer back to 17.17.

25. See von Rad, *Genesis*, p. 226; Westermann, *Genesis 12–36*, p. 333.

26. See Carol Meyers, *Discovering Eve: Ancient Israelite Women in Context* (Oxford: Oxford University Press, 1988), p. 112.

27. See John S. Kselman in James L. Mays (ed.), *Harper's Bible Commentary* (San Francisco: Harper & Row, 1988), p. 99.

28. For an illuminating comment on the laws of primogeniture, whereby the eldest son took a double portion of his father's estate, and on the social and economic purposes behind it, see Meyers, *Discovering Eve*, p. 193.
29. Phyllis Trible makes this point most powerfully in her essay, 'Genesis 22: The Sacrifice of Sarah', in Jason P. Rosenblatt and Joseph C. Sitterson Jr. (eds), *Not in Heaven: Coherence and Complexity in Biblical Narrative* (Bloomington and Indianapolis: Indiana University Press, 1991), pp. 189–91.
30. Trible asks the same question, ibid., p. 182.
31. See Trible, ibid., p. 181, commenting on 22.19. According to one rabbinic tradition, Sarah died from a broken heart when Abraham returned without her son (see Darr, *Far More Precious than Jewels*, p. 129, n 66; Darr quotes another legend of the rabbis, which also links Sarah's death with the events of Gen. 22 – see pp. 109–10).

3. Hagar: A Persecuted Madonna

1. Sharon Pace Jeansonne, *The Women of Genesis: From Sarah to Potiphar's Wife* (Minneapolis: Fortress Press, 1990), p. 18. ·
2. See Katheryn Pfisterer Darr, *Far More Precious than Jewels: Perspectives on Biblical Women* (Louisville, KY: Westminster/John Knox Press, 1991), p. 135.
3. See p. 42.
4. See Claus Westermann, *Genesis 12–36: A Commentary* (London: SPCK, 1986), p. 238.
5. See above, p. 43.
6. Conflict in such a situation was not inevitable. There is no mention of any rift between mistress and slave in Gen. 30, when Rachel and Leah offer their slave-women to Jacob. However, it does seem to have been common. The Code of Hammurabi, a collection of laws promulgated in the Babylonian empire in the eighteenth century BCE, includes a ruling on cases where slaves in Hagar's situation claimed equality with their mistresses (see Westermann, *Genesis 12–36*, p. 240).
7. Many of our versions have in verse 4 something akin to the NRSV's, 'she [Hagar] looked with contempt on her mistress', and in verse 5, 'she looked on me with contempt'. In fact, as our more literal translations on p. 44 of our chapter on Sarah demonstrated, the original Hebrew makes Sarai the subject of the verb in each case.
8. See Westermann, *Genesis 12–36*, p. 244.
9. See above, pp. 37–8.
10. The Exodus story contains a further verbal echo of the Genesis passage. The Hebrew word for Hagar's running away is the same as that used in Exod. 14.5 of the flight of the Israelites from Egypt.
11. See Trevor Dennis, *Lo and Behold!: The Power of Old Testament Storytelling* (London: SPCK, 1991), pp. 121–3.
12. The oracle Rebekah receives from God concerning the twins in her womb in 25.23 bears some similarity to God's promise to Hagar, but falls into a different category of divine pronouncement.

13. Phyllis Trible also calls her a madonna in *Texts of Terror: Literary-Feminist Readings of Biblical Narratives* (Philadelphia: Fortress Press, 1984), p. 25.
14. Unfortunately many of our versions mislead us by translating 'messenger' in such passages as Gen. 16 or Judg. 13 as 'angel', and so encourage us to import anachronistic notions into our interpretation of the texts.
15. Westermann, *Genesis 12–36*, p. 246.
16. It is possible to translate El Roi as 'The God of Seeing' or 'The God who Sees', but Westermann (*Genesis 12–36*, p. 247) rightly argues that the context demands the translation 'The God who Sees Me'.
17. Westermann, *Genesis 12–36*, p. 247.
18. The name is often translated in our versions, 'The Lord Provides', or 'The Lord will Provide'. I have called it 'The Lord Sees' to make clear that the same Hebrew verb lies behind both Hagar's name for God and Abraham's name for the mountain.
19. See Westermann, *Genesis 12–36*, p. 248. He applauds the emendation, while himself preferring a less radical one which translates, 'I have seen God after he saw me.'
20. Trible, *Texts of Terror*, p. 19.
21. Jeansonne, *The Women of Genesis*, p. 28.
22. See Dennis, *Lo and Behold!*, p. 154, commenting on Jonah 4.10.
23. Trible, *Texts of Terror*, p. 22.
24. See Gen. 17.20.
25. See Trible, *Texts of Terror*, p. 22.
26. The only further appearance she makes in the Bible is in Paul's allegory in Gal. 4.21–5.1.
27. Dennis, *Lo and Behold!*, p. 60.
28. The Hebrew verb used in 21.14 occurs in Exod. 4.23 and twice in 5.2. It is also the one employed in Gen. 3.23 for the expulsion from the Garden.
29. Susan Niditch, 'Genesis', in Carol A. Newsom and Sharon H. Ringe (eds), *The Women's Bible Commentary* (Louisville, KY: Westminster/John Knox Press; London: SPCK, 1992), p. 16.
30. See, for example, the Septuagint, or the RSV (the NRSV returns to the Hebrew as we have it), Gerhard von Rad, *Genesis: A Commentary*, 2nd edn, Old Testament Library (London: SCM Press, 1963), pp. 226 and 228, or Westermann, *Genesis 12–36*, pp. 337 and 341.
31. Trible, *Texts of Terror*, p. 24.
32. The story's context would lead us to think Ishmael must be sixteen or so, since it suggests that fourteen years have elapsed between his birth and Isaac's (compare 16.16 and 21.5), and we have already seen Isaac weaned in what would have been his third year. However, we are clearly meant to think of him as a very young child, small enough to be lifted on to Hagar's shoulder by Abraham as he sends them away. Interestingly enough, in the drawing we have been considering, Rembrandt depicts Ishmael as just such a child, although in his etching and drawings of their dismissal by Abraham he makes Ishmael much older.

33. Trible, *Texts of Terror*, p. 25.
34. ibid., p. 26.
35. Niditch, 'Genesis', p. 18.

4. Unsung Heroines: The Women of Exodus 1–4

1. See Gen. 46.7, 15 and the story of the rape of Dinah in Gen. 34.
2. See Claus Westermann, *Genesis 12–36: A Commentary* (London: SPCK, 1986), p. 150.
3. See Gen. chs 41 and 47.
4. See Gen. 45.5–9; 50.20.
5. See Exod. 14.14, 25 and Charles Isbell's discussion in his essay, 'Exodus 1–2 in the Context of Exodus 1–14: Story Lines and Key Words', in David J. A. Clines, David M. Gunn, and Alan J. Hauser (eds), *Art and Meaning: Rhetoric in Biblical Literature* (Sheffield: JSOT Press, 1982), p. 46.
6. See Gen. 41.33–6, 46–9.
7. Alice L. Laffey, *An Introduction to the Old Testament: A Feminist Perspective* (Philadelphia: Fortress Press; London: SPCK, 1988), p. 47.
8. The Hebrew word translated 'stones' is obscure. Some translate it 'supporting stones', envisaging a pair of stones on which the mother would kneel to give birth, some 'birth stool'. Others think it refers to the genitals of the new-born babies, and in particular to the testicles of the boys, and the context would suggest that meaning. Certainly it is clear what the midwives are expected to look out for.
9. Brevard S. Childs, *Exodus: A Commentary*, Old Testament Library (London: SCM Press, 1974), p. 11.
10. J. Cheryl Exum, '"You Shall Let Every Daughter Live": A Study of Exodus 1:8–2:10', in Mary Ann Tolbert (ed.), 'The Bible and Feminist Hermeneutics', *Semeia* 28 (1983), p. 69. Celia Thomson revealed to me in discussion that the killing of the boys introduces an interesting ambiguity. We are used to stories of boys being regarded as more valuable and more welcome than girls, and we still hear of mothers in some communities discovering the gender of their unborn children and having them aborted if they are female. In Exod. 1, is the higher value put on the boys because they are to be killed, or on the girls because they are allowed to survive?
11. Everett Fox, *Now These Are the Names: A New English Rendition of the Book of Exodus* (New York: Shocken Books, 1986), p. 15.
12. See Exod. 3.11, 13; 4.1, 10, 13. Moses' question in 3.13 looks genuine enough, but Childs, *Exodus*, pp. 74–5, argues convincingly that it belongs to the series of objections and is part of his resistance to God's plan.
13. Westermann, *Genesis 12–36*, p. 164, quoted above on pp. 38 and 41.
14. Childs, *Exodus*, p. 13.
15. ibid., p. 17.
16. Exum, 'You Shall Let Every Daughter Live', p. 74.

17. See Childs, *Exodus*, p. 23.
18. ibid., p. 17.
19. See Carol Meyers, *Discovering Eve: Ancient Israelite Women in Context* (Oxford: Oxford University Press, 1988), p. 106.
20. Jonathan Magonet, *Bible Lives* (London: SCM Press, 1992), p. 7; Cheryl Exum, 'You Shall Let Every Daughter Live', p. 74, interprets the joke as being made at the expense of the Egyptian women.
21. See Gen. 27 (Rebekah); 31.19, 30–5 (Rachel); 38 (Tamar). Susan Niditch, 'Genesis', in Carol A. Newsom and Sharon H. Ringe (eds), *The Women's Bible Commentary* (Louisville, KY: Westminster/John Knox Press; London: SPCK, 1992), pp. 19–23, provides excellent comment on these passages. On p. 18 she suggests that Sarai should be added to the list, because she acts as a co-trickster with Abram in 12.10–20, but since that passage allows Sarai no initiative, and nowhere informs us of her attitude to the deception, I believe such a description goes beyond the text.
22. In raising this possibility to do with authorship – and it must remain only a possibility – I am not wishing to beg any questions about the historical accuracy of the passage. That is another matter altogether, and one which does not fall within the bounds of our discussion.
23. George Coats, *Moses: Heroic Man, Man of God* (Sheffield: JSOT Press, 1988), p. 45.
24. Exum, 'You Shall Let Every Daughter Live', p. 72. (See also her p. 73 for a continuation of the discussion.)
25. ibid., p. 73.
26. In the Septuagint she appears earlier in 6.20, alongside Moses and Aaron, but that looks suspiciously like an attempt on the translators' part to correct what they saw as a curious omission. That apart, it is always possible that the Miriam of 15.20–1 is not the same sister as the one in ch. 2. However, we know of no other sister Moses had, and Miriam is mentioned alongside him again in Num. 12.4 and 26.59, 1 Chron. 6.3, and Mic. 6.4.
27. The Hebrew word which I have translated 'ark' (and which is generally translated 'basket') is the same one as is used of Noah's ark in the Flood story. It is a most unusual word for the narrator to choose, and this is, in fact, the only time outside the Flood story that it occurs. It would seem clear that he intends us to make the link.
28. See Childs, *Exodus*, pp. 8–10, and Coats, *Moses*, pp. 46–7. Both quote parts of the relevant passage of the Sargon legend (Coats gives considerably more of it than Childs), and both are keen to point out the differences between it and the Exodus story with regard to content and function.
29. See Exum, 'You Shall Let Every Daughter Live', p. 79; Fox, *Now These Are the Names*, p. 19.
30. See Childs, *Exodus*, pp. 10–11.
31. See George Pixley, *On Exodus: A Liberation Perspective* (New York: Orbis Books, 1983), pp. 11–12.
32. See Coats, *Moses*, pp. 51–2.
33. Robert Alter, *The Art of Biblical Narrative* (London: George Allen & Unwin, 1981), p. 57.

34. See, for example, Ps. 23 and Ezek. 34.
35. The translation of verse 26b is taken from Childs' commentary and reflects his discussion of the verse – *Exodus*, pp. 91 and 99–100.
36. See my discussion of the Genesis passage in Trevor Dennis, *Lo and Behold!: The Power of Old Testament Storytelling* (London: SPCK, 1991), pp. 49–54, and, for this particular point, p. 50. It is also possible to compare Exod. 4.24–6 with the story of the binding of Isaac in Gen. 22, though that does not stem from any demon story.
37. See, for example, Childs, *Exodus*, pp. 100, 101, 104.
38. See, for example, Childs' detailed discussions in *Exodus*, pp. 95–101 and 103–4.
39. Athalya Brenner, *The Israelite Woman: Social Role and Literary Type in Biblical Narrative* (Sheffield: JSOT Press, 1985), pp. 71–2.
40. That is what Brenner, in *The Israelite Woman*, calls him. In doing so she is attempting to go beneath the text as we have it to a more primitive level. In the final form of the text the god or demon is clearly identified as Yahweh, 'the Lord' (as most of our versions call him), the God of Israel. That identification is, of course, one of the more disconcerting features of the passage.
41. See Westermann, *Genesis 12–36*, p. 265.
42. See Drorah O'Donnell Setel, 'Exodus', in Carol A. Newsom and Sharon H. Ringe (eds), *The Women's Bible Commentary* (Louisville, KY: Westminster/John Knox Press; London: SPCK, 1992), pp. 30–1.
43. ibid., p. 31.
44. With regard to the larger context, Fox observes that if Moses is   the one under attack, the passage balances the description of his flight from Egypt in 2.15–16. There he goes to Midian because his life is threatened; here he is set upon as he leaves Midian to return to Egypt. Fox also points out that it would have another parallel in 2.1–10, where women again save Moses' life. Thus, he says (*Now These Are the Names*, pp. 33, 35), the pattern of the narrative suggests the early phase of Moses' life has come full circle and is now complete. The storytellers of the Old Testament certainly took great delight in creating such patterns and parallels in their narratives, and the Jacob stories in Genesis provide an example remarkably similar to the first one Fox detects here: Jacob flees to Haran because Esau is out to kill him, and is attacked by God on the way back (Gen. 27.41–5; 32.22–32). There is no doubt that Fox's observations deserve to be taken very seriously, and we might indeed claim they come close to solving this particular ambiguity in our passage, and reveal that it is Moses, not Gershom, who is attacked.
45. For discussions of the possibility of Miriam's authorship of the song in Exod. 15, see Setel, 'Exodus', pp. 31–2, and Brenner, *The Israelite Woman*, pp. 51–6. Both those discussions also deal with the wider and more important question of whether Miriam might have exercised a leadership role comparable with that of Aaron or Moses himself. If she did, then that fact, too, has been suppressed by the documents, while leaving traces of itself behind in such places as Num. 12 and Mic. 6.4.

46. See Exod. 4.21; 7.3–4; 9.12; 10.1, 20, 27; 11.10; 14.4, 8. The incident of the snakes and the first few plagues leave the question open, or suggest the pharaoh is in control of his reactions (see 7.13; 8.15, 32; 9.34), but I am convinced the later texts, together with the predictions of 4.21 and 7.3–4, make plain what is going on all the time: God is behind it all.

47. For the phrase 'prayer of protest' I am indebted to Gordon Mursell, *Out of the Deep: Prayer as Protest* (London: Darton, Longman & Todd, 1989).

48. Isbell, 'Exodus 1–2 in the Context of Exodus 1–14', p. 42.

5. Hannah: How the Feeble Gird on Strength!

1. See Jo Ann Hackett, '1 and 2 Samuel', in Carol A. Newsom and Sharon H. Ringe (eds), *The Women's Bible Commentary* (Louisville, KY: Westminster/John Knox Press; London: SPCK, 1992), p. 85.

2. See John Mauchline, *1 and 2 Samuel*, New Century Bible (London: Marshall, Morgan & Scott, 1971), p. 42.

3. The footnotes in some of the versions, such as the NRSV or REB, give an idea of the extent of the problem, though for more detailed information we have to turn to the larger commentaries, or to S. R. Driver, *Notes on the Hebrew Text and the Topography of the Books of Samuel* (Oxford: Oxford University Press, 1913).

4. See P. Kyle McCarter, Jr., *I Samuel*, Anchor Bible (New York: Doubleday, 1980), pp. 59–60.

5. See the discussions of 1.5 in the commentaries. One of the most detailed is found in McCarter, *I Samuel*, pp. 51–2. See also Driver, *Notes on the Hebrew Text*, pp. 7–8 (non-Hebraists should be warned that his discussion includes many untransliterated Hebrew words).

6. McCarter, *I Samuel*, p. 49.

7. Robert Alter, *The Art of Biblical Narrative* (London: George Allen & Unwin, 1981), p. 83.

8. ibid., p. 83.

9. H. W. Hertzberg, *I and II Samuel: A Commentary*, Old Testament Library (London: SCM Press, 1964), p. 24.

10. I am not sure any biblical narrative means to assert such a narrow view. As we said in chapter 2 with regard to Sarah, we have to bear in mind the limitations imposed on a narrative by the narrator – see above, p. 42.

11. Hackett, '1 and 2 Samuel', p. 89.

12. The NRSV has 'a male child' instead of 'offspring'. The rest of the vow, with its male pronouns, makes clear that that is what Hannah means, but it is not what the Hebrew text actually says.

13. The clause about the drinking of alcohol is introduced from the Septuagint. McCarter, *I Samuel*, pp. 53–4, gives a detailed discussion of the difficulties of this verse. He thinks the Septuagint's addition was once part of the original text, and includes it in his own translation on p. 49.

14. See Tobit 3.11–15 (Sarah, daughter of Raguel); Judith 9.2–14; 13.4–5, 8 (all prayers of Judith herself – and see her psalm of thanksgiving in 16.1–7); Daniel and Susanna, vv. 42–3 (Susanna).
15. In Old Testament narrative we hear of: Abraham in Gen. 15.2–3; 17.18; 18.23ff.; Abraham's servant in Gen. 24.12–14, 26–7; Jacob in Gen. 32.9–12; Moses in Exod. 5.22–3; 32.11–13, 31–2; 33.12ff.; 34.9; Num. 12.13; 14.13–19; 27.15–17; Deut. 3.23–5; 9.25–9; Joshua in Josh. 7.7–9; Gideon in Judg. 6.22, 36ff.; Manoah in Judg. 13.8; Samson in Judg. 15.18; 16.28, 30; David in 1 Sam. 23.10–12; 2 Sam. 2.1; 7.18–29; 15.31; and in 1 Chron. 17.16–27; Solomon in 1 Kings 3.6–9; 8.22–53; Elijah in 1 Kings 17.20–2; 18.36–7; 19.4; Elisha in 2 Kings 6.17–18; Hezekiah in 2 Kings 19.14–19; 20.2–3; Jabez in 1 Chron. 4.10; Asa in 2 Chron. 14.11; Jehoshaphat in 2 Chron. 20.6–12; Ezra in Ezra 9.6–15; Nehemiah in Neh. 1.4–11; Daniel in Dan. 2.19–23; 9.4–19; and Jonah in Jonah 2.1–9; 4.2–3.
16. Alter, *The Art of Biblical Narrative*, p. 84.
17. See above, pp. 105–6.
18. Mauchline, *1 and 2 Samuel*, p. 47.
19. Hackett, '1 and 2 Samuel', pp. 89–90.
20. Even if the clause about 'wine and strong drink' did not belong to the original text of Hannah's vow – see note 13 above – and she is not quoting her own words, she is still referring to the terms of the nazirite vow as laid out in Numbers: the phrase 'wine and strong drink' appears in Num. 6.3.
21. Alter, *The Art of Biblical Narrative*, p. 86.
22. As usual, the popular etymology of the Old Testament gets it wrong! 'Samuel', instead of meaning 'Asked of God', probably means 'His name [i.e., the name of the God he calls upon in worship] is El'. Furthermore, the Hebrew root, *sa'al*, is much closer to the name Saul than to Samuel, and, indeed, in 1.28 is used in the form *sa'ul*, which is precisely the name of the future king. This has encouraged some commentators to suggest that in the formation of the text, birth stories to do with Saul have been combined with Samuel's (see, for example, McCarter, *I Samuel*, pp. 62–3). Ralph Klein, *1 Samuel*, Word Biblical Commentary (Waco, TX: Word Books, 1983), p. 9, puts forward the interesting alternative that the puns on Saul's name are introduced deliberately to indicate that the true leader of Israel, the real 'Saul', the one truly asked of God and given by him, is to be Samuel, not king Saul (see also Hertzberg, *I and II Samuel*, pp. 25–6).
23. Hertzberg, *I and II Samuel*, p. 28.
24. The second sentence follows the lead of the Septuagint. The Hebrew text, with its 'may the Lord establish his word' (which is what the NRSV gives), makes no sense in the context.
25. See R. P. Gordon, *1 and 2 Samuel: A Commentary* (Exeter: Paternoster Press, 1986), p. 77; Hertzberg, *I and II Samuel*, p. 28.
26. See McCarter, *I Samuel*, p. 56.
27. See ibid., p. 78.
28. Drorah O'Donnell Setel, 'Exodus', in Carol A. Newsom and Sharon H. Ringe (eds), *The Women's Bible Commentary* (Louisville, KY: Westminster/John Knox Press; London: SPCK, 1992), p. 29.

29. The translation 'dedicated' is Kyle McCarter's – see *I Samuel*, pp. 50 and 63. More familiar to us from the versions is the translation 'lent' (see the NEB and REB, the RSV and NRSV), but that weakens the force of Hannah's statement considerably, and does not fit the context. There is no suggestion here or in any subsequent passage that she means one day to take Samuel back.

30. McCarter, *1 Samuel*, p. 73.

31. Walter Brueggemann, *First and Second Samuel*, Interpretation, (Louisville, KY: John Knox Press, 1990), p. 16.

32. My phrase is taken from the first line of Fred Kaan's hymn, 'Sing we a song of high revolt'. The hymn can be found in *100 Hymns For Today* (London: Hymns Ancient & Modern, 1969).

33. Driver, *Notes on the Hebrew Text*, p. 23.

34. McCarter, *1 Samuel*, pp. 71–2.

35. An additional phrase, 'no one besides you', occurs in the Hebrew text before this line (and appears in the NRSV). However, stylistic considerations, and the evidence of the Septuagint, which has a different order, suggest it is an intrusion that did not belong to the original (see Driver, *Notes on the Hebrew Text*, p. 24). If it is included, it expresses a notion that is weaker than the one immediately before it. Hebrew poetry invariably works with crescendos, not with such diminuendos; second or third clauses in a series intensify or add colour to what has gone before.

36. 'Has become sterile' is our translation of a word which means 'become feeble' or 'languish'. Here, and in a similar verse in Jer. 15.9, the balance of the poetry would suggest the particular meaning we have given.

37. Alice L. Laffey, *An Introduction to the Old Testament: A Feminist Perspective* (Philadelphia: Fortress Press; London: SPCK, 1988), p. 107.

38. Brueggemann, *First and Second Samuel*, p. 18.

39. Laffey, *Introduction to the Old Testament*, p. 107.

40. Claus Westermann, *Genesis 12–36: A Commentary* (London: SPCK, 1986), p. 327, quoted above, p. 70.

41. The same words are used in Gen. 21.1, when Sarah conceives Isaac.

6. Bathsheba: From Rape Victim to Queen Mother

1. David M. Gunn offers a brilliant and thought-provoking study of Saul's demise and David's rise to power in *The Fate of King Saul: An Interpretation of a Biblical Story* (Sheffield: JSOT Press, 1980).

2. See Walter Brueggemann, *David's Truth in Israel's Imagination and Memory* (Philadelphia: Fortress Press, 1985), ch. 1.

3. This is a straightforward translation of the Hebrew. Most versions and commentaries put the direct speech that follows into the mouth of a third, unidentified party, presumably the messenger sent to make the enquiries, who is envisaged as reporting back to the king. Hence the

NRSV's 'It was reported . . .' However, as Randall Bailey points out, in that case we would expect the Hebrew to indicate a change of speaker and to insert 'to David' or 'to him'; see Randall C. Bailey, *David in Love and War: The Pursuit of Power in 2 Samuel 10–12* (Sheffield: JSOT Press, 1990), p. 85.

4. We have to concede that the Hebrew text is slightly corrupt here, and that its sense is not entirely certain. P. Kyle McCarter claims that 11.1 looks back to the campaigns of ch. 10, and translates, 'When the time of year at which the kings had marched out came round again . . .'; see his *II Samuel*, Anchor Bible (New York: Doubleday, 1984), p. 277 for the translation, and pp. 284–5 for the discussion of it. However, the vast majority of commentators and versions translate as we have done.

5. J. P. Fokkelman, *King David (II Sam 9–20 & 1 Kings 1–2)*, vol. 1 of *Narrative Art and Poetry in the Books of Samuel* (Assen: Van Gorcum, 1981), p. 51.

6. See Alice L. Laffey, *An Introduction to the Old Testament: A Feminist Perspective* (Philadelphia: Fortress Press; London: SPCK, 1988), pp. 119–20.

7. See John Mauchline, *1 and 2 Samuel*, New Century Bible (London: Marshall, Morgan & Scott, 1971), p. 248; Robert Alter, *The Art of Biblical Narrative* (London: George Allen & Unwin, 1981), p. 76.

8. H. W. Hertzberg, *I and II Samuel: A Commentary*, Old Testament Library (London: SCM Press, 1964), p. 309.

9. Bailey, *David in Love and War*, pp. 84–90. The two phrases we have quoted appear on pp. 86 and 88 respectively.

10. ibid., p. 122.

11. ibid., p. 86.

12. For this last point, see Fokkelman, *King David*, pp. 52–3.

13. See Bailey, *David in Love and War*, p. 87; also McCarter, *II Samuel*, p. 285.

14. Bailey, *David in Love and War*, pp. 87–8.

15. See above, pp. 95–6.

16. See Bailey, *David in Love and War*, p. 100 and p. 177, n 80.

17. See ibid., p. 100.

18. See ibid., pp. 105–6; for a more detailed and measured discussion, see Gwilym H. Jones, *The Nathan Narratives* (Sheffield: JSOT Press, 1990), pp. 98–100. Jones himself does not agree with those who think the parable is at odds with its context.

19. David M. Gunn, *The Story of King David: Genre and Interpretation* (Sheffield: JSOT Press, 1978), p. 97.

20. See George W. Coats, 'Parable, Fable, and Anecdote: Storytelling in the Succession Narrative', *Interpretation* 35 (1981), p. 376.

21. Hebrew has no neuter, and the verbs used of the ewe lamb are all feminine in form – the lamb is 'she', not 'it'. That makes the correspondence with Bathsheba even easier to spot, of course.

22. Coats, 'Parable, Fable, and Anecdote', p. 371.

23. Coats, ibid., p. 371, also lists three more passages from Numbers, Ruth, and Kings, but of the four only 1 Kings 3.20 has the complete phrase 'lying in the bosom'.

24. See David M. Gunn, '2 Samuel', in James L. Mays (ed.), *Harper's Bible Commentary* (San Francisco: Harper & Row, 1988), p. 295.

25. This represents a translation of the ancient Syriac version of the passage. The Hebrew text as we have it reads, 'I gave you your master's house, and your master's wives into your bosom'. The NRSV follows the Hebrew, but McCarter (*II Samuel*, p. 295) argues that the Syriac more probably represents the text as it was originally written. Other scholars agree with him: see Jones, *The Nathan Narratives*, p. 105 and p. 168, n. 59.

26. Jones, *The Nathan Narratives*, p. 105.

27. This is McCarter's translation (see *II Samuel*, p. 293). The NRSV has 'the Lord has put away your sin', but McCarter comments (p. 301), 'The sin cannot simply be forgotten. It must be atoned for. Thus, if David himself is not to die, the sin must be transferred to someone who will.'

28. The NRSV has 'he named him', but the margin of the Hebrew text has 'she named', and McCarter (*II Samuel*, pp. 298 and 303), Jones (*The Nathan Narratives*, pp. 112–3), and Bailey (*David in Love and War*, p. 118) all argue that the marginal reading is more likely to represent the original text.

29. Mauchline, *1 and 2 Samuel*, p. 256.

30. Hertzberg, *I and II Samuel*, pp. 316–7. In the notes on Chapter 5 we gave 1964 as the date of Hertzberg's commentary, but that is when the English translation appeared. The German original was published in 1956.

31. See note 28 above.

32. See Athalya Brenner, *The Israelite Woman: Social Role and Literary Type in Biblical Narrative* (Sheffield: JSOT Press, 1985), ch. 2. She argues that it was very difficult for women to attain any great political power in ancient Israel, much harder than it was for their royal counterparts in some of the neighbouring Near Eastern states. The cases of Jezebel, who is portrayed as the power behind Ahab's throne in Samaria (see 1 Kings 18–21), and Athaliah, who seems to have reigned as sole regent for a time in Jerusalem (see 2 Kings 11), were exceptional.

33. Gunn, '2 Samuel', in Mays (ed.), *Harper's Bible Commentary*, p. 303.

34. ibid., p. 301.

35. Again Jezebel and Athaliah provide exceptions to the rule. 2 Kings 9.30–7 gives us the gruesome story of Jezebel's death, and 2 Kings 11.13–16 tells of the death – also violent – of Athaliah.

36. See Gwilym H. Jones, *1 and 2 Kings*, vol. 1, New Century Bible (London: 1984), p. 89; idem, *The Nathan Narratives*, p. 37; John Gray, *I and II Kings: A Commentary*, Old Testament Library (London: SCM Press, 1964), p. 77.

37. See S. Szikszai, 'King, kingship', in G. A. Buttrick, et al (eds), *The Interpreter's Dictionary of the Bible*, vol. 3 (Nashville: Abingdon, 1962), pp. 14–15, section entitled 'Divine kingship in the ancient Near East'.

38. See Gray, *I and II Kings*, pp. 79–81; Jones, *1 and 2 Kings*, vol. 1, p. 90.

39. See Jones, *The Nathan Narratives*, pp. 51–3; *1 and 2 Kings*, vol. 1, pp. 93–4; Gray, *I and II Kings*, p. 88.
40. Jones, *The Nathan Narratives*, p. 43.
41. ibid., p. 50.
42. Gen. 27 makes it quite plain that Rebekah is chiefly responsible for Jacob's successful attempt to gain Esau's blessing from his father Isaac. Isaac, too, is old and frail in that story, and the parallels between the two passages are well worth exploring, though we do not have the space to do so here.
43. Celia Thomson's remark was made in a personal communication she sent to me.
44. Alter, *The Art of Biblical Narrative*, p. 98. See also, Burke O. Long, *1 Kings with an Introduction to Historical Literature*, The Forms of the Old Testament Literature, vol. 9 (Grand Rapids, MI: Wm B. Eerdmans, 1984), p. 37. Like Alter, Long is quick to point out the artistry and sophistication of Bathsheba's speech.
45. Richard Nelson, *First and Second Kings*, Interpretation (Louisville, KY: John Knox Press, 1987), p. 19.
46. See Long, *1 Kings*, p. 50.
47. See Gunn, *The Story of King David*, p. 137, n 4.
48. Long, *1 Kings*, p. 51. Celia Thomson, in a personal communication she sent me, draws our attention to Bathsheba's initial greeting of Adonijah in 1 Kings 2.13, 'Do you come peaceably?' She remarks, 'Her question to Adonijah suggests a honed wariness, and implies she knows only too well what a threat he still presents to Solomon, and even possibly to herself, if he is attempting another bid for power through her as David's widow.'

Index of Authors

Index of Biblical Characters